T·H·E C·O·M·P·L·E·T·E BASEBALL PLAYER

THE COMPLETE BASEBALL PLAYER

DAVE WINFIELD
WITH ERIC SWENSON

Illustrations by Bob Cram

AVON BOOKS ⬦ NEW YORK

To Arline Winfield and the past from which we learned
so much,
and Gulliver Swenson and the future in which we have
such hope.

We are indebted to the following individuals and organizations for permission to use photographs in this book: Louis Requena; Jack Balletti; Bob Olen; Ron Kuntz; Gordy Jones; Corky Trewin/Seattle Mariners; New York Yankees; Minnesota Twins; San Diego Padres; Jim Mense/*Redbird Review*; University of Minnesota; Pat Kelly, National Baseball Library, Cooperstown, New York; UPI Bettmann Archives.

THE COMPLETE BASEBALL PLAYER is an original publication of Avon Books. This work has never before appeared in book form.

AVON BOOKS, INC.
1350 Avenue of the Americas
New York, New York 10019

Copyright © 1990 by Winfield Enterprises, Inc.
Text illustrations by Bob Cram
Front cover photographs courtesy (left to right): Bill Smith/*Sports Illustrated*; Chuck Solomon/*Sports Illustrated*; *Focus on Sports*
Published by arrangement with the author
Library of Congress Catalog Card Number: 89-92475
ISBN: 0-380-75830-X
www.avonbooks.com

First Avon Books Trade Paperback Printing: April 1990

AVON TRADEMARK REG. U.S. PAT. OFF. AND IN OTHER COUNTRIES, MARCA REGISTRADA, HECHO EN U.S.A.

Printed in the U.S.A.

ARC 10 9 8 7 6 5

CONTENTS

**8   COACHING AND MANAGING
       (AND PARENTING)**

9   MEASURING ACHIEVEMENT

**10   FROM THE SCOUTS'
        PERSPECTIVE**

ACKNOWLEDGMENTS

To my brother Stephen, many of whose contributions came years before this book was ever contemplated. It was with Steve that I shared the longest and most frequent discussions about baseball. Sometimes adversaries, more often partners, we dreamt, strategized, and competed together. We have always been a winning combination.

To my former agent and mentor, the late Al Frohman, who sharpened my hunger for excellence.

To all those people who improved my game, notably: Bill Peterson, one of my first baseball coaches, who really did teach me just about everything I had to know; Jim Dietz, coach of the Alaska Goldpanners, and a friend 3,000 miles from home; John McNamara, one of my first managers in the bigs, who had the patience (and insight) to play me every day; Bob Watson, for his hints on power and the occasional loan of the lumber to back them up; Charley Lau, a supportive hitting instructor who introduced me to his absolutes; Mike Barnett, video coordinator for the Yankees, who proved you don't have to play the game to analyze and teach it; Lou Piniella, who emphasized balance and extension in my stroke.

Then there were the players who, knowingly or unknowingly, influenced me and contributed to my style of play: Willie McCovey, who took me under his wing on and off the field; Dick Allen, whose kind words from a slugger I respected bolstered a young man's spirit; Steve Garvey, for his unwavering intensity; Joe Morgan, George Hendrick, and Billy Williams, who demonstrated that it's not the size of the bat nor the man that determines the damage he wreaks; Pete Rose, for his fire; Tony Perez, for his gruff but playful taunts.

To Tommy John and the rest of *The Complete Baseball Player* all-star consultants: Johnny Bench; Dave Righetti; Don Mattingly; Ozzie Smith; Harold Reynolds; Gary Gaetti; Kirby Puckett; and Vince Coleman. Thanks also to the baseball people—players, coaches, trainers, brass, scouts, and managers, current and former—who shared their special insights and insider's tips that strengthen our book: Don Baylor; Willie Stargell; Donnie Reynolds; Sparky Anderson; Jim Lefebvre; Tony LaRussa; Dave Valle; Jim Palmer; Johnny Sain; Peter Shmock; Jeff Mangold; Woody Woodward.

There were others, in and out of baseball, who made our job easier, including Dave Aust, Ethan Kelly, Pete Vanderwarker, and Abby Stern of the Seattle Mariners' Public Relations Department. Randy Hecht helped with research; Gordy Jones with photographs; Mel Schneider contributed his computer expertise; and the versatile Mario Casciano provided intermittent inspiration and assistance.

Our agent for this project, Sam Mitnick, delivered us to the right publisher. At Avon Books, we found working with our editor, Michael Bradley, to be stimulating and pleasurable. If your read is as enjoyable as was our write, we're both going to come out winners.

Thanks finally to our wives, Gail Swenson and Tonya Winfield. The relations between writers and their relations can be a big factor in what kind of manuscript is produced. Tonya provided unwavering support, and even when Gail's criticism wasn't particularly constructive, it was usually right-on.

PREFACE

We live in an age of specialization, and this generalization applies to sports as much as to life. Long gone from football are single-platoon teams, two-way players, and triple threats. We now have players who only come in on third down and long. In baseball, we have the designated hitter; short, middle, and long relievers; defensive specialists for the late innings, and a host of other devices. In part, this is because there are not more complete players. Players who can't field stay in the lineup because of their bats, and players who can't hit stay because of their gloves.

One goal of this book is to inspire its readers to aim to be complete players, and to suggest techniques that allow them to accomplish that goal. Whether you are a rookie or a veteran, young or old, whether you are quick or strong or both or neither, there are tips in this book that will help you. They represent the culmination of what Dave Winfield has learned in three decades of playing organized baseball (seventeen years as a professional).

The advice comes not only from Dave but also from a team of complete players and all-stars who have proven to be the best in the game. They will coach you in the three components of winning play: Attitude, Conditioning, and Technique, all that you need to better perform the ACT of playing baseball. These players can beat you running, catching, throwing, thinking, hitting—and several of them by hitting for power. They are all motivated, disciplined gamers who deliver in the clutch. They have played through all sorts of injury and adversity. Every player on the Avon Books All-Star Team is a hard worker. The necessity of dedicated effort to achieve excellence is one of this book's messages.

We want to stimulate your responsibility and your ability to respond. Baseball is a game of action and reaction. If you can respond immediately, if your reflexes are sharp, if you can anticipate correctly, you will have an edge over your opponent.

Successful players must train both the body and the mind while sustaining the spirit. This book covers every aspect of the game. It aims to be inspirational, informational, and to the point. We believe that you will find the text in hand to be the most comprehensive, succinct guide to playing baseball ever published.

DAVE WINFIELD
ERIC SWENSON

Note: While this book was a collaboration between friends, indeed the work of many hands, it is written in the first person and reflects the experience of David Winfield.

FOREWORD

If you believe in fate, as to a large extent I do, you will see how I came to believe that I was destined to become a ballplayer. Of course, I had no idea that I would be well known, a perennial all-star, a professional player for two decades, but I had an inkling that baseball was in my future.

To begin with, I was born on October 3, 1951, a famous day in baseball history. That was the day that Bobby Thompson hit "the shot heard around the world." His dramatic home run beat the Dodgers and allowed the Giants to win the one-game National League Playoff. Then there is my surname: WIN FIELD. That's a baseball name if I ever heard one.

Nature and nurture also played roles in my development as a player. I was blessed with an athletic build. I grew up in a supportive community with a family, neighbors, and coaches who cared about me and the other kids and gave freely of their time. I was lucky enough to grow up just a half block away from a playground.

In Saint Paul, Minnesota, where I was born, the seasons are short (except for winter), but there are lots of sports to participate in. We even took advantage of that long winter by flooding our baseball diamond and turning it into a hockey rink.

Our baseball field was a real source of pride to our neighborhood, however, because all of us had pitched in to build it from scratch. It still gives me joy and pride when I go back home and pass Oxford Playground and see kids playing on the field that I helped build. Seeing those kids brings back memories of my own youth.

I started playing ball when I was eight years old and went through the ranks—Pee Wee, Midget, Little League, Junior, American Legion. What a thrill wearing that first uniform was! I remember walking to that first game with Steve in the sky-blue uniforms Grandmother Jessie had lovingly washed and pressed for us. I told my mother and grandmother that I wanted to be tall and strong—the tallest in my family—so I could be a better athlete.

By the time I was twelve, I had announced to anybody who would listen that I was going to become a professional baseball player. My mother thought this would be fine just so long as I finished high school and went to college. So pretty early in life I had set my sights high and began to work toward my goals.

Between studies and sports, I had to use my time wisely. Some of my friends drifted into using alcohol and other drugs and became ex-friends. Peer pressure of the negative sort had little effect on my determination or direction. I kept my mind on the challenge and the rewards. I wanted to play, have fun, win, and travel. I worked hard, didn't take anything for granted, and seldom made excuses. I'm not pretending to be a Boy Scout; I'm just telling you the route that I took.

There were a multitude of factors that helped to produce the player I am today. Some were within my control and others weren't. It all began with the interest and desire. When added to my aptitude and ability and the fact that I had support and guidance at home, I had a solid foundation for whatever I found outside my family. I was lucky. There were various programs and good coaches available to me. The neighborhood was behind its players. With achievement on the field of play came recognition and reinforcement. We

1962 Oxford Playground Team, St. Paul City Pee Wee Champs. Dave Winfield, second from left, kneeling next to brother Steve.

consistently won championships. The little articles in the paper grew longer. Then came a scholarship to play ball at the University of Minnesota. A rewarding collegiate career was followed by an immediate introduction to the majors and, eight years later, by the largest contract ever offered to a ballplayer.

Baseball has been good to me and I have always tried to give something back to the game that has given so much to me. Please accept *The Complete Baseball Player* as another payment on account.

CHAPTER ONE

Attitude and Psychology: The Sound Mind

A GAME OF MANY PARTS

So Simple, So Complex

One of the characters in the movie *Bull Durham* defines baseball as the simplest of games. Someone throws the ball, someone catches it, and someone hits it. You either win or you lose or it rains. I suppose, reduced to its elements in that fashion, baseball *is* simple, but part of the delight of the game for me is its complexity and variety. Although there are certain situations that are predictable, like a sacrifice bunt in the late innings when you're down a run with runners on first and second and no outs, and although the pitcher and catcher both know what pitch was called for, once that ball leaves the pitcher's hand nobody really knows what will happen. There are many possible permutations and combinations— and plenty of time to consider them. In a game that usually takes close to three hours, the ball is seldom in actual play for much more than five minutes. This makes base-ball the quintessential game of anticipation, a most cerebral sport, a physical form of chess matching player against player.

I try to never lose sight of the fact that baseball is first and foremost a game. Even though I make well over a million dollars a year, I'm being paid to *play*. This is not to say that a lot of hard work isn't involved but if you can't have fun when you're playing a game then you might as well hang it up, which is what I will do when baseball stops being fun, if that day ever comes. Baseball is also a multi-billion-dollar business followed closely by millions of Americans. I work hard on the job. I've earned a reputation as someone who consistently delivers, who gives 100 percent and then a little extra, whether at the plate, in the field, or on the base paths. Baseball is also a team sport made up of a continuous round of individual contests. It is a science that combines elements of physics, optics, mechanics, physiology, and aerodynamics, among other disciplines. Baseball is also an art to be pursued gracefully. Watch Vince Coleman steal a base, or Kirby Puckett climb a

1

Anticipating your opponent's moves and avoiding mistakes are keys to winning on the chess board and the baseball diamond.

wall to steal a home run, or Tommy John pitch himself out of a jam, or Don Mattingly turn an 0–2 pitch into a game-winning hit, or Ozzie Smith pick and throw, and you are watching an artist at work. So baseball is a lot of things rolled into one.

The Levels of Play

The layers of baseball that I have just described pertain to playing the game at its highest level. At most times during the regular season, there are only 624 people who do this in the major leagues (twenty-six teams with twenty-four-man rosters). But whether you are watching baseball at Yankee Stadium or at a neighborhood sandlot, you can observe different levels of play that separate players. Athletes bring varying physical skills to the game, but this is not what I am talking about. Let us assume that a certain degree of *physical ability and coordination* is the first level of play. Certainly in professional ball everybody has the physical tools. Next comes *knowing and understanding the fundamentals* and techniques and rules of play. Any serious player

can reach this level; this is largely an intellectual process. The next step is one that winnows out a lot of players. Once you know the techniques, you must internalize them. They become like reflexes for you. You don't have to stop and think, you simply act. *Application*, *execution*, and *adaption* become automatic.

The next level of play is achieved by those who, in addition to the first three levels, bring to the game a *superior fitness and conditioning* allowing them to outlast opponents at the first three levels. Finally, to achieve the highest level of play you must demonstrate a *relentless and aggressive mental discipline*. Here is where the thinking comes in. Top players are always looking for what it takes to win the game. They can concentrate and focus their thoughts, their attention, their strength on the task at hand. From the first pitch to the last, at bat or in the field, game after game, week in, week out they're bearing down. If they have one hit they want two; got three, get four.

Whether their teams go on to win or not, these players are winners. I've been fortunate to play with and against some of the best gamers in the business: Donnie Baylor, Steve Carlton, Lou Brock, Carl Yastrzemski, Willie Mays, Steve Garvey, Willie Stargell, Joe Morgan, Pete Rose, Don Mattingly, Bob Gibson, Tom Seaver, Willie McCovey. These are the kind of players you want in your dugout when the going gets tough. So many players enter the game with the same approximate skills. Some excel, some get by, and some—regardless of talent—don't make it. The difference is not aptitude, it's attitude.

The ACT of Playing Baseball

Eliminating the role of luck, which most often is just a case of preparation coinciding with opportunity, I find that winning boils down to achieving the advantage in three areas: Attitude, Conditioning, and Technique. The right attitude should come first. It certainly facilitates achieving excellence in the other two areas. Attitude is where excellence begins. It's the hunger, the desire within, the intensity and determination that gives you the edge. Keep in mind the primacy of the mind, the importance of attitude; it's the A in the ACT of playing baseball.

WINNING AND LOSING

Keeping Your Balance

In the pages that follow, I hope you note how important balance is to just about everything connected to baseball. Balance is the essence of choosing a bat, taking your stance at the plate, and making your swing. At several points in the delivery, the pitcher must literally be able to balance his body. Fielders and runners must maintain their balance in the midst of a headlong dash. A good team is a balanced team. Balance is the one great key to everything I am trying to teach in this book, and I don't mean just physical balance. If you can bring spirit, mind, and body into balance, you will have made a tremendous achievement in life. Baseball can be a means to that end. The balance that you learn through baseball, the excellence you achieve on the diamond, can become a way of being and extend to every other field of endeavor.

Particularly important is the balance with which you respond to failure. There is more failure in baseball than in any other sport I can think of. Average hitters fail three out of every four times they go to the plate. The very best hitters, and I'm talking about the ones in major league baseball you can count on the fingers of a single hand, fail two out of every three times they try. Those statistics in any other sport would get you booed off the court or the field—if you had, by some oversight, even managed to get there. If you don't learn to live with failure, it will kill you as a player. If you're still thinking about how you went hitless in your last game, or the crucial error you made, or how this team chased you in the first inning the last time you faced them, you're on your way to failing again.

Over the long haul and the short haul, baseball holds many setbacks, both individual and collective. You must keep on keeping on and go with the flow. Don't get too high or too low. Mental consistency, stability, equilibrium—in a word, balance—will allow you to adjust to hard times and stay even during good times. These qualities enable you to lose with dignity and win with aplomb, perhaps the game's

Bad Call! I give up! I gave the umpire credit for this game-ending strikeout. You can't let plays like this get to you, though; they're part of the game.

hardest lessons. Athletes are often told how important courage is to sport. It means more than being able to break up that double play with your body or not being afraid of that fast one, high and inside. Courage is the trait that keeps you from getting dis-*couraged* and allows you to be en-*couraged* when things look bad.

Set goals for personal achievement and accomplish them. If your philosophy is "winning is the only thing that counts," you've got no escape hatch. I am not preaching defeatism but realism. There have been a very few undefeated champions in individual sports, but I'm not familiar with a single *team* that had a lifetime winning percentage of 1.000. Failure and losing are a constant in baseball. You will never be balanced if you cannot accept this as part of the equation. You can, however, be a consistent winner if you compete within.

THE INNER GAME OF BASEBALL

Training to Win

When most people hear the word *training* applied to sport, they tend to think of running and weight lifting and calisthenics—in short, a program or regimen to strengthen the body. Well, that's an essential part of becoming a complete baseball player, and we will discuss that aspect in the very next chapter. Before we get there, however, I want to sketch the ways in which you should train your mind. In some ways they are not all that different from what is required to get your body into shape. To begin with, in both cases, you must exercise discipline. To eat properly and do repetitive exercises, the basics of physical conditioning, requires self-con-

Sometimes, however, you have to let the ump know he was WRONG!

trol. To get your mind in shape, you also need control. We stretch to give our muscles flexibility. Unless you are already there, you will have to do some mind-benders to achieve mental fitness. In strength training, you overcome resistance, sometimes that of your own body, to become more powerful. To become mentally strong, you must overcome mental flabbiness and often the resistance of your own mind. What follows is a brief discussion of the components of mental training.

Defining Goals

I not only want to sketch how to set goals, I also want to suggest a mindset that will help you play ball and enjoy an active, healthy, playful life. It's your responsibil-

ity to acquire the lifetime fitness skills needed to promote a sound mind in a sound body, and you may have to do it without the benefit of many good examples. Many professional athletes and coaches, to cite but two groups, are not particularly good role models. Achieving mental discipline and physical fitness is the first major choice you face as an athlete. A coach, trainer, or manager can assist you, but nothing happens until you commit yourself to the goal. Whatever that goal is—doing thirty push-ups, losing thirty pounds, or adding thirty points to your batting average—I predict that in the course of striving for one goal you will realize others. It all begins with setting the goal.

Set your sights high. Shoot for the stars and fall back to the moon if you have to. For youngsters, the odds may be tremendously long against long-term athletic success. Discipline yourself through baseball, however, and who knows what other intellectual or physical pursuits you will be better equipped for. Although it's possible that only a few reading this guide will ever play professionally, some readers still might win a college scholarship. You might be long past any league except the parks and recreation co-ed slow-pitch division. You can still use baseball as an incentive to achieve or maintain fitness.

Goal setting is a continuous process. As you reach one goal, you set the next. You define, refine, and redefine your goals as you go along. Begin by taking stock. Where are you now? Where do you want to be? What are your short-, mid-, and long-range goals? How long will it take you to achieve them? Challenge yourself, but be realistic. Be as specific as you can be. Where possible, your goals should be quantifiable. This is not to say that intangible benefits won't result, just that you must have a way of measuring your progress. Write your goals and timelines down. This will allow you to review and renew your commitment to something that's there in black and white for all to see. Of course, you do not have to share your goals with anyone. They are *your* goals, but you may find that the simple act of sharing them with someone you trust and respect adds incentive.

Determining Strategies

Once you have definite goals on paper, your next task is to determine *how* to reach them. You need a game plan. Identifying obstacles and resources will help you decide what methods are appropriate. What are your strengths and weaknesses? How can you minimize those elements that will hinder you and maximize those that will help you? Are there resources that you have never tapped before or can you combine old resources in new ways? Can other people be of assistance? The techniques and tactics that form your action plan must include steps for monitoring your progress, evaluating your success, and eliminating your errors. You need to complete the loop with accurate feedback. You're not a starry-eyed Pollyanna operating in a vacuum. You need to perform reality checks and issue yourself report cards.

Affirming, Visualizing, Repeating

The more researchers delve into the study of the brain, the more they realize its amazing force and how untapped this potential power is for the overwhelming majority of us. This power can be spelled out in life-and-death terms. One of the most brilliant intellects of our age was Buckminster Fuller, the creator of geodesic domes, among other design breakthroughs. He shared such a wonderful bond with his wife that he had decided that if she died he would quickly follow. Literally hours after she passed away in a California hospital, Fuller died of natural causes. He died not by his own hand, but by his own mind.

Medical science cannot explain the opposite phenomenon, people who live when they should be dead, except to call it "spontaneous remission" and speak of the powers of the mind. What people can accomplish once they put their minds to it is truly astonishing. There are several well-documented cases, for example, of mothers who single-handedly lifted cars to rescue their children trapped underneath.

"Self-fulfilling prophecy" is a frequently heard term. It is usually applied to failure. "I knew I couldn't do it, and see, I didn't." What you have to do is turn it around and make a self-fulfilling prophecy work for you positively. If you have negative thoughts and images about yourself, you must reframe them and make them positive. You learned these negative things about yourself, now you must unlearn them. The way you visualize yourself is a large factor in how you perform. Researchers have confirmed that imagery alone can alter you physiologically and affect such functions as blood flow, brain waves, and heart rate.

One way to train your mind is to visualize yourself again and again doing well at baseball. In effect, you become not only the star but also the director of your own mind movie. You see yourself pitching strikes or getting a crucial hit and you rerun that video until the image is firmly implanted. Rewind and replay. It may help to

A positive approach helps to create positive results.

with us, and mental housecleaning cannot be accomplished overnight. An essential of mental training is to practice positive self-statements called affirmations. We all talk to ourselves. Affirmations channel and direct this interior monologue. Make your statements in the present tense and avoid qualifiers. Go beyond telling yourself "I can pitch with control today." Say, "I am powerful and in control. I am as strong as anyone on this field. I pitch strikes when I want to." Repeat these statements over and over. Remember that they are exercises; the more you perform them, the stronger you get. Review your goals and compose your affirmations based on them. Write your affirmations down so that you can see them with your eyes and not just hear them in your mind. Read them out loud.

slow the motion down and study your form as you perform perfectly. Make your movies vivid and appeal to all your senses. Hear the encouragement of your teammates, smell the summer air, feel the stitches of the ball in your hand, wipe the sweat from your brow. You are not just watching this movie; you're feeling it—because you are in it.

Of course, nothing succeeds like success when it comes to visualizing desired results. You won't really know what it's like to retire a feared batter or get a game-winning hit until you actually do it. This is where the confidence you've built up comes into play. Faith in your ability is increased every time you succeed, and increased faith leads to increased success. Be confident, then work to deserve your confidence.

Most people must do a lot of work to rearrange their interior landscapes. We carry an array of negative baggage around

Concentration and Relaxation

I would not have a professional career if I did not have the power to go within myself when I hit, that is, to tune out all distraction and negative thoughts; to forget fans, family, friends, and anything else except the immediate task at hand: to hit the ball. Various players have different names for this ability. Rod Carew called it an "altered state." For Wade Boggs, it's a "cocoon." Dave Stewart calls it his "tunnel." I simply call it "my world." As a hitter, this is what you have to aim for: total concentration on the ball. Time and time again, the primary flaw I see at all levels of play, but particularly with young hitters, is failure to follow the ball. How can you "see the ball, hit the ball" if you've already turned your head away? As a fielder, total concentration will help you focus on the hitter and allow infielders, for instance, to pick up when a bunt is coming. It will also

There's a lot of time in baseball to cool your heels. Relax when you can as Don Mattingly does here, watching a reliever's warm-up throws.

help you focus on and deliver your throws. A pitcher, if he cannot achieve total concentration consistently, will probably not be in the game for long. Simply delivering the ball to the target requires tremendous focusing of your mental energies.

It may seem curious that I have in this section linked concentration and relaxation. You might assume that they are opposites, and in a sense they are, but they are opposite sides of the same coin. Both are exercises in mind control and focusing. To achieve the highest level of performance, you must learn to concentrate and relax at the same time. As you stand at the plate awaiting the pitch, or on the mound preparing to deliver the ball, you must be relaxed. Gripping the ball or bat too tightly is one of the most common flaws in baseball. The tenseness moves right up your arm to the rest of your body, and tension diminishes your chance of success.

Ironically, learning how to relax might prove to be hard work. It is easier to accomplish if you are already a confident, centered, contented individual, at peace and in harmony with yourself and your world. In our competitive, fast-paced society, such people seem rare. So how do you promote relaxation in your mind and body?

Begin with your breathing. When you are tense or angry or afraid, your breathing is shallow, quick, and irregular. Breathing that helps you become calm is just the opposite—rhythmic, slow, and deep. Instead of breathing with the chest alone, you must involve your stomach, indeed your whole torso. This is called diaphragmatic or abdominal breathing, in contrast to the thoracic (high in the chest) breathing that most of us use. Until it becomes natural, you will actually have to practice deep breathing. It starts with your diaphragm moving downward, contracting to suck air into your lungs. As you begin to inhale, your lungs fill from the bottom, expanding first your abdomen and then your chest. You also exhale from the bottom up, starting with your abdomen and finishing with your upper lungs.

Deep breathing can be practiced anywhere at any time, and is the basis of most other relaxation techniques such as meditation. Meditation requires a relatively quiet place (ideally solitude) and enough time to reach and benefit from the calm state you achieve. It also lowers your body's metabolism and should not be undertaken before physical exertion. Seat yourself comfortably and concentrate on establishing deep but quiet rhythmic breathing. As you establish this pattern, begin to say a word or sound over and over again, timing it to coincide with your breathing. As you repeat this word, lose consciousness of all else. Drain your mind of all ideas and distractions. You may find meditation so restful that you become drowsy, although it can also be used to refresh yourself.

I'm able to take quick catnaps in the clubhouse before many games. Particularly in the final stretch of a long season, these short rest sessions give me a boost. I follow the nap with some stretching, sprinting, and swinging the bat, and I'm ready to go. On the field, I stretch and flex to become and stay relaxed.

Other forms of relaxation often require manual or mechanical assistance. Floatation tanks can put you into a state of deep relaxation and help open your subconscious better than any other device with which I am familiar. Massage is a wonderful relaxation treatment, and after being under the hands of a skilled masseur, I can come off the training table feeling like a new man. It not only eliminates soreness, it also can revitalize you physically and mentally. Pitchers, in particular, benefit from deep-friction massage of the neck, shoulder, and arm, especially the elbow. Lower limb massage and the traditional back massage are also common in the training room. Massage is usually done before a game, but not always. If professional massage is beyond your means or not available in your area, a friend or relative might be able to fill the bill for you. There are right and wrong ways to go about rubbing the body, however. If you opt for an amateur, invest in a massage guidebook.

The Mentally Fit Athlete

A player who has prepared himself by mental training will accomplish results thought to be extraordinary by athletes without this training. Players after players report that when they are performing at their peak there is no thought involved, that they seem to be operating on automatic pilot. Everything is slowed down. The ball comes to the plate slower and fatter. Impossible catches become possible as actions and movements are anticipated. The player is supremely confident and enjoys a sense of awesome power. Totally immersed in his activity, the athlete is barely conscious of the outside world.

What I have described does not occur just in professional sports. It can happen to you if you make it happen. Let us review the qualities required to reach this glorious state. To begin with, you have assumed total responsibility for your progress and success. You control, motivate, and direct yourself. You are the only one who can master your fate. Your emotions are in check, and you can remain calm under pressure. Your confidence is high; you are realistic but positive. You are determined and can focus both your physical and mental energies. For good reason, you expect success. Now all you have to do is go out and achieve it. To borrow Nike's advertising slogan, "Just do it!"

RECOMMENDED RESOURCES

H.A. Dorfman and Carl Kuehl. *The Mental Game of Baseball: A Guide to Peak Performance.* (Diamond Communications, 1989).

Charles Garfield and Hal Bennett. *Peak Performance.* (Houghton Mifflin, 1984). $8.95.

Dorothy and Bette Harris. *The Athlete's Guide to Sports Psychology: Mental Skills for Physical People.* (Leisure Press, 1984). $7.95.

Kay Porter and Judy Foster. *The Mental Athlete: Inner Training for Peak Performance.* (Ballantine Books, 1986). $3.95.

CHAPTER TWO

Fitness and Conditioning: The Sound Body

NEEDS FOR OPTIMUM PERFORMANCE

It is probably harder to stay in shape for baseball than other team or individual sports. Most sports require greater or more sustained physical exertion. This is why an exercise program is essential for baseball players who seek to excel.

Before anybody can properly design a fitness and conditioning program, they should have a firm idea of the physical qualities they must enhance in order to play at their highest level. What follows is a list of those abilities. While some of us are more blessed physically than others, all of the skills below can be improved through steady work. Where we start off is less important than where we end up.

Strength and Power

Strength is the ability to exert or withstand force. Power is the ability of the muscles to contract repeatedly and explosively.

Speed and Quickness

Speed is velocity or rapid rate of movement. Quickness is the ability to accelerate, to move fast from a standing start.

Flexibility and Agility

Flexibility allows a joint to twist and turn through a full range of movement without strain. Agility is the ability to change directions quickly and still retain control of the body.

Balance and Coordination

Balance is stability achieved through equality of opposing forces. Coordination is the harmonious interaction of forces.

Endurance

Endurance is the ability to withstand stress and stay strong over a long period of time.

For purposes of definition, we have separated the physical qualities listed above.

11

Parts of your training program can focus on these individual components, but you will not be able to advance far in your pursuit of one component unless you also advance in other components. They must be integrated. Peter Shmock, a member of the U.S. Olympic Track Team in 1976 and 1980, now strength and conditioning coach for the Seattle Mariners, in addressing the two major elements of a training program, puts it this way: "The stronger you get, the more flexible you must be. Weight training and flexibility go hand in hand. A muscle that's loose and relaxed gives you greater range of movement, decreased chance of injury, and increased quickness." Seeing how the parts fit together to form the whole is the first important lesson of good conditioning.

THE GOALS OF A TRAINING PROGRAM

Becoming an Athlete First

People reading this book—youth, their parents, and their coaches, primarily—are naturally interested in improving baseball skills. The majority of youngsters have presumably already decided what position(s) they want to play and may therefore be particularly interested in what exercises could help them become better pitchers, for instance. Our approach is that if you want to be a good pitcher you have to be a good baseball player. And if you want to be a good baseball player, you first must be a good athlete. Certainly there are sport-specific skills that you should hone to advance as a baseball player, but all of them depend on your first achieving a certain level of athletic ability on the program we recommend.

As a baseball player, you are going to be expected to sprint, jump, swing, and throw regardless of what position you play. (The pitcher in some college and professional ranks is the exception, not being called upon to hit.) Naturally, some positions will require some activities more than others, but no player can afford not to strengthen certain abilities such as throwing. Often different activities overlap or require strength in the same areas. Everybody requires strength in the upper body and legs. The goal of this book is to give you the tools to be a complete baseball player, and in this chapter we contribute to that goal by suggesting the kind of conditioning that produces all-around athletes.

Defense Against Injury

Baseball consists largely of long periods when no demands are made upon the player alternating with brief periods when extraordinary demands are made upon him. During these short bursts of dynamic physical movement and explosive muscle contraction, the risk of injury is heightened. Injuries occur because muscles are weak, out of balance, or lack flexibility. Muscle pulls are perhaps the most common injuries on the baseball diamond, and they most often occur because the muscle has not been properly stretched or lacks the necessary strength to withstand stress. Injuries also happen more often when players are tired. Conditioning delays or precludes the fatigue that is almost an inevitable consequence of a long season (162 games in the major leagues, not counting preseason and postseason play).

To reduce the risk of injury, the muscular frame and connective tissue (tendons, ligaments, and cartilage) must be strengthened to produce and withstand quick force and rapid acceleration. The strengthening must, however, be done so that proper muscle balance is achieved or else the chance of injury will be increased, not decreased. Each muscle group is stabilized by a supportive partner. There are muscles that move a body part (agonists) and those that oppose the movement (antagonists). If one group is significantly stronger than its opposing group, injury is more likely. Some of the common complementary muscle groups are:

Hamstrings versus Quadriceps
Abdominals versus Spinal Erectors
Biceps versus Triceps
Back versus Chest
Adductors versus Abductors

The exercises we recommend are meant to achieve and maintain balance. Make sure you complete all exercises—and in the order stipulated. You cannot mix and match or pick and choose and maintain the integrity of your program. Naturally, if you have access to a professional coach or trainer, alternative programs can be designed for you, but unless you have that option, stick to a proven regimen.

Psychological Edge Through Physical Advantage

A sound body is the product of a sound mind. To be physically fit is the conscious choice of a thinking person. Indeed, you could hardly start and stay on a regular training program without firm personal commitment. Pushing yourself to new limits requires mental toughness. Beyond the blending of physical and mental discipline derived from a training program, however, other benefits accrue.

Your exercises should prevent injuries, not cause them. Weight training can be dangerous if you do not know what you are doing.

By constant hard work, you should reach a point where you know you can handle game situations that draw upon your physical abilities. You have worked as hard as possible to prepare yourself physically and there's a good chance that your opponent hasn't. The knowledge that you are in peak condition instills tremendous confidence. And by being in that state, you will find that you sometimes can go *beyond* that state. One-upmanship on the field begins off the field.

WARMING TO THE TASK

First Things First

Unless you perform exercises in the proper sequence, they are not only counterproductive, they can also be dangerous. Strength training must be preceded by stretching exercises that require warming up to be safe and effective. Warm-ups are aptly named. If they are correctly performed, they raise your core body temperature and warm your muscles so that you don't begin stretching from a cold start.

Your body temperature should be raised between two and four degrees above the normal 98.6 degrees. Warming up also elevates your heart rate and gets the blood pumping to the muscles you are about to use. In your normal state of rest, 85 percent of your blood is centered in your torso. Before stretching, you want to open capillaries throughout your body and circulate blood to your extremities.

Aerobic Exercises

Aerobic exercises are those that are performed at such a pace as to allow for the free circulation of oxygen within the system. They consist of rhythmic, continuous action and constitute the best way of warming up. Jogging or long, slow, distance running; running in place; brisk walking; bicycling (stationary or free); using a rowing machine; and skipping rope are all examples. Ten minutes of aerobics is generally sufficient to bring your body to a state of readiness for stretching. If you have worked up a light sweat, you're there.

Aerobics also develop body tone, facilitate your breathing, and help you lose weight or control body fat. They are the best exercises for improving your cardiovascular fitness and building your general stamina. If aerobics are to be used for these purposes, they must be performed a minimum of three times a week for at least a half hour each time. Daily practice is even better. Exercise needs to be worked into your life-style and daily schedule.

Unfortunately, many people who think they are doing aerobics, burning fat, and losing weight are doing no such thing. Their exercise is intense; lactic acid, the waste product of the fuel burned, builds up, but they do not lose any body fat. They lose none because in this state they are drawing on the body's sugar, not on its fat. "No pain, no gain" is a motto that has probably been seen on more gym and locker room walls than any other. When it comes to aerobic exercises, however, just the opposite is true. If you feel pain during or after these exercises, you're doing them wrong. Fat-burning aerobics are mild exercises, producing no more than a slight sweat. Your heart rate should be constant and your breathing steady.

GETTING FLEXIBLE

Long and Strong

The aim of training for flexibility is to increase your range of motion and make movement easier by lengthening the muscles. Slowly the muscles are stretched and held in the extended position for several seconds before being returned to their accustomed position. If these exercises are performed regularly, preferably daily, greater elasticity gradually results. There is no rushing here. You cannot expect quick results. Changing your muscular structure is slow, incremental work. Extremes of concentration and relaxation can expedite the process, but even the hardest working athletes will find that patience is probably the most valuable quality to bring to flexibility training.

You should use stretching in two ways: to limber up and loosen the muscles before and after practices and games, and as a required prelude to weight training. I cannot stress this relationship too much. Lengthening the muscle must precede strengthening the muscle. The more you want to lift, the more you have to stretch.

Stretching Exercises

The two kinds of stretching exercises are ballistic and static. With ballistic stretching you bounce against the muscle to increase length, whereas with static stretching you simply hold the muscle in an extended state for ten seconds or so and then relax it. I consider static stretching to be far more effective and safe, and it is the only flexibility training that I recommend. Keep in mind the wide range of flexibility that people exhibit naturally. When doing these exercises, compete against yourself, not anyone else.

Once you are properly warmed up, you can begin to stretch. It's important to avoid a common mistake. Don't hold your breath while stretching. If you're not breathing you're not relaxing; and if you're not relaxing, you're not stretching properly. Breathe in easily and exhale any tension. Your breathing and your thoughts, what you visualize as you exercise, should promote ease, release, and relaxation. All muscles not directly involved in the stretch should be at rest.

One way to organize your stretching is to begin with the head and work your way down. Unless directed otherwise, hold each stretch for fifteen seconds and repeat five times. If the exercise is described for one side of your body, make sure you perform the same actions on the other side as well. You need not do every exercise suggested, but you should stretch every muscle group.

Begin by making full clockwise circles with your head, then reverse direction and repeat. Shrug and roll your shoulders, up and down, back and forth. Hold the stretch for a few seconds in each of the four directions and repeat. Extend your arms straight out at your sides and make ten circles forward and then ten backward. With your arms in front of you, rotate your wrists and hands ten times in each direction. Bring one arm across your chest and grasp its elbow with your other hand. Pull until you can feel a good stretch, hold, release, reverse, and repeat. Move your feet farther apart, bend at the waist, and touch your right toe with your left hand, then reverse. Alternate sides until you have reached a total of twenty bends. If you cannot touch your toes, reach as far as you can.

Sit on the ground with your arms behind you. Bend your elbows and lean back. Next, lie on your stomach with your arms outstretched. Roll one leg over the other. Your torso will follow, and you will roll back over your arms. Repeat with your arms in the three-quarters position. These exercises will work your shoulders. Kneel; bend forward, supported by your arms with your hands pointed outward; then lean back. Your wrist and forearms will benefit from this activity. Hang from a vertical bar or other stationary object and hold your stretch. All these exercises benefit your upper body. You're now ready to move down your torso.

Sit with your legs in front of you and twist your trunk as far as you can to one side and then the other. Lie on your back with your legs straight up. Lower them together to the side, alternating sides. While still on your back, raise one knee and pull it toward your chest. Repeat with the other knee. Hang from a chinning bar, rotate your hips and legs to each side, kicking your lead leg relatively high. These exercises will loosen your lower back. Lie flat on your stomach with your hands at your

Quadriceps (Quads), the muscles at the top of your legs, are stretched with this exercise.

Extend your leg and pull on your toes to loosen calf and hamstring.

shoulders. Lift your upper body to work your abdomen. To stretch your groin, stand, place your feet wide apart, lean far to the right, and with the left hand apply downward pressure to your left leg. Reverse directions and repeat. Sit with your hands on the ground for balance; flex one leg beneath and behind you while you stretch the other in front of you. Sit with the soles of your feet together and your knees as far apart as possible. Your upper and lower leg should form a V. Clasp your feet with your hands and push down on your knees with your elbows. Now loosen up your legs.

From a kneeling position, stretch your thighs by leaning back slowly. To flex both your thighs and your hips, kneel on one knee, reach behind you, and bring your foot toward your backside. Sit with your legs in a wide V in front of you. With toes up, grasp one foot and pull your body forward. Switch to the other leg and repeat. Finish these exercises for the hamstring by simply lowering your upper body between your outstretched legs. Stay seated, bend one leg until its foot touches your other knee, then touch your nose to that knee. Hold, return, reverse, and repeat. To loosen both hamstring and calf, kneel on one knee, extend the other leg in front, and pull back on your

toes with your hand. Stand up and work your calves by taking a stride with one foot while keeping the heel of the other foot down. Bend your front knee and lower your body. Change striding foot and repeat. With legs fully apart and arms folded, bend from the waist until your elbows almost touch the ground to exercise the back of your legs. Finish with the ankle. While sitting, bring one foot to a position above your opposite thigh. Cradle your ankle in both hands and turn it as if you were "reading" the sole of your foot. Stand with one foot two or three feet in front of the other. Keep your weight on the back foot and bend your knees. You should now be stretched from head to toe.

Buddy or partner stretching allows you to achieve extensions that you cannot do alone. Two athletes sitting opposite each other with their legs in a V form a diamond. Muscles throughout the body can then be contracted and relaxed through pulling motions back and forth initiated first by one partner then the other. Additional pressure can be applied with the legs, and you can combine a twist and a pull by putting increased pressure on either side. You can stretch your hamstrings and back by sitting with your legs straight in front of you. Hold your toes with your hands and have your partner place his hands on your shoulder blades and push you forward. If you spread your legs before applying pressure, you will work your groin. An exercise that stretches your entire trunk is performed with the partners back-to-back, their arms straight above their heads and their hands joined. One partner bends forward, bringing the other player onto his back and off the ground.

You can use stretching and related exercises during a baseball game as well. Simply tighten, then loosen. Find the point that allows you to be wound but relaxed, the ideal state of preparation. I tense and then release before batting and while I'm in the field. I'm looking for the range of balance that signals being prepared. Baseball is a game of waiting punctuated by short bursts, and stretching while on duty helps you to stay ready. Some major league teams even recommend formal stretching exercises about halfway into the game.

BUILDING STRENGTH

Old Myths and New Realities

For years, weight training was absolutely scorned in baseball circles. The thought was that if you used dumbbells, you were one. Strength training was fine for other sports, but would make baseball players muscle-bound and unable to perform the basic movements of their craft such as swinging a bat or throwing a ball. Well, a new age has dawned, and although there are still a few old fogies around who stick to their old myths, strength training is here to stay in baseball. Most major league clubs , have a strength and conditioning coach and well-equipped facilities.

A new breed of young players who have grown up using free weights is setting records and proving the value of strength training. California Angel pitcher Mark Langston and Kansas City Royal outfielder Bo Jackson are two prominent examples. Langston regularly leads the league in strikeouts and is a two-time All-Star. Jackson continues to amaze the sporting world with his feats on both the diamond and the gridiron. These young players and others like them are setting a pace that requires others to try to keep up—and that means strength training.

Calisthenics and Machines

Calisthenics (also called body-resistance exercises) is the classic way to increase strength. These simple exercises, many of them used by Greek athletes 2,500 years ago, are still an excellent way to develop your muscles and promote physical well-being. An added advantage is that push-ups, chin-ups, and sit-ups can be done anywhere at any time. You need only a few feet of floor space, not access to expensive equipment and a gymnasium. Lastly, there is no major muscle group that calisthenics can't strengthen.

One of the best exercises you can do, considering the importance of the stomach, is the sit-up. Although it is a simple exercise, it is often done incorrectly. Do not hook your legs or feet under an object to gain leverage or ask another person to hold your feet. Keep knees bent and feet flat on the floor. Don't cheat by using your upper body strength or rocking. Roll up slowly, keeping your lower back in contact with the floor. In a variation on the sit-up called the crunch, you cross your feet and with your arms behind your head bring your shoulders six inches off the ground. Sit-ups strengthen your stomach and give you a better sense of how a tightened stomach feels. You should keep your stomach contracted as a matter of course and form. Suck it in and keep it in, all the time. Your whole body will be better off. Many people with back problems really have front problems. A tight belly will eliminate a multitude of troubles.

The "Dying Warrior" develops several parts of your body essential to baseball simultaneously, notably the upper back, arms, shoulders, and wrists. Lower yourself to a push-up position and then hold your body two inches from the ground. Begin by sustaining the hold for twenty seconds and work yourself up to the point where you can stay in position for several minutes. To strengthen your fingers, do this on your fingertips. These and other calisthenics, such as jump-ups, chin-ups, leg lifts, and squats, are some of the oldest exercises in continuous use for the good reason that they work. Incorporate them into your regimen.

Among the newest ways to exercise your body is the use of strengthening machines such as the Nautilus. This equipment is built for high-intensity, short-duration, full-range exercise. If you have access to mechanical apparatus of this sort, by all means take advantage of it. Keep in mind, however, that machines will not allow you to work several muscle groups together. They are most useful in working small muscle groups in isolation. For this reason, I recommend machines for supplementary exercises, after you have completed your primary large muscle exercises with free weights.

The curl is *the* basic exercise for increasing bicep strength.

Pumping Iron

The most common way baseball players develop their strength is through exercising with free weights—barbells and dumbbells. I don't recommend that youngsters begin lifting weights until they are at least fourteen years old, and then only under the supervision of a qualified trainer. Injuries can occur, but the risk is lessened if technically correct methods are used to perform the exercises and a spotter/trainer is on hand to assist. Also remember that you must warm up with a minimum of ten minutes of running and ten minutes of stretching before doing any lifting. You should work large muscle groups in your legs, shoulders, chest, lower torso, and arms before moving on to small muscle groups in the same areas. Lastly, breathe properly. Your breathing should be exaggerated. Inhale prior to work movement and exhale forcefully during action. Develop a rhythm that becomes automatic.

The principle underlying strength training is progressive overload. Your body adapts to any resistance you apply to it. To increase your strength, you must constantly add resistance and force your muscles to work harder than they are accustomed to. You can accomplish this by increasing poundage and increasing the number of sets you perform.

Begin your strength program by testing yourself in various areas. Refer to the "Monitoring Progress" section on page 24 for methods of testing. To measure upper body strength, see how much you can bench press with no more than one repetition. For lower body strength, use the squat or leg press. If you are not experienced, for safety's sake it might be wise to simply make an educated but conservative guess at these weights. Once you've established your benchmarks, you can design an accurate program and also set short- and long-range goals for motivation.

If you always use the same weight during your workouts, your strength will level off and then begin to decrease. In order to eliminate muscular burnout and promote a smooth transition of overload, your strength training should include intensity phases. The chart below provides a way of varying your intensity for bench presses and squats/leg presses over a six-week period.

Week 1	3 sets × 10	70% of maximum weight
Week 2	4 sets × 8	72% of maximum weight
Week 3	5 sets × 5	82% of maximum weight
Week 4	4 sets × 4	85% of maximum weight
Weeks 5 and 6	1 set × 10	70% of maximum weight
	1 set × 8	72% of maximum weight
	1 set × 6	82% of maximum weight
	1 set × 4	85% of maximum weight
	1 set × 2	91% of maximum weight

Increase arm and shoulder strength and protect against rotator cuff injuries with this exercise. For balance, turn over on your stomach and raise the weights from floor to shoulder level.

The squat is one of weight training's most useful exercises, working several major muscle groups.

Determine your secondary exercises through trial and error and in consultation with a trainer. You'll want to repeat leg and bicep curls, lat pulldowns, and tricep extensions eight or ten times. Experiment to find the right poundages. Once you have completed your six-week routine, retest yourself to determine new maximum lifts and start the program again.

For those of us who worked regularly with weights, the Yankees recommended three-day-a-week, full-body workouts done in the following order:

1. Bench presses
2. Lat pulldowns
3. Seated military presses
4. Squats/leg presses
5. Tricep extensions
6. Bicep curls
7. Toe raises
8. Abdominal work

Although they are usually reserved for off-season training, four-day split routines are also an option. They provide additional exercises for the same muscle group while resting others.

Monday and Thursday	Tuesday and Friday
1. Bench presses	1. Squats
2. Inclines	2. Leg presses
3. Seated military presses	3. Leg curls
4. Dips	4. Lat pulldowns
5. Lateral raises	5. High pulls
6. Tricep extensions	6. Bent over rows
7. Bicep curls	7. Shrugs
8. Reverse curls	8. Calf raises
9. Abdominal work	9. Leg extensions

Circuit Training

If you're squeezed for time, or need a change-of-pace workout to avoid becoming stagnant, or are just beginning a longer program, circuit training might be just the ticket. The exercises emphasize cardiovascular and muscular endurance and involve lighter poundages, more repetitions, and shorter rest periods. Jeff Mangold, former Yankees strength and conditioning coach, recommends the following ten-exercise workout:

1.	Bench presses	10 times
2.	Jumping rope	30 seconds
3.	High pulls	10 times
4.	Sit-ups	30 seconds
5.	Jumping jacks	30 seconds
6.	Leg presses	10 times
7.	Bicep curls	10 times
8.	Lat pulldowns	10 times
9.	Run in place	30 seconds
10.	Dips	10 times

You should perform three sets before moving on to the next exercise and rest no longer than thirty seconds between each set or exercise.

OTHER EXERCISES

Anaerobic Training

Anaerobic exercises are performed at a much greater intensity level than aerobic exercises. They train your body to draw on quick sources of energy needed for short burst activity and they strengthen your cardiovascular capability. You should perform them at 80 percent to 100 percent of your maximum capability, and for this reason they need to be interspersed with short rest periods that allow your body to recover. When the weather doesn't allow you to train outside, you can skip rope at a rapid pace or sprint inside if a gym is available. Sprinting is the best anaerobic exercise for baseball players. Whether you are exploding off the mound or toward a base or the ball, many short sprints make up the game. An exercise called the "giant walk" is a good preparation for sprinting. Run in a slow-motion, highly exaggerated fashion complete with continuous deep knee bends on every stride and elbow swings up to your head.

Although sprinting can be done anywhere, if you have access to a baseball diamond, I recommend that you "bat" and run the cycle. Or you can set up your own diamond with markers for bases.

Take your position as if at the plate, swing, and sprint ninety feet, the distance to first base. If you are playing in a youth league with a shorter distance between bases, make the necessary adjustments. Jog back from first, resume your position at the plate, swing, and sprint to second. Return to home and repeat the procedure, but this time go to third. Rest a moment or two and then dash home as if coming in on a sacrifice. Finish the exercise by "hitting" an inside-the-park home run and making it around the bases as fast as you can. You can vary this exercise by leading off from first and sprinting to third or coming home from second. In essence, you're exercising and simultaneously practicing the situations you face in an actual game.

To help improve your running speed, practice sound mechanics. Eliminate any wasted motion. You want to achieve a smooth and easy stride. Your arm swing should be relaxed with rotation at the shoulder, not the elbow. Don't cross your body with your arms. Swing your arms straight ahead. Make sure your hands go no higher than your forehead on the foreswing and that your elbow goes no higher than your shoulder on the backswing. Your elbows should almost be grazing your hips. Short, quick, regular, powerful arm pumps will help you to drive your legs. You should be pushing as you run, getting good leg extension with your rear leg driving you. Run on the balls of your feet with your weight forward. Keep the force you generate going forward, not laterally or vertically.

Sprinting is not only a way of training, it should also be the way you get from one place to another once you're in the game.

By sprinting to and from your position in the field, you'll help keep your body warm and reduce the chance of pulling or straining a muscle. Sprinting should be the exercise that concludes your pregame warmups and a mainstay of your preseason training when you are building up speed. If you are combining anaerobic, bounding, and aerobic exercises, make sure you save the aerobics for last because they require the least intensity.

Bounding and Jumping Exercises

One of the best ways to develop strong, explosive legs is through bounding exercises and jump drills (also called plyometrics). You can think of continuous single-leg bounds as high-energy skipping where you are aiming for maximum hang time. For double-leg bounds, place your feet together and explode forward. Single-leg hops over stationary objects or up stairs help develop calf and ankle strength. Lateral hip strength is important on the mound,

High bounds with lots of arm action and long hangtime improve your anaerobic and leaping capability.

Jumping over a stationary object is one of the simplest plyometric exercises.

at bat, and when you want to change direction quickly. To strengthen your hips, place markers two and a half feet apart. With your feet together, jump sideways back and forth quickly from the outside of one marker to the other. With an exercise called the "skater's lunge," you imitate the movement of skaters trying to gain speed. Use hard push-offs to achieve a rapid zig-zag motion forward. Before you initiate single-leg exercises, make sure you have strengthened both legs through double-leg movements.

Some of these exercises gain by being performed in a swimming pool. The water softens your landing while increasing resistance. Vertical jumps, where you reach as high as you can, are a good example. If you're in a pool, you can also do repeated power push-offs, as if you were beginning a backstroke race. Another way to develop the leg muscles strengthened through bounding and jumping is by running up steep hills or flights of stairs.

Medicine Ball Training

Long relegated to the attic or to garage sales as a relic of a bygone era, the medi-

cine ball is enjoying a renaissance among trainers. Performing exercises with a two-to-twelve-pound medicine ball can increase your strength and explosiveness. Using both hands, throw the ball to a partner from both sides of your body. You can emphasize torso development by kneeling during these exercises and exaggerating the rotation of your hips and upper body. Instead of throwing to a partner in front of you, catch the ball thrown from your side. Rotate to the other side, and then return the ball forcefully, trying to use your midsection and not your arms. This variation will limber up your lower back and abdomen in particular.

Some medicine ball exercises resemble movements on the basketball court. Passing the ball to your partner with a push away from your chest will strengthen your wrists and fingers. A high-energy set shot starting from your chest will help develop explosiveness. Put your entire body into the throw and lift off the ground. Throw the ball as far as you can from between your legs like an old-time foul shot. You can also throw the ball over your head and behind you. To work your legs, flex your knees, lower your body, and spring upward, throwing the ball as hard as you can straight up. Three sets of five throws, trying to increase the distance each time, is an appropriate regimen.

Medicine ball exercises are excellent for strengthening the torso.

FINISHING UP

Cooling Down

After the heat of competition or the exertion of exercise, most athletes are eager to shower, dress, and get home. The smart ones, however, will take a few minutes to ease back into a state of rest. Light jogging and some mild stretching or slow, rhythmic movement of some sort will do the job. You want the blood to circulate and help flush from your system the waste products your body has produced. Then, to get the blood back into your trunk, you can lie on the floor with your legs straight up and resting against a wall. In essence you are reversing the dynamics begun with your warm-up. In the majors, we have whirlpools, and some players take a short lukewarm bath as part of their cooldown. You could substitute a lukewarm or even cool shower. If you are lucky enough be near a swimming pool or lake, jump in. Swimming is an excellent way to reduce soreness, increase flexibility, and prepare your body for the next day's workout.

MONITORING PROGRESS

Measuring and Testing Your Body

During the last decade, fitness evaluation has become the norm in professional baseball. The Cincinnati Reds and their head trainer, Larry Starr, introduced physiological testing, like many of the other innovations in training (they were, for instance, the first team to use the Nautilus machine), to baseball. Testing is done in both the preseason and the regular season, and measures five areas: aerobic fitness, anaerobic fitness, body fat, muscular strength, and flexibility. Establishing baselines allows a team to have physiological profiles of its players and to have measurements to compare for athletes returning from an injury.

I advise testing for younger players because it provides a good way to monitor improvement. Test results do not vary much for individuals at the professional level. Year-round fitness is the norm, and pros have already reached a high level of attainment. Younger players, though, are still developing, and the name of the game is getting better. In the major leagues, machines such as dynamometers and computerized stationary bicycles are used to test athletes, but there are inexpensive alternatives for those without access to such sophisticated machines.

To measure aerobic fitness, time a mile-long run or measure a fifteen-minute run. A timed 30-to-60-yard dash can gauge speed. Anaerobic fitness can be measured with a timed 300-yard run. Test strength through bench presses and leg presses or chin-ups, push-ups, and sit-ups. To determine flexibility, Larry Starr recommends five tests:

1. Hamstrings, gluteals, lower back: From a sitting position with legs and knees straight in front of you, reach for your toes. Measure distance to go or length beyond.
2. Back: Lie on your stomach with hands behind head and someone else holding down your hips and legs; raise your up-

per body as far as you can. Measure from floor to chin.

3. Shoulders: Lie on your stomach with arms extended in front of you and grasp a yardstick, dowel, metal rod, or similar object; lift it as high as you can. Measure from floor to object.

4. Groin: With your legs resting against a wall, do a split by spreading your legs as far apart as you can. Measure the distance from the inside of one knee to the other.

5. Trunk: With your back against a wall and your hands clasped behind your head, spread your legs 36 inches apart a foot from the wall. Bring your head slowly forward and see how close you can come to touching the ground. Measure from floor to forehead.

As with all stretching exercises, it is imperative that you warm up first. In fact, because you are trying to measure maximum flexibility, you should take a little extra time to warm up for these stretches.

NUTRITION

Eat to Compete

When I first came up to the big leagues, the prevailing wisdom was that baseball players needed a steady diet of steak and potatoes to fuel their bodies. Candy bars were recommended as a good source of quick energy. We're much more knowledgeable now, and both of these beliefs have been shown to be false (except for the potatoes, which, if they aren't fried, *are* good for you). Heavy foods, high in protein and fat, raise your cholesterol level and are hard to digest. And that candy bar, rather than giving you a burst of energy,

does just the opposite. After briefly raising your blood sugar level, it rapidly decreases it, and like all food, forces blood to your stomach, away from where it is actually needed.

Yankees head trainer Gene Monahan recommends an easy way to remember the essentials of a good diet. He's reduced it to a number code, 44432, that refers to the basic food groups. Each day you should have four servings of fruits, vegetables, and cereals or grains; three servings of protein; and two servings of dairy products (more for youngsters). He's so big on fruits and vegetables that he assigns each one its own number. They are high in vitamins, minerals, carbohydrates, natural sugars, and water. Cereals and grains provide more vitamins and minerals, fiber, and carbohydrates, particularly starch. Proteins give you body builders such as amino acids. Milk and other dairy products are rich in calcium and phosphorous.

The tendency to be fat develops early. Youngsters should not assume that being overweight is just a problem of the future. Healthy males should have a body fat level of 14 percent to 16 percent; women, 22 percent to 24 percent. Sensible athletes aim for a 10 percent to 14 percent level. Many athletes condemn themselves to injuries and take years off both their playing and actual lives by having too much fat and being out of shape. Excess weight requires excess energy to move. Fat almost always shows up in your midsection, where it slows you at your core. This is the center of the body in motion; you must be able to move it with ease and efficiency. Poor diet is the principal cause of obesity, with lack of exercise being the other main culprit. If you are serious about being a good baseball player, then let it show in your diet. I think it's probably too much to ask that you eliminate fatty, fried, or oily foods; highly processed products; sweets; and all those tasty delights that are properly called "junk food." These are the items that you must limit, however, if you aim to perform at your highest level.

In general, people should eat more lightly. For athletes, particularly before a game, it is essential. I try not to eat much for several hours before a game so that I can pretty much play on an empty stomach. It helps to have your last food before a game be high in carbohydrates. If you load up on these compounds, you raise the glycogen level in your system and expand your energy reserves. Unlike simple sugar, the complex carbohydrates release their energy slowly and allow an athlete to draw continuously upon these reserves over the length of a game.

Fluid Replacement

The human body is about 60 percent water. Our body has evolved some fairly ingenious methods of circulating liquids that allow it, among other functions, to control body temperature. For instance, sweating and its evaporation cool the skin and help it absorb heat from within, regulating our core temperature. Hot, humid conditions can upset this mechanism and interfere with the continuous balance our body needs. In bad cases, cramps and exhaustion occur, and in the worst cases heatstroke can result.

Playing outside in the heat of summer, there is very little we can do about the weather. Sometimes the conditions can be brutal. One reason that I'm glad to be playing in the American League is that I no longer have to play at Saint Louis's Busch Stadium, where temperatures on the field can reach 140 degrees. Even with its waterfall behind the outfield, Royals Stadium in Kansas City is the hottest place to play in the American League. On a hot day, baseball players in positions requiring heavy exertion, such as pitchers and catchers, can drop up to fifteen pounds.

While we can't do anything about the weather, we can do something about replacing the fluids we lose through sweat. Drinking water is absolutely the best thing to do. Electrolyte-carbohydrate drinks (Gatorade is perhaps the best known) have gained great popularity in recent years. They work best for high-exertion and endurance athletes—football players, marathoners, and the like. For baseball players, these drinks and sodas are counterproductive. Salt tablets also work against the hot and sweating body that they supposedly help. Stick to water; plain water is what you need for effective rehydration. Eight to ten glasses of water help to keep your system regular and flushed.

Drink water before games or practices. A few glasses twenty minutes or less before game time is appropriate. The need to urinate shouldn't be a problem because the kidneys tend to slow down markedly during exercise. Every half hour or so during the game or practice, drink another glass of water. Do not just drink water when you feel thirsty. Your body doesn't tell you when it needs water until it is too late. After your exercise or game, you should drink a lot of water to replenish lost supplies and to help flush your system. Youth league coaches who do not let their charges drink water during competition or practice are enforcing a misguided discipline and should revise their methods to conform to modern scientific evidence on the body's needs.

For adult players, I want to say a word of wisdom about alcohol consumption after a game. I'm not approaching this from a temperance angle, but strictly from a physiological viewpoint. Going out with the guys and gals after a game and downing a few beers is fine, but it won't do anything to replace fluids. Like all caffeine drinks, including some sodas, alcoholic beverages dehydrate the body. You urinate more frequently and lose even more body water. Alcohol also inhibits the release of the antidiuretic hormone that helps your body retain water. In addition, it depresses the central nervous system and disrupts your cellular structure for muscle rebuilding. So, if you must drink alcohol, do it in moderation and chase it with more than moderate amounts of water.

BEYOND THE DIAMOND

Lessons for Life

Although you will not be playing baseball year-round, you may find yourself cross-training for and playing other sports. If you don't, you should play tennis, handball, practice the martial arts, swim, or dance. Yes, dance! To develop flexibility, timing, balance, and coordination, take a class in modern dance. Dancing will also strengthen your small muscles; most athletics develop only the major muscle groups. Perhaps most importantly, dance will give you an awareness of your body difficult to achieve through other activities. You have to know what's happening to your spine, your knees, and your pelvis as you move. Too many players learn the moves of baseball by imitating others and then spend the rest of their careers just going through the motions.

I hope that by this time readers will be aware that fitness has a 365-day-a-year season. It is far easier to stay in shape then to get into shape. Develop good work habits and use them the rest of your life. There's a lot of living beyond baseball, and by staying fit you are giving yourself the best chance of extending and enjoying those years.

RECOMMENDED RESOURCES

The Trainers of Major League Baseball with Lee Lowenfish. *The Professional Baseball Trainer's Fitness Book*. (Warner Books, 1988). $12.95.

You can also get an absolutely first-rate videotape on baseball strength and conditioning featuring Mark Langston of the California Angels and Peter Shmock, conditioning coach for the Seattle Mariners. Seeing the exercises done properly and learning the whys and hows from a professional trainer gives you a good basis for designing your own program. Order *Training with the Stars* for $32.50 from Proformance, 4802 Dayton North, Seattle, WA 98103 (Washington residents add $2.43 sales tax).

Players twelve years of age and younger will benefit from *The Official Little League Fitness Guide*, by Frank W. Jobe, M.D., and Diane Moynes, R.P.T. (Simon & Schuster, 1984). $5.95.

CHAPTER THREE

Equipment:
Choice and Care

THE BAT

Weight, Length, and Shape

Baseball is a game of continual choices, and the first one to be made by the hitter is which bat to use. The size of your hands and the length of your arms, your height and weight, and your quickness and strength are all factors in choosing the bat that is best for you. During my career I've used bats ranging from 32 to 38 ounces and from 34 to 36 inches. I'm a big man and can handle a relatively heavy bat (although I'm still amazed that sluggers like Babe Ruth used a piece of lumber that weighed three pounds!). There is no doubt that quickness, rather than weight, is the major element in hitting for both power and consistency. A light bat that hits the ball is infinitely better than a heavy bat that doesn't.

I emphasize the obvious here because at every level of play I've observed hitters using bats too heavy for them to control. Beginning players in particular have the tendency to choose too heavy or too long

a bat, hoping this will improve their power. The result is a loss of balance and control, slower wrist action, and impaired timing. If you manage to hit the ball, you may get a few more long hits, but assuredly you'll get a lot fewer hits.

One key to hitting is waiting as long as you can before you swing, learning as much as you can about the pitch before you commit yourself. Then you must swing quickly. The heavier the bat, the harder this is. Of course, the heavier the bat, the denser the wood, and the farther and faster it will drive the ball. Good wood in the bat imparts good jump to the ball. Look for a bat with the wide grain characteristic of older wood. Such a bat will be more resistant to flaking and chipping, and hard-hit balls will not dent it.

A rule of thumb for beginning batters is to choose the heaviest bat you can handle easily. Then to be on the safe side, step down from there. The best hitters of the modern game for both average and power—Musial, Mays, Williams, Aaron, Mantle, Banks—all used light bats. Most batters

Many players, hoping to be heavy hitters, use bats that are too heavy. Be smart and make sure your bat is quick.

prefer a 32-to-34-ounce bat with lengths in the same range. Younger batters should naturally use lighter bats.

Such variables as different pitchers or game situations, injuries, and the time of season at which you're playing also affect your choice of bat. As the season wears on, some players opt for a lighter, shorter bat than the one they used to start off the year, when they were at their strongest. Where you hold the bat is an additional factor; a 34-ounce bat held with a choke grip will feel like a 32-ounce bat held with an end grip. Your position in the batter's box is also a consideration. With my size, strength, and arm length, I can cover the strike zone standing far from the plate. Smaller hitters may swing from a position closer to the plate and should choose a shorter, ''quicker'' bat.

Aluminum bats are automatically quicker. They have come into use at every level of play except professional ranks. I understand the economics of aluminum versus wood. Most leagues simply can't keep up with replacing broken bats. Wood bats have a weak spot and aluminum bats don't. The laws of physics also make aluminum bats a better choice. Their center of gravity is lower than that of wood bats, and the hitting surface is not tied to weight. Aluminum gives the ball a better ride than wood except when a batter using a wooden bat hits the ball directly off the ''sweet spot.'' Although the aluminum sweet spot is not as effective as that of the wooden bat, it is an inch or two larger.

So aluminum is here to stay, and players must use metal to stay competitive. Don't be fooled, however, by your hitting with aluminum if you aspire to play professionally. Those home runs and hits off inside pitches are just outs with a wooden bat. If you don't use a wood bat in games, at least use it in practice so that if you do get a chance to play in the minors, your transition will be smoother. One tip regarding aluminum bats: Before using one, strike the head with a hard object. It should ring. If it doesn't, the bat is dead and should be discarded or slipped into your opponent's bat bag.

In the last few years ceramic and graphite bats have come on the market. These new products carry a big price tag—up to $180 apiece. They sound more like a wood bat, but otherwise appear to offer no advantage over aluminum. In fact, the report is that the new bats sting the hands more.

Finally, don't be swayed in your choice of bat by color, a cosmetic treatment, or whose name is on the bat, a promotional device. Experiment with different bats in your effort to find just the right one. Even in the majors, players borrow bats from each other and switch around in their search. Make sure you are comfortable with your selection. The right bat is not only your first choice as a hitter, it may also prove to be one of your most important.

Balance

Concentrate on achieving a quick, easy, fluid, balanced swing. View the bat as an extension of your body. You must maintain control and balance to be a good hitter. Your bat must also be balanced. Shape is almost as important as weight or length in determining the balance of a bat. When I first broke into the majors there were still a few players using "bottle" bats, with handles almost as thick as their heads. Manny Sanguillen, a member of the Pirates' feared "Lumber Company," was one of them. The bats I see now are cone-shaped, tapering down from the head to the handle. The diameter of the handle is important in choosing the right bat. Players with smaller hands should use bats with thinner handles. You can adjust the thickness yourself by sanding or scraping the handle of a bat that otherwise suits you.

This may allow you to choose a bat with a larger barrel and hence more hitting surface. Just make sure that with your personal adjustments, you don't produce a bat that is top-heavy.

A recent development in bat design helps reduce the weight of the bat at a critical point, the end, without reducing hitting surface. Cupped or dimpled bats are a legal way to gain the advantage ascribed to "corked" or other doctored bats. The depression at the end of the bat can be two inches in diameter and up to one inch deep. Along with the shaved bat handle, this is the best way to decrease the weight and moment of inertia of the bat. While the advantage may be small, it is real, and a smart hitter will try to gain the edge in every little way.

Care

Once you have found the right bat, keep it in good condition. Bats should not be left on the ground to pick up moisture—and hence weight. If you do get a bat wet, dry it off and rub it with linseed or a similar oil. You can keep the surface of your bat hard by manually compressing or "boning" it. Use a piece of bone, a thick glass bottle, or another bat to rub the hitting section of your bat along the grain. If there are any little nicks or chips, sand them down to keep your bat smooth.

Pete Rose, who is one of the most serious students of the game I ever met, used to clean his bat with alcohol after every game. This allowed him to study his bat and see where the ball was making contact. He could adjust to the pitcher's speed in the middle of an at bat. If you use pine tar, alcohol is a good solvent to remove the tar from your bat and batting gloves. Another way to avoid tar building up or caking on your bat is to tape the bat in the area where you apply tar.

Store your bats vertically, big end down, in a dry place, especially in the off-season. At home I keep mine in the furnace room. Rod Carew used to store his in a box filled with sawdust to absorb any moisture. During the season, he'd keep them next to the sauna in the clubhouse. As you can see, a lot of us professionals, once we've chosen our weapons, keep them in shape.

THE GLOVE

A Personal Item

Although professional players can go through boxes of bats in a season, they tend to hang on to the same glove for years. You almost establish a personal relationship with this piece of equipment, and it's a rare player who can't tell you one or more stories about his glove. My first glove story happened years before I entered the majors. It was my sixth birthday, and I had asked for a glove as my big present. My mother splurged and bought a nice one for me, and waited expectantly as I took it out of the box and unwrapped it. She certainly didn't get the response she had anticipated. You see, I didn't know anything about baseball, but I knew I was right-handed, and here was this glove that only fit my *left* hand. I was most disappointed.

Your glove should be your most important piece of baseball gear. I have three of them, actually. One is eleven years old, another nine, and the youngster is three. My favorite, the old guy, looks like he's been on the losing end of a couple of wars. I take a lot of ragging from my teammates on how raggedy my mitt is, but I've got it broken in just the way I want it. It's as flexible as an omelet, and anything I can reach, it can snag.

The Varieties of Gloves

All gloves are strictly regulated by size according to the official rules of baseball. The largest glove allowed, as you might imagine, is the catcher's mitt. It can be up to 38 inches in circumference and $15\frac{1}{2}$ inches from top to bottom. When I first broke into the majors, some catchers still used the well-padded, doughnut-shaped glove with the round pocket. If the ball didn't hit right in the pocket, it often popped out. Receivers used to have to hold the ball in with their "meat" or throwing hand, and were referred to as "two-handed catchers." This kind of glove has passed from the scene, however, and the major glove companies don't even make them anymore.

Catchers today use a glove with a hinge, wing, or break in it that allows the mitt to fold over the ball. You can get gloves with either one or two hinges. The single-break glove allows your hand to fold at the base of the thumb. The double-break glove adds a hinge at the base of the little finger. I have never seen the double-break glove used in the major leagues, and suspect the manufacturers have simply produced one more option we don't need. Hinged gloves have allowed receivers to catch the ball with one hand and lessen the chance of injury, although with men on base catchers use a modified two-handed style to speed their throw in case the steal is on. Catchers also use a special mitt for knuckleball pitchers. The thing is about as big as a pizza pan, flexible as a tortilla, and must just barely skirt the maximum allowable circumference.

The first baseman is also allowed to wear a mitt larger than those of other fielders. It is hinged, and in this sense resembles the catcher's mitt. Other infielders and the pitcher use smaller gloves, although, compared to those of even a few years ago, today's models look huge. Pitchers like the big glove to better hide their pitches and give them maximum protection on hard drives back through the box. Some pitchers prefer closed webbing over open webbing because they believe the ball is better hidden. If you keep the ball deep in the pocket, this shouldn't be a factor, and closed-webbed mitts may prove a bit harder to break in properly. Make sure that the glove you choose is not so large as to throw off your delivery or your balance on defense.

Third basemen, having to field those smashes at the ''hot corner,'' also favor big gloves with tight fingers. It's a reflex position, and the more glove you can lay on the ball, the better your chances of at least knocking it down. Most shortstops and second basemen wear smaller gloves with shorter fingers and flatter pockets. (The second baseman generally has the smallest glove on the diamond.) They need the dexterity this kind of glove gives them to get the ball out quickly and turn those double plays. Even so, you still see middle infielders using these big fielding machines. Personal choice cannot be dictated. Whatever feels comfortable, whatever works, use it. Compared to the infielders, outfielders use outsized gloves with longer fingers pulled tight. We need to be able to reach and grab, sometimes over a fence or off the shoetops. Most players like an open webbing, which lets them watch the flight of the ball all the way into the glove.

Breaking In the Glove

Although all major leaguers use leather gloves, there are less expensive vinyl gloves on the market that certainly do the job for younger players. If you can afford leather, though, go for it. Buy your glove out of season and you will probably save enough to get leather or purchase a better model. Regardless of the glove you buy, take care to break it in properly. One key is patience. I've seen some players beat a pocket into their glove with the end of a bat. This method moves the padding around and gives you a pocket that does not conform to the ball.

Break in your glove by catching with it. If it's the only glove you have, you'll have to use it in game situations before it is fully ready. You can speed the process by oiling your glove, which softens the leather and helps to form the pocket. Saddle soap and shaving cream can also be used. When the glove is not in use, put a ball in the pocket and wrap a rubber band around the glove to keep the ball in place. If by chance you get your glove wet, do not try to speed dry it by placing it near a heat source. You can crack the leather and ruin a glove in this fashion. Younger players will have to replace their gloves as their hands grow larger; more mature players will be able to use their mitts for years if they take care of them.

SHOES

Protecting Your Wheels

In contrast to bats and gloves, where there are dominant manufacturers who make a clearly superior product, the shoe market is more up for grabs. To my mind there is no Louisville Slugger or Rawlings of shoes. Oh, sure, there are endorsements, and one Japanese manufacturer has secured the services of nine out of the ten best base stealers in baseball. But let's face it, that shoe can't make *you* a speed demon. The shoe market is a very competitive one, meaning that there are lots of good shoes out there and lots of model changes out there.

The right shoe will lessen your chance of injury and should be chosen carefully. Shoes that fit poorly or provide inadequate support can contribute to pulls and tears in the connective tissue of the lower leg and foot. Particularly if you have flat feet or fallen arches, you must make sure that your shoe compensates for the failing of your foot. If, when you stand up, there is no space between the floor and the inside middle portion of your foot, you have flat feet. Instead of the foot absorbing the pressures it should when you run, your lower leg/knee is forced to assume an additional burden, and this can lead to injury. Flat feet are easily corrected by inserting into your shoes a soft orthotic device that gives you an artificial arch. Some shoes have these devices built in, or you can buy them at a shoe store.

Durability is important to a shoe. Press down on the top of the heel of a shoe you are thinking of buying. A good shoe will have a sturdy heel counter and will resist the pressure. A cheaper shoe will bend easily. A supporting last within the shoe should run the entire length. A good shoe will feel comfortable right from the start. There might be some stiffness, but this is to be expected with a new shoe. As with your glove, a period of breaking in is necessary. Most shoes will stretch during the year, so to avoid loose shoes and the blisters that

often accompany them, many players choose athletic shoes smaller than their street shoes. I know that for young players, with fast-growing feet and considering the cost of shoes today, there is a temptation to buy shoes that are too large and to let the feet grow in to them. You'll play better in snug shoes, so resist the temptation.

EXTRAS

Batting Gloves, Tar, Sweatbands

Most major league players, including me, use batting gloves—and for good reason. For me, playing day in, day out, and taking batting practice seven months in a row, the glove is a welcome option. A glove protects my left hand from stinging, calluses, and blisters. (I never use a glove on my right hand). Also, I use resin, pine tar, and other sticky substances on my bat, and gloves keep my hands clean. In addition, batting gloves can protect your hands from cuts and scrapes when you are on the base paths and sliding into bases. Fielders often use a batting glove underneath their mitt to help reduce the sting of hard balls. Some batters use one glove, others two, and a few, like George Brett or George Hendrick, don't use them at all. For young hitters playing a limited schedule, batting gloves are mostly for show but probably don't do any harm. Sweatbands for the wrist are, on the other hand, a sensible accesory for players who sweat a lot.

The important thing is that your batting glove contribute to, or at least not detract from, your comfort and your grip. You should be able to retain your sensitivity to the bat and it should feel good in your

Showboats, hot-dogs and other "me only" players are often enthralled with the game's "extras."

hands. The same holds true for using the pine tar rag on your bat before going up to hit. I've seen some players use so much tar that I was amazed they could even drop the bat. My old batting coach and manager, Lou Piniella, went to the other extreme. He'd actually rub dirt on his hands and the bat to make them slippery. It worked just fine for "Sweet Lou" and it might work for you.

CHAPTER FOUR

Pitching

THE IDEAL PITCHER

Most people think of Dave Winfield as only an outfielder. Few realize that I was drafted out of high school by the Baltimore Orioles as a pitcher. I went to college instead and hung up some pretty impressive numbers hurling for Minnesota. When I eventually went into the majors, however, it was as an outfielder. I must confess a yearning to return to the mound—certainly not for more than a few innings, and only in a game that is already won or lost (in such a situation, the Yankees have even let *Rick Cerone* pitch!). Before I retire, I'd love to get out there to face some major league hitters.

With my extensive background—and dubious future—as a pitcher, I felt I had better turn the chapter on pitching over to a more experienced hand. I have seen thousands of pitchers since I began to play ball. Several in the major leagues taught me some hard lessons and made me a more formidable adversary: Bob Gibson, Tom Seaver, Jerry Koosman, Juan Marichal, Jim Lonborg, Steve Carlton, the Niekro brothers, Don Sutton, Mike Marshall, Jack Morris, John

Candelaria, Vida Blue, Ferguson Jenkins, J. R. Richard, Bert Blyleven, Rollie Fingers, and "The Goose." Of all the hurlers I could have asked to write the chapter on pitching, I asked an all-star who, in addition to his pitching, has shown me a lot about courage, kindness, and leadership.

Tommy John has been a major leaguer for more than twenty-five years. He's pitched longer than anyone else in the history of the game. He's seen it all, done it all, knows the game thoroughly, and can explain it clearly. He's versatile; I saw the Yankees use him as a starter, a long reliever, and a closer. He threw as broad a range of fine-tuned pitches as I've ever seen.

Tommy's not a pitcher out of the textbook; his is an unorthodox pitching style—mechanical and fluid at the same time. His unique delivery begins when he leans back and rocks. As he proceeds with the windup, release, and follow-through, it's almost like a stop-action camera has broken each stage of his pitch into segments.

Compared to many all-stars in the game today, TJ is not a "natural" athlete. He made himself into an all-star pitcher, and worked hard to stay one. He was flexible

37

Tommy John was one of the best control pitchers I've seen. He could operate on hitters like a surgeon.

and adaptable. Do you know of any other ballplayer who didn't start weight training until after he was forty? Tommy was a good team man who brightened up the clubhouse and remained steady through the most incredible personal disasters. After a "career-ending" injury to his pitching arm and an operation to rebuild it, he astounded the medical and sports worlds by coming back to pitch his best baseball. An amazing story, an amazing man, and my all-star pitcher.

BEFORE THE FIRST PITCH

The Four C's of Pitching

Years ago, the grand old man of baseball, Connie Mack, estimated that pitching constituted 70 percent of the game. Observers since then have revised that figure, usually upward. While I am reluctant to assign a precise value to a process that so combines probability and chance, we should be able to agree that the pitcher enjoys a level of influence not found in other sports. It is, for instance, possible to pitch a "perfect game." In contrast with other sports, the defense begins with control of the ball. Only when the pitcher or his teammates fail is that control temporarily relinquished. To a large extent, the game is literally and figuratively in the pitcher's hands.

Control is the first and foremost of the four C's that characterize a successful pitcher. In order to control the game, he must control the hitter, which means controlling the ball, and that results from the pitcher's ability to control his own mind and body. If the pitcher allows the ups and downs of the game to get to him, if he gets angry when he gives up a hit and continues to dwell on his mistake or otherwise fails to hold his emotions in check, he is out of control, and his game will suffer.

Control as it relates to the pitched ball has never been better defined than by Casey Stengel. He said that the pitcher should aim to put the ball "as close to the plate and as far from the bat as possible." To do this on a regular basis requires mastery of pitching mechanics and great control of the body.

Confidence is also an essential ingredient of pitching. If you don't believe you can do the job, you probably won't. The positive can-do attitude is more important for the pitcher than for other players simply because it must be brought into play more often. A pitcher cannot be constrained by the fear of failure. Confidence, poise, and even grace under pressure will keep the pitcher up when the hitters momentarily have him down. In an otherwise evenly matched competition, confidence can give you the edge.

Consistency is necessary to be an effective pitcher. Good pitchers get "into the groove." Their mechanics are sound, their movements are coordinated, and they establish a consistent rhythm and timing. In terms of mechanics, they do not have to think about what they are doing. They do it the same way and they can count on the results.

Concentration is the last of the four C's, but certainly not the least. No other person on the field is required to concentrate as hard or as frequently as the pitcher. The fielder making a play or the batter about to swing are also studies in concentration, but they are reacting in a split second and instincts play a greater role than with the pitcher, who has more time to focus his mental energies. In addition, the hitter comes to the plate four times a game or so and some fielders may touch the ball only a few times in a game. The pitcher needs to summon his powers of concentration on every pitch.

Getting and Staying in Shape

My off-season throwing has a short season. I don't begin throwing until the first of the year, and even then I start slowly and build gradually to spring training. During the season, there are no exercises that I use specifically for my arm. Pitching in regular rotation is exercise enough. Of course, I throw between starts to stay loose and warm up before games I pitch. How long I warm up depends on how loose my arm is to begin with and the temperature. Muscles loosen easier in warm weather. I gradually increase my distance and tempo as I begin to work up a sweat. Only then do I start to throw hard and add breaking pitches. Throw all the pitches you intend to use in the game during your warm-up

and throw some of your pitches from the stretch. Different pitches use different parts of the arm, and you want everything to be ready.

I keep to a regular year-round fitness and conditioning program. If your total body is not in shape, you and your arm will wear down as the innings pile up. Your legs are almost as important as your arm, hence the importance of running to build strength and stamina. In season, run on your off days. Your ability to pitch well, particularly in the late innings, is largely dependent on your legs and your stamina. Every pitch you make, you'll lift and land on one leg and drive off the other. To improve your wind, get into the habit of sprinting regularly. This will pay far greater dividends than jogging. Come early to a ball game and you will see the pitchers doing wind sprints in the outfield. Generally, major leaguers sprint about seventy-five yards fifteen times or so on off days. The day before they pitch, they'll do no more than ten, and on game day none.

Regular calisthenics are also part of the pitcher's regimen. Straight-leg and bent-leg lifts, deep knee bends, leg and groin stretches, and crossovers help your lower body. Windmills, sit-ups, and trunk twisters are good for keeping your upper body in shape. Tom Seaver recommends arm exercises with three-to-five-pound weights, and Steve Carlton practices the martial arts. If you work with weights, I strongly advise that you do so only under the direction of an experienced trainer. You can do real damage to your arm if you don't know what you're doing. Choose your own methods and vary them to reduce boredom, but accept that pitching is hard work—and not just when you're on the mound.

The important thing to remember when

Right-hander with no one on base.

considering how to prevent and heal injuries to the arm is that pitching is an unnatural motion. It's unusual for the arm *not* to get injured. And the only cure for most arm injuries is to stop pitching. The two essential ingredients of forestalling injuries are to develop as fluid and easy a motion as possible and to stay in shape.

Windup Stance

There is no such thing as *the* correct way to stand as your prepare to deliver the pitch. Pitchers' stances vary almost as much as those of hitters and probably for the same reason. Whatever you find comfortable, whatever works, use it. Comfort is the key. You should be relaxed as you take the sign and begin your windup. It really doesn't matter whether you have one foot or two on the rubber (you must, of course, have your pivot foot touching the rubber). Most pitchers place their striding foot in back of the rubber and their pivot foot so at least the front cleat is in the dirt. The feet are generally six to twelve inches apart and the

pitching hand comfortably at the side. Face the plate squarely and you will be able to put more into your pivot. To achieve the best angle on the pitch, left-handers should place their pivot foot toward the left end of the rubber and right-handers toward the right end. To make the pivot easier, this foot is generally angled to the side of the field from which you throw.

Stretch Position

With runners on base you must alter your stance and throw from the set or stretch position. Instead of facing the plate, you are now sideways to it, your front shoulder aligned with the plate. Your rear foot is on the rubber or resting against its front edge, and your other foot is in front of it. From this position, the left-hander can look directly at the first-base runner; and the right-hander, by turning his head and shoulder slightly, can see both first and home. Simply closing the hands from their resting position or stretching the arms above the head and then bringing them to rest at the belt (or chest or straight in front) substitutes for a full windup. I don't recommend bringing the hands to rest below the belt. Remember that in this situation you need to be quick and you should always be striving for a delivery that conserves energy.

Some pitchers, mostly relievers, actually pitch from the stretch all the time. The mechanics of the pitch are similar to those you would use with a windup except that there is less of a kick and pivot and more of a push-off. Your aim is to shorten your motions a bit and speed them up without rushing or destroying your rhythm. Keep in mind your primary object: to get the *batter* out. The runner is going to try to distract you, break your concentration, and upset

Right-hander with men on base.

your rhythm. The more successful the runner is in accomplishing these goals, the more successful the batter will become.

Taking the Sign

As they await the sign from the catcher, most pitchers already have their weight on their striding foot. Some pitchers even bend

Left-hander with men on base.

down to take the sign, automatically transferring their weight to their front foot. Your pivot foot or both feet must be touching the rubber as you take the sign. Hide the ball in your glove or behind your back at this time. The less the batter sees of the ball, the better off you are. You may choose to shake off one or more signs, either to get to the pitch you want or just to give the batter more time to think.

THE DELIVERY

Basic Types

The four methods of delivering the ball to the plate are overhand, three-quarters, sidearm, and submarine or underhand. Most major leaguers throw three-quarters, fewer sidearm, even fewer overhand, and only a couple underhand.

The overhand pitch tends to be straighter with less motion than other pitches. It's a hard pitch to throw, and when overhand pitchers tire they have an even greater tendency than other hurlers to hang the ball high in the strike zone, where hitters like to see it. Certain pitches, such as the slider, are hard to throw from this delivery.

The three-quarters delivery, which I use, is the most frequently seen, lends itself to a larger variety of pitches, and allows the pitcher to impart more movement to the ball. Generally, three-quarters pitchers can also keep the ball down low, forcing the batter to hit more grounders. It's the delivery that puts the least strain on the arm.

Sidearm pitchers are hard to hit if they come at the batter from the same side of the plate the batter is standing on. The ball seems to come from behind the batter and is harder to see. Some batters' initial reaction is to bail out for safety's sake. On the other hand, many hitters like facing sidearmers who pitch from the opposite side of the plate. The pitch is on a single plane, it's flat, and when it breaks it goes only one direction. The pitches are easier to anticipate and adjust to.

Pitchers who use the submarine delivery are rarities. Dan Quisenberry and Kent Tekulve are about the only ones who practiced this delivery in the majors recently. Submarine pitches can break on several planes. They are deceptive, lively, and mighty hard to control. Batters are probably pretty happy that very few pitchers master the technique.

Whatever delivery you choose, and some pitchers use more than one, the motions you use to get there, the point of release, and your follow-through should be about the same. You don't want to signal the batter what's coming by changing the way you throw.

The Windup

Keep in mind the reason for the windup and it should be easier to achieve an efficient one. To put full force behind the ball, you want to shift your weight backward. It's like the batter's starter mechanism or the golfer's backswing. You're gathering momentum. You actually begin this rocking motion by taking a short step back or to the side (but fully behind the rubber) with the striding foot. As your weight begins to go back, you have already reached into the glove and gripped the ball. By the time the shift is complete, your hands and arms have moved toward the plate and upward to a position as low as your shoulder or as high as above your head (or even behind your head, which I prefer). Make sure your movements do not block your view,

Get into your rhythm and gain momentum with a balanced windup.

because your eyes should be focused on the target during this time.

Most pitchers also use variations on the standard windup. The no-pump windup begins with the hands together at the waist or higher. The hands go up as the striding foot goes back, but the movements are shorter and the delivery is more compact. Very few major leaguers use the full pumping action, where the arms begin at the sides and go back before they come forward, which was standard procedure when I broke into baseball in 1963. Some pitchers do not bring their hands above their heads at all, which may be useful with men on base, although it is easier for the batter to follow the ball. Others sometimes use a double pump whereby the hands go up, drop down, and go up again as the pitcher prepares to deliver the ball. This move is helpful in breaking the hitter's concentration and throwing off his timing.

Pivot and Kick

By the time your hands start down, you have already shifted your weight to the pivot leg, which is bent slightly for greater flexibility and balance. You have begun to lift your striding foot and bring it forward. It is essential that you not delay bringing the hands down, as this will throw off the timing of everything to follow. Get them up and bring them down. You have begun to pivot on the ball of your foot, which will turn until it is perpendicular to the rubber. At about the time your hands reach belt level, your striding leg will have crossed your body and be lifted to the point where the thigh is approximately parallel to the ground. How you raise your knee determines what kind of hip action you achieve. The leg leads the rest of your body around until your hips and shoulders are cocked with the front shoulder closed to the hitter. If you have rotated correctly, the hitter should have a good view of your rear pocket and at least a partial view of the numbers on your back. If the hitter can read your numbers clearly, you have pivoted too far. Overhand pitchers will not be able to pivot as far to the rear as those using other deliveries.

Pitchers lift their knees or kick their legs to different heights. Juan Marichal had the highest kick of any pitcher I have seen. Sometimes young players trying to imitate professionals will kick high. Perhaps they also think that this will give them more power. It won't, and an easy test for determining the highest you should kick is whether you can balance and hold the position once you reach it. The high kick can deceive or bother the hitter and allow the pitcher more arc to his arm, but the key here is to stay balanced and to keep your weight back. If the body moves forward prematurely, your delivery will be rushed, you will not be able to explode into your push-off and forward thrust, and your power and control will suffer.

It is during this sequence of movements that you will take the ball from the glove and "break" your hands. As with so many other elements of pitching, there is no correct spot for this to happen. Some pitchers do it above their head and others below their belt. I recommend breaking in the middle of the body. Regardless of what height you choose, the action should occur roughly above the knee of your pivot leg.

Begin the delivery by raising your front leg, bending your back leg, and starting to turn your body.

Continue your pivot, take the ball from the glove, and begin to move your striding foot forward.

The one absolute of breaking your hands is to do it quickly. Don't dawdle. Get your arm into the throwing position quickly. When you take the ball from the glove, your palm should be facing down and your wrist bent forward slightly. Once your hands break, your glove hand will not begin to move forward until your throwing arm reaches the point from which it moves forward. Some pitchers almost touch the mound with the ball, while others don't bring it below their waist.

You begin to open your hips, your striding foot lands, and you lower your body as you drive off your back foot.

Thrust and Stride

As with the rotation backward, the striding leg, now coming forward, leads the action as you begin to open your body and prepare for the stride. Do not kick out with your leg or you will misdirect your movement and slow down arm action. You should bend your pivot leg even more at this time and begin to lower your body into a better position to thrust forward. This is the beginning of the move known as "drop and drive." There are pitchers who drop so low that the knee of their pivot leg scrapes the mound (Tom Seaver was most famous for his dirty pant leg, now it's Mark Gubicza). Most pitchers stay higher and achieve a greater angle to the ball's trajectory. You push off the rubber hard with your hips and shoulders still in a closed position. To achieve maximum force you will rapidly open first the hips and then, as your hand approaches the point of release, your shoulders. This movement is explosive and culminates in your entire body's getting behind the pitch.

The toe of your striding foot is pointing down, and by the time the stride is complete your foot is pointing toward the batter. It has landed close to an imaginary line between your pivot foot and home plate. If you do not come close enough to the line, you will lose power as your hips and shoulders open up too early and at the wrong angle. If you go too far over the line, you will lock your hips and be forced to throw across your body.

You have touched down on the ball of your foot, although the heel will not be far behind. If you land on your heel, you will tend to straighten your leg, which must be avoided. It is essential that your front leg be bent so that it can absorb the force of your thrust and stride, accommodate the rest of your body, and facilitate a smooth follow-through. As your body comes forward, your bent striding leg will almost form an L. The more flex there is to your lower body, the less jar and strain there will be to your upper body. Your pivot foot, push-off completed, will now be three to six inches in front of the rubber.

The length of your stride depends on your size, physique, and what is comfortable for you. Many young hurlers tend to overstride, thinking this adds power to the pitch. Correctly executed, the stride has nothing to do with power, although you will reduce your power by striding too far or not far enough. What is important is that you stride to the same point on every pitch. If your stride varies, there is no way your control will be consistent.

Arm Movement and Release

Once your striding foot has been planted, you have established the firm base that allows full force to be put into the pitch. Your throwing hand has reached far behind you and, as if you were preparing to cast a fishing rod, you have flicked your wrist backward. As the ball comes forward, your glove hand comes forward palm up. This helps you keep your front shoulder closed until just before your release, when you open it forcefully. Keep the glove hand above your front arm elbow so that your front shoulder will be down and your rear shoulder up as it should be for you to get on top of the ball.

In moving down, back, up, and over, your throwing arm is tracing as wide an arc as you can manage easily. The speed of the pitch increases with the width of the arc, but you should aim for as smooth a motion as possible. The greatest mechanical advantage occurs with the greatest arm angle downward. Hence, the farther away from the head the pitcher's hand is when he releases the ball, the less advantage he will have. Except for sidearmers, the elbow should be at or above shoulder level. The forearm should be kept parallel to the ground as the elbow leads the rest of the arm into action. As you prepare to release the ball, your fingers are on top of the ball, ready to drive it downward toward the strike zone.

The moment of release requires the greatest force and concentration of any stage of delivery. Despite this degree of intensity, the arm, wrist, and hand must be free of tension and relaxed to allow the maximum snap to be imparted to the ball. The arm is acting like a whip at this point, and if it isn't loose the action will be constrained. The ball is released off the index and middle fingers and spun downward by the sharp action of the wrist. Although the ball is released above the head, the pitcher should envision releasing the ball well out

Stride completed, you continue to thrust forward and, elbow high, accelerate your arm.

With your head over your striding leg and your arm fully extended, you release the ball.

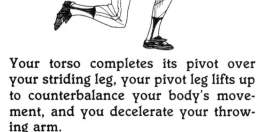

After release, your palm rotates away from your body, thumb down, your pivot foot leaves the rubber, and your throwing arm leads your torso forward over the striding leg.

Your torso completes its pivot over your striding leg, your pivot leg lifts up to counterbalance your body's movement, and you decelerate your throwing arm.

in front of his body and low. This will facilitate the downward trajectory of the ball that effective pitchers strive for. You must achieve a consistent point of release or control will always elude you.

The Follow-through

Just as a batter must follow through with the swing after he has hit the ball if he wants to drive it, the pitcher must follow through with the delivery after he has released the ball to impart maximum power to the pitch. Correct follow-through also assists your control and puts you in a good fielding position. Your weight has shifted to your striding foot, while your pivot foot continues to come forward, heel up, forcing the hip to explode toward the plate and help drive the pitch. At the end of its motion, the pivot foot will have swung around until it is parallel or slightly in front of the striding foot, leaving you square to the plate, knees bent, on the balls of your feet, and ready to handle anything hit in your direction. Some pitchers have such an explosive follow-through that they almost fall

off the mound. Bob Gibson used to end up off balance and on one leg like a crane striding into a pool of water. These hurlers must make an adjustment after they land to get into good fielding position or depend solely on quick reflexes.

Your glove arm continues its descent (begun before release) diagonally across your body. Lead with your elbow and your front shoulder will lower while your throwing shoulder rises, helping you to direct the pitch downward. Imagine trying to drive your elbow into someone standing behind you and you won't be far off. Some pitchers bring the glove hand in toward the body at this time and simply rotate it outward to get it up for fielding. Your throwing arm, meanwhile, follows a similar diagonal path across your body, ending on the other side of your striding leg at about knee level. It's almost as if your two hands are connected and the glove hand helps to pull the throwing hand down. Finishing the whiplike movement of your throwing arm with a smooth sweep will cut down on the arm strain that is an inevitable consequence of pitching. Indeed, if you master the mechanics of pitching and achieve a consistently easy delivery, you will minimize the chance of injuring yourself.

PITCHING FLAWS AND HOW TO CORRECT THEM

Rushing and Overthrowing

The most common flaw affecting pitchers at every level of play is rushing the pitch. Basically what happens is that the weight shift forward occurs prematurely, and the upper body moves forward ahead of the arm, which tries to catch up, rushing the throw. An eagerness to get the ball to the plate quickly, an early stride, straight legs, and delay in getting the arm back, down, and up can all contribute to rushing. The pitcher cannot get on top of the ball and ends up throwing with just the arm and not the rest of the body. The result is loss

If your body leads your arm into the throw, the pitch will be rushed and may quicken your departure.

of control and power, a shorter arm arc, and more frequent injuries. Pitches will generally be high and breaking balls flat.

Overthrowing is similar to rushing in that there is too much arm movement and not enough body behind the pitch. Tense arm muscles are often involved in this flaw.

Correction Coordinating the upper and lower parts of your body is the key here. Concentrate on your first balance point, when your weight is on your pivot foot and your striding leg is at the apex. Your throwing arm should already be up and coming forward while your weight is still back. And don't be afraid to talk to yourself. Remind yourself, silently or out loud, to slow down and relax.

Short Arming

When the pitcher fails to extend his throwing arm fully his arm movement is restricted and takes a shorter path to the release point. The advantage of a long arc with its increased power and greater downward angle is lost. Often short armers are also rushers.

Correction Follow the correction for rushing. Also make sure your stance is correct and you are not overrotating.

Arm Hooking

Hooking the throwing arm is similar to having a hitch in your swing: extra movement at a critical moment throws off your timing. Hooking occurs after the hands break, when the throwing arm goes down and sideways instead of down and back. Because the arm takes longer to get to the release point, the pitcher may drop his elbow and rush the pitch.

Correction Bring the throwing arm straight down and back toward second base after you break your hands. If this proves difficult, you may wish to delay slightly your move forward so that your arm and body will be synchronized by the time the ball is released.

Throwing Across the Body

When the pitcher strides too far across his body before planting his foot, he is forced to overcome the resistance of his lower body to deliver the pitch. This creates extraordinary strain on the arm and shoulder and has ended the careers of several pitchers.

Correction Remember that imaginary line between your pivot foot and home plate. Don't cross it. Draw a line in the dirt or place a batting glove or rosin bag beyond which you should not stride.

Overstriding

When you stride too far you tend to land on your heel, your leg is straight instead of bent, your upper body is too upright, and you cannot complete the delivery with the proper arm and shoulder action.

Correction   As with striding too far across the body, place a marker or draw a line in the dirt beyond which you do not step. It may help to start back by increments from where you overstride to where you should land. Concentrate on landing on your toes.

THE PITCHES

The Elements of the Pitch

Every pitch, regardless of type, is characterized by three elements: placement, movement, and speed. The most important of these is placement, or control. If you cannot get the ball over the plate, a fast lively pitch will do you little good. But control is more than the ability to pitch strikes; sometimes you can be "wild in the strike zone." Control means being able to put the ball where you want to, sometimes out of the strike zone. Without control you will not be able to deceive the batter or work him by selecting different pitches and locations. Liveliness is the next most im-

Overstriding can be embarassing.

portant element. A flat pitch that does not move is an invitation to the hitter to drive the ball. A pitcher who masters control and movement can go far, even in the major leagues, without velocity. A pitcher who has speed but nothing else is usually destined to fail.

Having said this, let me add that the most important pitch in the game is the fastball. You could even say that it is also the second most important pitch. Next comes the change-up, but your off-speed pitches cannot work unless you can set them up with the fastball. Everything works off the fastball, and you cannot teach a player how to pitch one. You either have it or you don't. Control and movement can be taught, velocity can't. Through improved mechanics, a pitcher might increase his speed, but only slightly.

I'm not known for my fastball, and when I throw it, it is not an overpowering one, but it is the pitch I go to 80 percent to 90 percent of the time. It makes my money pitches, such as the sinker, effective. The other side of the coin is that my off-speed pitches make my fastball more effective. I hope you understand by this time that the ability to change speeds is at the heart of pitching.

Control and movement are products of good mechanics and can be achieved through practice. So can a wide repertoire of pitches. There are nine basic pitches in baseball and a number of variations. You need a minimum of two pitches to be effective at all but the lowest levels of play. These pitches should break down and to each side. Beginning in high school, pitchers can usually throw the fastball, curveball, and change-up. College and professional players generally master one or more other pitches. Relievers often use fewer

pitches—say, just a fastball and curve—and a rare one will throw just one kind of pitch if he doesn't expect to see any of the hitters more than once. Novice players can get by with a single pitch: the fastball. Pitching the fastball is also the best way to stretch and strengthen a young arm, so beginning players should concentrate on pitching this one ball well.

What follows are directions on how to hold the ball, and descriptions of baseball's nine basic pitches and the variations of grip, spin, release, and wrist action that are necessary to produce them.

Coming to Grips

There are only two basic ways to hold the ball: with your fingers across the seams or parallel to the seams. Holding the ball across the seams where they are narrowest produces a two-seam rotation. If you grasp the ball across the seams where they are widest, your ball will have a four-seam rotation and more "bite" as it spins. Most curves and fastballs are thrown from this grip, and it seems to be preferred by power pitchers. Although control is the result of many factors, it is thought that the cross-seam grip enhances control. This is why I recommend that young pitchers grip the ball across the seams.

A pitcher gripping the ball with the seams can do so in two ways: so that your fingers either touch a seam or not. The placement of your fingers determines whether your thumb will be in contact with a seam. Generally, throwing with the seams produces more pronounced movement.

I hope by starting my discussion of grip with seams that I have not exaggerated their importance. A very few pitchers, most notably Mickey Lolich, don't use the seams at all. And different pitchers, through the process of trial and error, throw the same pitch in very different ways. Sometimes the same pitcher will throw the same pitch with or across the seams. You will find that other aspects of the grip are more important, but focusing on the seams gives you something to hang on to in the beginning.

With the exception of the change-up and knuckler, you should hold the ball with the tips of your fingers, which are comfortably flexed. Except for the forkball, you do not want your fingers to be widely separated. Both the index and middle fingers serve as pressure points and play prominent roles in the grip and release. The index finger is usually the stronger of the two. Because the middle finger is longer, pitches are usually released off this finger. The thumb is also a pressure point and is important in imparting spin. How you grip the ball is the most important factor in how you release it.

While a degree of tightness is essential to give a tight spin to the ball, you must be careful not to hold the ball too tightly. A tight grip moves right up your arm and produces tension in the rest of your body. The tighter your grip, for instance, the stiffer your wrist, and for most pitches you need great flexibility. At least from when you first grasp the ball to when you are bringing the ball forward, your grip should be loose enough so that a hard tap would dislodge the ball. Just as the batter's grip on the bat increases in the course of his swing, the pitcher's grip tightens as he approaches release. Don't start with a tight grip. Maybe this little mind game will help: pretend that what you are holding in your hand is not a ball but an egg. This should help you achieve the right amount of pressure.

Fastball

Here's where it all begins, with what is sometimes called the "king of pitches." Other names applied to this pitch are more descriptive. "Pill," "aspirin tablet," or "BB" indicates the apparent size of the ball. "Heat," "heater," "smoke," "hummer," "gas," and "high octane" all speak to the velocity. Perhaps the funniest term for the pitch is "radio ball" (because the batter hears it, but doesn't see it).

A good fastball does not have to have overpowering speed. How the ball moves, in fact, is far more important. If all the ball has is speed, the hitter can time or "groove" his swing to the fastball; he can "turn his dial up" and catch up to your fastball. So the first thing to learn about the pitch is how to make it move and the second is how to pitch it at different speeds. You should have a fast fastball and a faster one. To pitch a fastball, you can grip either across or with the seams.

Before going any further in my explanation of the fastball, I would like to depart from the vast majority of pitchers, coaches, and commentators and debunk a myth. There is no such thing as a rising fastball! In fact, there is no way *any* pitch thrown by a human can defy gravity and rise. I know that just about every guide to the game in general and pitching in particular refers to the rising or "riding" fastball, but the pitch is a physical impossibility. Some writers even provide a pseudoscientific explanation for the phenomenon by referring to Bernoulli's Principle. They claim that the spin and centrifugal force of the ball is sufficient to overcome air pressure and gravitational force. The physical facts simply don't mesh with the theory. Even a pitch from a sidearm hurler pitching high

Fastball

in the strike zone will come down, and the farther it goes the more it drops. The greatest spin that a human can impart to the ball is 1,600 revolutions per minute. This means that the maximum that a ball could rotate on its way to the plate is about a dozen times. All pitches drop on their way to the plate, regardless of spin. Some simply drop more than others. You can make a ball move to either side, but not up. The rising fastball is an illusion created by the hitter's expectations, the relativity of perception, and a skillful pitcher.

Having clarified the true nature of the "rising" fastball, let me share with you how to pitch so that the ball doesn't drop as much as with other pitches. If you want the ball to stay high, grip it across the seams where they are widest. This way, all four seams will "bite" the air. Your thumb is underneath the ball, crossing the bottom seam, and your ring and little fingers are curled on the side of the ball. If your index and middle fingers are touching, it is easier for the pitch to slide from your grasp and cause control problems. If they are too far apart, your wrist might lock and limit the necessary wrist action. I recommend these fingers be no more than a half inch apart.

Grip the ball with your fingertips, well out from the hand. You should be able to

move a finger easily in and out of the space between the ball and your palm. The ball is released in front of the body off your first two fingertips and given a backward rotation with a sharp snap of the wrist. Experiment with your pressure points. Because the middle finger is longer and thus is the last to leave the ball, you may find that this is the natural one to exert more pressure as is required for this pitch. Delivered by a righty, the cross-seam fastball moves to the right, hence in to right-handed batters and away from lefties.

Sinker

The sinking fastball is my favorite pitch. Properly thrown, it is almost impossible for the batter to hit anywhere but on the ground. The ball breaks low and drops "off the table," as they say. One night in 1987, when my sinker was really cooking, I kept the infield busy gobbling up grounders and Don Mattingly set a major league record for putouts with 22. Pitchers frequently go to this pitch when they need a groundout or a double play.

The usual way to grip the sinker is along the two narrow seams, although you can also grasp the ball across the narrow seams. This variation will give more sideways motion to the ball. There is less velocity and spin with a sinker than with a riser because the ball is released not with a snap of the wrist but with a turn of the arm. The index finger applies the greatest pressure and then the thumb, with the middle finger figuring little in the action of the pitch.

Just prior to release (well in front of the body), the ball is rotated inward and downward so that the back of the hand faces the pitcher. While the wrist does turn, let me emphasize that the action originates be-

Sinker

cause the forefinger is applying pressure. The pitch is sometimes called the "turn-over fastball" because the pitch turns over the thumb as it is released. It is best to deliver the sinker from a three-quarters delivery or lower because the wrist is in an ideal position to turn. Most pitchers also deliver the sinker from a lower position than other pitches. A bit more bend in the pivot knee causes the body to lower and then drive forward in what is called the "drop and go" movement.

Other Fastballs

By experimenting with different grips, pressure points, wrist actions, and deliveries, you can discover fastballs that will run, tail, and sail. I encourage you to try different kinds to find out what works best for you. I recommend against incorporating different fastballs with different grips into your repertoire unless you are an experienced pitcher with good control. If you have to change deliveries and throw from different positions, you will get out of sync, out of your groove, and your control will suffer. There is tremendous value to consistency in a pitcher. With all the things you must think about on the mound and

with the degree of concentration that is required, it helps to have certain aspects of your game be automatic.

Curveball

The curveball is the pitch that separates the sheep from the goats whether they are pitchers or hitters. If you can't throw one or hit one, advanced levels of play are probably not for you. The pitch is often called the "deuce" (the catcher calls for it with two fingers), the "hook," or the "jug," (like in jug handle), and less often the "yakker" or "yellow hammer" (alluding to the dipping flight of a bird). For some reason, it's also called an "Uncle Charlie."

Most people do not understand the trajectory of the curveball on its way to the plate. For starters, there is very little horizontal movement to the pitch. The ball moves mostly downward, and as it approaches the plate, the ball appears to break more sharply. In fact, the arc of the ball is a smooth, constant one from the moment it leaves the pitcher's hand, but because of increased gravitational force, the ball travels faster at the end of its flight. The illusion of the late break is enhanced by the fact that the batter views the ball from an angle that makes it hard to discern the gradual arc.

There are several ways to grip the curve. Perhaps the most common method in the big leagues is similar to the basic fastball grip with the fingers across the seams at their widest part. This gives the ball four seams to bite with and a tighter spin. The ball is farther back in the hand than the fastball, but you must be careful not to choke it or you will not be able to give it the necessary spin. You simply use more

Curveball

of the surface of your fingers. You throw the curve with topspin so that the ball rotates toward the plate, in contrast with the backspin of a fastball. Your middle finger applies most of the pressure to the pitch, with the index finger resting more loosely on the ball. The thumb helps spin the ball by flipping up upon release. Your ring and little fingers should be curled into the palm so as to not impede the spin.

Good wrist action is essential to the curve. The wrist is cocked as it comes forward and then rotates inward. As your hand passes your head, your palm and the ball should be facing you. Your wrist will be twisted so that, with your forearm, it forms an L. Just prior to release your wrist will have turned completely over and snapped down, and you release the ball over the index finger. You pull down on the ball much like the action of pulling down a window shade sharply. If you have released the ball correctly, the back of your hand will face the batter. Your elbow must be high or you will not be able to pull the pitch down and direct the ball on a downward plane. To get a better idea of the motion, extend your glove hand in front of you and

bring your pitching hand into it with a karate chop.

If your arm action quits upon release and you do not have good follow-through, you may produce the notorious "hanging" curve and give some kid in the bleachers a souvenir to take home. Pitch your curve low. Although Nolan Ryan has a 90-miles-per-hour curveball, the velocity of other pitchers' curves is slower. You may be able to get away with a slower ball low, but up high, watch out. To make sure you have the proper wrist action, don't try to throw the curve too hard.

A correctly thrown curveball does not strain the arm, but I think too many youngsters try to throw this ball too soon and without good instruction. I certainly don't recommend that young hurlers throw this pitch until they are at least fourteen, and then only under the guidance of a knowledgeable coach, and not hard to begin with. Don't risk severe arm problems to acquire a pitch you won't need until later in your career. When you do begin to throw the curve, make sure you're warmed up and start off slowly.

Slider

The term "nickel curve" is sometimes used to describe the slider, but I feel this is a misnomer because it is a big money pitch for many hurlers in the majors today. "Fast curve" or "hard curve" is more accurate. In contrast to the curve, the harder it's thrown the better it works. The pitch looks like a fastball as it approaches the hitter and then appears to break at the last moment. The pitch breaks sideways, and while it doesn't move as much as a curve, its movement is faster and sharper. It is

Slider

easier to learn and to control than the curve, and harder for the hitter to spot.

The grip resembles that of the fastball or curve, with the index and middle fingers across the two widest seams. The ball is held farther out on the fingers than the curve, but not as far as the fastball. Your fingers should be off-center toward the outside of the ball, but still on top of the ball. The thumb and middle finger apply the pressure. Some pitchers raise the forefinger slightly to help achieve the off-center grip and correct pressure.

Coaches frequently compare throwing a slider to the motion of passing a football. There are similarities. You want to impart a tight spiral spin to the ball, and you may pull down the elbow more than you do with other pitches. What you should not do is throw the ball with a stiff wrist or you will put considerable strain on your elbow. At release, the degree that the wrist is turned in delivering the slider is approximately between that of a curve (palm toward pitcher) and a fastball (palm toward batter). Use a loose wrist and a fastball snap to deliver the ball. To help get the spin, pretend you are slicing through the ball with your middle finger upon release. Or you may think of the motion as if you were turning a

doorknob. Just don't open the door too soon. Keep your fingers on top of the ball until the very end.

Change-up

There are more ways to throw the change-of-pace than any other pitch, and all of them can be devastating against a hitter who is expecting a fastball. The biggest problem about the pitch is overcoming the reluctance of some pitchers to throw it. They fear that serving up a soft toss will just allow the hitter to launch a rocket, and if a batter is anticipating a change-up and gets one, he *can* drive it a country mile. The trick is to get the batter thinking fastball, and an essential part of the deception is to throw the ball with exactly the same motion as you would a fastball. You cannot tip off the hitter by exaggerating your windup, for instance, or slowing down your arm speed. Altering your grip and release are the principal means of slowing the ball down.

Once you have developed the pitch and gained the necessary confidence to throw it, the advantages are several. You've expanded the potential of your baseball career dramatically. No pitch is as effective in throwing off the batter's timing. Getting the batter out is your main object, but the best way to reach that goal is by disrupting his timing. The fastball makes the change-up work, but the change-up helps to establish your fastball as an effective pitch. Not only will it make your heater look faster, but if the batter has to worry about off-speed stuff he's got one more thing to think about at the plate. The change-up also gives you an option on those days when your fastball might not be working for you. Lastly, the change-up allows the pitcher to conserve

Change-up

energy. You put less on the ball; you can usually get out of situations that can tire a hurler, such as the batter's fouling off pitch after pitch; you throw fewer pitches and stay fresher.

Because there are so many different grips for this pitch, experimentation is essential, followed by practice. Some pitchers practice their change-up like some batters practice the bunt: indifferently or not at all. A grip I recommend that you start with is the three-finger delivery. The ball is held farther back in the hand than other pitches, with the first three fingers on top of the ball and across the seams at their widest. Even the pinky is in contact with the ball, helping to slow it down. In another variation, the index finger can be curled around the side of the ball until it connects with the thumb, forming a circle and reducing the pressure it can exert on the pitch. Another way of achieving this effect is to lift your fingertips from the ball, holding it with the thumb and middle joints of your fingers.

Your release also helps to deaden the ball. There is no snap to the wrist, which should remain relatively stiff. You bring the wrist straight down, heel first, like lowering a window shade. It might help you to think your wrist is going to reach the ground. Aiming the ball at the plate may also help you keep the ball low, as will keeping the arm and elbow high. Some pitchers alter their lower body action to slow the pitch. They do not push off the rubber as aggressively, and they shorten their stride. They "dead leg" their pivot foot, dragging it behind them and slowing their weight shift forward.

Palmball

Several major leaguers go to the palmball when they change pace. The ball is held deep in the palm and gripped with all the fingers to maximize drag. The joints of the thumb and ring finger are the pressure points. As with other change-ups, the fingertips do not figure in the action. You may or may not have to physically lift them from the ball. Some pitchers straighten out their fingers as they release the ball to ensure that they don't involuntarily hold the ball incorrectly. Upon release, the hand is behind the ball rather than on top of it. With the variation known as the slip pitch, the ball is not stuffed as deeply into the hand, which is rotated slightly to the outside. When the ball is released, it slips out between the thumb and fingers, hence the name.

Palmball

Forkball

Purists will argue that the forkball and split-fingered fastball are not the same pitch—and they're not, depending on who's pitching them. Mike Scott throws this pitch at an explosive 85 miles per hour. Other pitchers, such as Bruce Sutter, use it as an off-speed pitch. Some wit said, "It starts off like a fastball and ends up like a dead fish."

Forkball

For pitchers unable to master other change-ups the forkball can be a blessing. If you can spread your fingers wide enough to accommodate the ball, you will find that it is easier to throw than most other change-of-pace pitches. Long relegated to the specialty or freak pitch category, the pitch has gained popularity largely through the efforts of Roger Craig. Although Craig never used the pitch himself when he hurled for the Dodgers, he taught it to his pitchers as a coach for the Tigers and as manager of the Giants. His staffs have proven the effectiveness of the pitch. It is, for instance, the out pitch used most often by Jack Morris, the most successful pitcher of the 1980s.

Craig actually first recommended the pitch for Little League players to use so that they would not hurt their arms trying pitches other than the fastball. It's easy to both learn and throw. The ball is delivered exactly as a fastball is, including good wrist action, although its effects are different. There is less spin to the ball, which rotates backward and thus breaks down on the batter. Because arm speed and motion all say "fastball," the batter is fooled when a change-of-pace pitch arrives.

The ball is held with the seams and between the index and middle fingers. Jam the ball back as far as you can without discomfort. Pitchers with long fingers can hold the ball halfway down and right up against the webbing between their fingers. Few individuals will be able to achieve this depth, however, and it is not necessary to throw an effective forkball. Most players can get between a quarter and a third of the way down, and this is sufficient. To discover your comfort threshold, start by throwing your regular fastball and gradually work your fingers down the sides of the ball. While you do not snap your wrist as energetically as you do with a fastball upon release, you want to throw through the ball and give it enough wrist so the ball slides easily from between your fingers.

Screwball

Pitching the "scroogie" probably qualifies as the most unnatural act regularly performed on the baseball diamond. No pitch is harder on the pitcher's arm. Thrown as an off-speed pitch, the ball acts as a reverse curve. It rotates opposite to the curve's spin, and breaks down and away from hitters standing on the opposite side of the plate. It is, therefore, generally used by southpaws facing right-handed batters and vice versa.

Hold the ball as you would your cross-seam fastball so that you get four-seam rotation. As the ball approaches the release zone, your wrist, forearm, and, to a lesser extent, elbow turn inward, almost as if you were looking at a wristwatch. The corkscrew spin of the ball (clockwise for lefties, counterclockwise for righties) is imparted not only through rotation of the arm and wrist but also by the action of the thumb, which flips the ball upon release. The index finger is the other pressure point as the ball releases off the middle finger.

Left-handers, particularly overhanders, seem to have an edge in pitching the screwball, although Christy Mathewson, who invented the pitch and called it a fadeaway, was right-handed. Its greatest exponent was Carl Hubbell. Today, Fernando Valenzuela probably has the best one in the business. He is loose-jointed and with his great arm extension throws the ball as easily as anyone I've seen.

Knuckleball

Screwball

Knuckleball

The knuckleball is the most famous of the "novelty" pitches because it is so erratic in its flight. As the ball flutters toward the plate at a leisurely pace, it barely rotates and so responds more readily to factors such as temperature, wind, and humidity. The seams of the ball interacting with air currents are responsible for the knuckler's crazy behavior. One commentator compared it to a drunken butterfly. The ball swerves, darts, jumps, and dodges so that not even the pitcher can predict where it will go. It's probably small consolation to hitters that the pitch bedevils catchers as much as batters. Bob Uecker's advice on how to catch the knuckler was simple: "Just wait until it stops rolling, then pick it up."

The pitch can be thrown off the knuckles after the fingers have been folded over. If this hold is used, the thumb and last two fingers provide the pressure and the pitch, released with a snap, is faster than the floating knuckler. By far the more usual way to grip the ball is by digging the fingernails of your first two or three fingers into the seams of the horsehide. The ball is then pushed toward the plate with a stiff wrist. At the moment of release, the fingers are quickly extended, helping to push the ball forward.

The knuckleball puts very little strain on the arm, and pitchers who use it frequently enjoy extended careers. The best I ever saw was Hoyt Wilhelm, who was still pitching at forty-four. For a one-two punch, it would be impossible to beat the Niekro brothers, with whom I pitched for the Yankees. Phil didn't pack it in until he was almost forty-nine, and Joe was just a couple of years his junior.

Illegal Pitches

The whole issue of banned pitches is exaggerated, just as the pitches themselves are overrated. A few pitchers are occasionally caught red-handed. Gaylord Perry, a past master at the art, was finally apprehended in the act in 1982. At any given time, several pitchers and some teams as a whole (such as the Astros) are widely suspected of cheating. As a close student of the game and of other pitchers, let me tell you that the illegal pitch is rare in baseball today. I've occasionally been accused of knowing what to do with a scuffed ball. I do nothing to dispel the notion. If the batter thinks I might be doing something extra to the ball, it just gives him something extra to think about.

Most people have heard of the spitball. Some other names for doctored pitches are "shine ball," "mud ball," and "emery ball." Vaseline, K-Y Jelly, pine tar, pitch, sweat, and good old saliva are the substances most frequently used to load up the ball. Since baseball rules forbid the pitcher from bringing his hand to his mouth or spitting on his hands, glove, or the ball, great subterfuge is necessary to get away with a spitball. In fact, I think spitting is pretty much out. It's more common for other banned substances to be secreted somewhere on the body, uniform, shoe, or glove. The stuff is rubbed into one spot on

The spitball is baseball's most famous illegal pitch, but a doctored ball today is far more likely to be scuffed or nicked rather than loaded up with spit or other substances.

the ball as the pitcher pretends to be rubbing up the entire ball.

The ball can also be scuffed, nicked, scraped, or cut by either the pitcher or the catcher. A sharpened belt buckle, part of the catcher's gear, an emery board, small file, piece of sandpaper, or thumbtack can be used. In 1987, Joe Niekro was nabbed trying to discard an emery board from his back pocket and Kevin Gross got nailed with sandpaper. Scuffing is more popular than putting something on the ball because you need not keep reloading it and a scuff could be caused naturally.

Whether the ball is touched up with a substance or scuffed or cut, the effect is the same. The ball will move in the opposite direction from the defect, which is usually put in the same spot. If the spot is on the side when the ball is released, the ball moves sideways. If the spot is on top, the ball drops. This is also the action of the spitball, sometimes called the supersinker.

PITCH SELECTION

Getting Ahead

I cannot overstress the importance of getting ahead of the hitter in the count. The pitcher has a built-in advantage: he can give up four balls before losing the hitter, but needs only three strikes to get the hitter out. If you get behind in the count and squander this advantage, your options are severely constrained. You must play catch-up and fight a rearguard action instead of dueling on your best terms and with the fullest array of weapons. You want to be on offense and keep the hitter on defense. Statistics prove that a mediocre hitter ahead in the count hits for a better average than a good hitter with an even count. Don't strengthen the hand of the weak hitters you may be lucky enough to face.

Naturally enough, getting ahead in the count starts with the first pitch. Deliver that first pitch over the plate with some authority. Of course, there are exceptions. If you are facing a notorious first-ball hitter or someone who chases bad pitches, you have some room to play. Otherwise, start with a strike. Hitters behind on the count are only half as likely to drive in or score a run as a hitter who starts out 1–0. Eighty percent of the walks given up result from that 1–0 count. If you lose that first batter, there is a 50 percent chance that the opponents will score. If, on the other hand, you retire him, the chance of scoring drops to 16 percent.

Just as it is important to get ahead of the hitter, it's important to get ahead in the inning. That first out determines the strategy that follows. In a very real way, one out with no one on is a world away from no outs and a man on first. Oh, sure, the pitcher's best friend, the double play, can intervene, but do you want to count on a play that statistics show occurs about once a game? With one on and no outs, the team at bat can get a man in scoring position with a deliberate out. And if you open the inning with a walk, the chances are better than not that the runner scores. To stay ahead, get ahead; and avoid those walks.

Playing Lowball

Moving the ball around, up and down, in and out, is an essential dimension of pitch selection. The most important place to be able to put the ball, however, is down low. If you can consistently put the ball around the hitter's knees, you're on your way to mastering one of the biggest lessons of control. It's harder for most batters to hit low pitches with power, they see less of the ball, and you get more grounders off low pitches. All types of pitches are effective low, particularly breaking balls. The only pitch you want to throw high is the fastball.

If you make a mistake on a lowball, the chances are you'll soon be looking at a base runner. If you make a mistake up high, there's a good possibility that you'll see the base runner crossing home plate. The two pitches that account for more home runs than all the rest combined are high curves and sliders.

Starting at an early age, pitchers should work on delivering the ball low. It's harder to achieve vertical control than horizontal control. If you're having problems with pitches too far inside or outside, don't sweat

All balls should have a downward trajectory from the mound to the plate. The most successful pitchers can keep the ball low consistently.

it. Among other remedies, you can change your position on the rubber. Concentrate on pitching low strikes.

Capitalizing on Strengths and Weaknesses

The confrontation between the pitcher and the batter is the classic one-on-one duel on the diamond. To prevail, you must have a firm sense of your own strengths and weaknesses. To start with, you have to know your limits and your capabilities. A lot of failure in sport comes from trying to do more than you can. Can you overpower your opponent? Can you fool him? What is your best pitch? What can you get away with? A cliché of the game is that "good pitching stops good hitting." Some wise man improved the accuracy of the statement by adding "and vice versa." It's the vice versa that provides much of the fascination of pitching. Whatever you do, don't let a hitter's strengths dictate to your strengths. You've got to go with what you do best, even if this means challenging the hitter with a pitch that he traditionally handles well.

Assess the hitter's strengths and weaknesses. Have you faced him before? With what result? If you've never pitched to him, have any of your teammates? What can your catcher tell you about him? Most serious pitchers at advanced levels keep a

"book" on hitters, either a mental one or an actual written notebook. Major league teams have scouting reports with the most current information on hitters and pitchers, and some teams computerize data and can provide coaches and players with printouts. Even if all this is beyond you or if you are facing a mystery hitter, you and your catcher can learn a lot by just keeping your eyes open.

Start with stance. When Pete Rose was still playing, for instance, he and I would regularly get into pitcher-hitter gamesmanship. He'd back off the plate and close his stance, aiming to hit to right, and I'd feed him curves. When he went back into his more open normal stance and tried to pull the ball, I'd switch to pitching him away. When I'm on the mound concentrating, delivering the ball, and following through, I'm not always in the best state or position to observe the hitter closely. This is where a sharp-eyed catcher can help his battery mate. He's sixty feet closer to the subject and has a better opportunity to watch and then advise me that, for instance, the batter is pulling off the ball so let's keep the pitches outside.

Some hitter's characteristics to watch for and suggested pitches to use follow. By and large, the suggestions are based on a variation of Wee Willie Keeler's famous line, "I hit 'em where they ain't." You want to pitch 'em where they ain't or, to be more exact, where they are unlikely to hurt you even if they get the bat on the ball. You'll be pitching to what should be their weakness. Keep in mind that these suggestions are theoretical and must be modified by the specific realities of the game. Neither can you keep using them on the same hitters all the time. You want to be in a groove, not a rut.

- Closed stance: fastball inside unless he comes out of stance with stride.
- Open stance: breaking balls outside unless stride alters position.
- Crouch stance: high and inside if pull hitter; high and away if not.
- Erect stance: low balls unless he strides and drops; then high balls are in order.
- Batter holds bat up: inside fastball.
- Batter holds bat flat: low balls.
- Long strider: high fastball and change-ups.
- Short strider: low balls.
- Head turner: outside curves.
- Lunger: fastballs up and in or change-ups away.
- Batter strides away from plate: low and outside, particularly breaking balls.
- Batter strides toward the plate: fastballs up and in or curves low and away.
- Batter drops rear shoulder or uppercuts: fastballs up and in.
- Batter turns his hands: fast or breaking balls low and outside.
- Batter hitches his hands: pitches up give this batter trouble.
- Batter with sweep swing: fastballs up and in if he's close to the plate; outside change-ups if he's not.
- Batter hits off heels: breaking balls low and outside.
- First-ball hitters: fastballs out of strike zone and change-ups.

Working the Hitter

Some of the essentials of working the hitter have already been recommended. If you can get ahead of the hitter, for instance, you don't have to give him anything too juicy to swing at. You can nibble at the corners and hope for the call or that the batter swings at a bad ball to hit. The successful batter is one who has his timing down. If you can consistently disrupt that timing, you will be a successful pitcher. This means being able to move the ball around and change speeds on the hitter to throw him off balance. A satisfying moment for a pitcher is when he sets up the batter to expect a fastball and then pulls the string on him with a change of pace.

Pitch selection can be compared to a chess game. You should never make a move without a reason on the board or on the mound. There should be a purpose to each pitch you throw. And just as the best chess players don't simply react to their opponents' moves but plan their strategy several moves ahead, you and/or your catcher must have a sequence in mind before you begin pitching to a batter. Before the game, my catcher and I will go over the game plan and then I delegate authority to him. I do my homework in preparation for a game and then some. I not only read the reports and box scores, I also pitch the game in my head to the point of visualizing specific pitches. I know this is way beyond the preparation of many pitchers, but it works for me.

Without a doubt, the best pitch in the game is the one-pitch out. It's not often that it takes only a single pitch to get an out, and the play may or may not come off your best pitch. Far more frequently, the pitcher must work for the out. Building to the out pitch is what sequence and pattern are all about. The batter is going to expect, guess, and anticipate. Your job is to surprise him and, if you're good at it, to disappoint him. If you set up the hitter properly, your out pitch should work.

I want to caution you about using your best pitch too often or too early or when it may not actually be needed. If you show the batter everything you have, the element of surprise is gone. You may have exposed the best card in your hand when a lesser one would have sufficed. Generally there are only a handful of potential turning points during a game, when what happens really matters. One of your jobs as a pitcher is to make sure you have the right stuff for these critical junctures.

Turf Wars at Home Plate

Home plate is seventeen inches wide. Warren Spahn used to observe that he was only interested in five inches of that span: the two and a half inches on either side. He didn't use the rest. Good pitchers will follow Spahn's example and let the hitter claim the middle of the plate, but only rarely pitch him anything there. What the good pitcher cannot allow is for the hitter to stake a claim to the middle *and* both sides of the plate. Most pitchers feel that they have a territorial imperative to the outside of the plate and the ammunition to defend it. Pitches low and away can be tremendously effective if the batter is not crowding the plate or if he isn't dug in and ready to let 'er rip. If he has taken a toehold preparatory to teeing off or if he's leaning toward your turf, you must move him back.

The brushback is the appropriate response when a hitter crowds the plate. Also

Down I go for an unexpected push-up, but that pitcher better realize that once is enough.

called a duster (the hitter sometimes tumbles into the dust to escape the pitch), the pitch is an inside fastball between the edge of the plate and the hitter. The brushback is a legitimate part of the pitcher-hitter battle. In contrast, the deliberate hit—or worse yet, the beanball—has no place in baseball. The "purpose" pitch is used to nail a hitter who has previously gotten a homer or to retaliate against the other team for some reason. The baseball is a lethal weapon, and it amazes me that the majors have only seen a single death as the result of a beaning. Intentionally throwing at the hitter is illegal and, thankfully, headhunters, pitchers who play chin music, are not as big a part of the game as they once were.

DEALING WITH BASE RUNNERS

Holding Runners On

Once you have given up a single or a walk, you have an additional responsibility: you don't want the other team to get its man into scoring position without even touching the ball, so you must prevent the steal. The steal is far more important to the game today than when I first came up. There were more than twice the number of thefts last year than there were in my first year. I've seen the havoc Rickey Henderson can cause when he gets on base, and I am glad I don't have to pitch against him. While he's the best in the business, there are many others who cause more than enough trouble for pitchers. This dramatic increase in speed is one of the big changes I've observed during my twenty-five years in the game.

The duel between the batter and pitcher is often referred to as a cat-and-mouse game, but that term is more applicable to the battle between pitcher and runner. There are feints, thrusts, and parries. Quickness is essential if you are to beat your opponent, but the match boils down to a waiting game to see who commits first. Once the opponent has committed, the other player can either dash or pounce.

Keeping these speedsters on base is a challenge, but the pitcher is not without weapons. If he expects a steal attempt on the next pitch, he can pitchout to his catcher. He can try to pick the runner off base with a quick throw. Even if these methods are untried or unsuccessful, the pitcher can keep the runner close to the bag

and, through various techniques, make base stealing a riskier proposition.

Reading the pitcher is the starting point for a successful steal. Avoid giving the runner any information that makes his job easier and, more than that, try to misinform him. You must have the same move to first base as to home. Ask your coaches and teammates if they can spot tipoffs that you are going to throw one way or the other and then eliminate them. If you are a right-hander, you might move your back heel or open your shoulder a bit before your move to first. Left-handers often vary the height of their leg lift depending on whether they are going to home or first. They can also reveal their intentions by moving their head or eyes. Conventional wisdom is that left-handers have an easier time with runners on first because they are facing that direction. I'm not sure the advantage is always to the pitcher. The runner has a full view of the pitcher, making him easier to read. Deception on the move to first, therefore, is more important for lefties than righties.

Keying on the pitcher's rhythm is the most common way the runner tries to get a jump when stealing. Consistency is important to the pitcher, and we tend to be creatures of habit. This can hurt you with a runner on. Just as you try to disrupt the hitter's timing by changing speeds, you must upset the runner's timing by changing your rhythm. Change how you move into the set position and the amount of time between set and break. Vary the intervals at the various stages. Don't fall into the habit of looking over to first the same number of times before you throw. Pitch quickly one time and hold the ball the next. Step off the rubber, bluff a throw, avoid being predictable.

The runner is trying to read you; do the same to him. For right-handers, keeping the runner in view may be hard if you do not have good peripheral vision. You can turn your shoulder and head slightly and rotate your eyes to the left as far as possible, but don't dip or lower your head to look toward first. If you do this, you will have to raise your head to go to the plate, and this will give the runner an advantage on getting his jump.

You should have some information on the runner before he even gets to base. To begin with, know whether you are dealing with a serious threat. If the guy has one stolen base in the last two years you can't ignore him, but you sure don't have to pay a lot of attention. Then begin your observations. Does the runner tip off his intentions? Is his lead longer or is he leaning more? Has he already opened up a bit with his right foot? Does he seem anxious as he begins a walking lead or is he trying to fake you out by feigning nonchalance? The runner has his mark from which he launches his steal. You should have a mark too, a point beyond which you will not let him pass without throwing to first. I have two different speeds when I throw to first, one to deke or set up the runner that also serves to keep him honest and another faster one that I use when I really need or want the out.

The Pickoff at First

The elements that contribute to an effective pickoff move are quickness, speed, and accuracy (and to a greater degree for left-handers, deception). Your throw to first must be a good one—at or a tad below the knees and on the inside part of the bag. The throw must have speed. You can't ex-pect a lazy toss to nail the runner. Most pitchers should be able to meet these requirements without too much difficulty. After all, a large part of what they regularly do is deliver the ball with some velocity to a specific location. It's the last requirement, quickness, that proves the stumbling block for many pitchers. You've got to get the ball to first quickly, and that means not reaching back too far with the ball before you bring your arm forward. Neither the full-arm extension or the follow-through of your regular pitch is necessary for your pickoff throw. A quick release is. Lefties might find that a sidearm snap throw proves best for pickoffs.

The right-hander must have a quick upper body and feet for his regular move to first. He must pivot off the rubber with his right foot and step toward first with his left foot, or he can speed the process up with what is called a jump pivot. The maneuver is a combination of a small jump just barely off the ground and a quick turn. The rotation is quicker than a regular pivot, and the movement gets your striding foot into its step toward first. At the same time, you must open up your upper torso so that you do not have to throw across your body. Remember, if you make *any* move to first base except with your head, you must step toward and throw to first.

Any time you are off the rubber, you can try to pick off the runner. Sometimes, a throw to first as soon as you get the ball back from the catcher will nab an inattentive runner. Pitchers usually begin their pickoff from the set position, but going into or coming out of the stretch also presents good opportunities. The pitcher's arm is up and in a good position to throw, and the runner is establishing his lead and often moving in the wrong direction to get back

In making a pickoff move to first, the right-hander steps off the mound and pushes off with his back foot while pivoting/stepping toward first with his front foot.

to base. To be smooth, quick, unpredictable, and to avoid balks, you should practice your pickoff move and try different kinds.

As the southpaw breaks from the set and lifts his striding leg, he has the option of going to either first or home unless his kick breaks the back plane of the rubber, in which case he must pitch to the batter. The left-hander needs good balance and leg control to skirt the plane, making it hard for the runner to determine which way the ball is going. If the pitcher can get to the point where his leg lift is completed and his hands have broken without the runner starting to steal, the theft will probably not be attempted on that pitch for the window of opportunity has been closed. A factor that helps determine a lefty's effectiveness is his head movement and how he looks at the runner. The key is to not fall into a predictable pattern, such as looking to home and then throwing to first. Alternate your looks. You may even find that looking *between* home and first as you begin your delivery makes you harder to read.

The Pickoff at Other Bases

Most runners say that third base is easier to steal than second base. The theft is not attempted more often because the man on second is already in scoring position and many managers do not consider the extra base worth the risk of having the man thrown out. Still, the base is stolen frequently enough, and you want to limit the runner's lead from all bases, so you must learn pickoff moves to all bases.

Before a pickoff attempt, the left-hander keeps his eyes on home and retains the option to pitch there. He then adjusts his stride toward first and fires the ball to the sack.

Because no fielder is holding the runner on, the pickoff to bases other than first has the added elements of timing and sometimes signals. Usually, but not always, the shortstop is the fielder taking the throw at second, because he plays behind the runner and can surprise him by breaking for the bag. The pitcher must lead the fielder with his throw. The jump pivot from the set is the usual way the pitcher gets into position for the pickoff at second, although it can be accomplished further along in the delivery.

The play at second is initiated in various ways. The pitcher or shortstop can signal the other player, either can use simple eye contact, or the pitcher can see daylight between the shortstop and the runner (which occurs when the fielder is closer to the bag). The catcher can also start the play with a signal. Sometimes a 1-2-3 count is employed whereby the pitcher and shortstop signify the play when the pitcher checks the runner. The pitcher turns back to the batter for one count. On two, the pitcher whirls around and the shortstop breaks for the bag. The pitcher throws the ball on three—at the knees and over the bag.

There are fewer pickoff throws to third than to any other base. One main reason is simple enough: a bad throw will inevitably yield a run. The third baseman and pitcher use a sign-and-break system like the one used in the pickoff at second. The left-hander going to third uses the mechanics of the right-hander going to first, while the right-hander going to third can use the simple step move of the lefty's move to first. You cannot balk to second or third base by stepping and not throwing. So if you see you do not have a chance to get the runner, hold up on the throw.

The Pitchout

When a steal, hit-and-run, or squeeze play is expected, or when the catcher thinks he can nail a runner taking a long lead off base, the pitchout is called for. The aim is to throw a ball that the hitter will find impossible to hit and the catcher easy to catch as he comes out of his squat and prepares to fire the ball. Throw the ball far outside and high, and make your release quicker and snappier than your usual throw. Less of a leg kick will also shave a split second off your time to the plate. Your catcher will indicate where it's best to throw the ball: down toward the chest or up around the shoulders. Deception is important with the pitchout. If you give it away, the runner won't go and you will have just wasted a pitch.

Avoiding Balks

The balk is probably the most frustrating way of seeing a player advance. If you walk a man, it may be a free pass but at least you worked on him. If he gets a hit or steals a base, he worked on it. A balk is a mechanical error by the pitcher or, recently in the majors, an almost impossible call for the umpires to make fairly. After Bert Blyleven's pitching in the 1987 World Series, Cardinal manager Whitey Herzog complained so loudly and effectively that a new approach to the balk rule was instituted. It was a bad decision, and many of the new balk calls changed the outcome of many games in 1988. There was too much pressure on the umpires, inconsistent enforcement, and real distraction for the pitchers. I'm glad that after a year that set balk records in both leagues, the rule has been reinterpreted again, pretty much back to its earlier form.

If you let a runner rattle you and alter your delivery, a balk frequently results.

To avoid having a balk called on you, observe the following precautions:

- Keep your foot on the rubber while pitching.
- Pause a full second in your stretch position before continuing your delivery.
- Don't drop the ball during delivery.
- If you swing your striding foot past the back edge of the rubber, pitch to the batter.
- Step toward a base before throwing to it.
- Don't make any motion toward a base below your head without throwing to that base.
- Make no pitching motions without the ball.

Be comfortable in your stretch position and if you see anything you don't like, step back off the rubber. Don't let the runner shake you up and force you into movements that will advance him without risk.

STARTING AND RELIEVING

Determining Rotation

While this section might be more appropriate in the chapter on managing, this might be one of my best chances to share my opinions, so I will. I realize that the rotation based on ''Spahn and Sain and pray for rain'' is something we will never see again. (In the heat of the 1948 pennant race, Johnny Sain pitched nine complete games in twenty-nine days, going 7–2.) Baseball has changed a lot since then, and even the four-man rotation has given way to the five-man rotation. I guess the thinking is that we pitchers need four days of rest between starts, but I don't and neither do many of the hurlers I've talked to. Some pitchers claim that you can get too strong from too much rest and your control suffers.

Another reason I don't think the change to a five-man rotation was for the better comes down to pure percentages. How many teams have five firstline pitchers, or even four? I think a realistic appraisal of mound staffs around the majors would show that many clubs are lucky to have three top pitchers. If this is the case, would you rather have them pitching for you 60 percent of the time (five-man rotation) or 75 percent of the time (four-man rotation)?

Given that the five-man rotation, for better or worse, is the way we play in the majors, it's important that there be a balance between right-handers and left-handers. That way no club, in the course of a series, can continually unload on a staff tilted in one direction. So mix it up with, say, two lefties and three righties alternating.

The Varieties of Relief

When I first entered baseball, pitchers were expected to work not only more frequently but also longer. The philosophy has changed and so has the way pitchers pace themselves. Throw as hard as you can as long as you can and then we can take you out is the prevailing wisdom. As relievers have begun to play a more important part in the game, their numbers have increased and so have the roles that they play. A reliever is not just a starter on an off-day or the guy who comes in when the going gets tough. Today the reliever is a specialist. The mop-up man comes in when the starter has been bombed and the team is hopelessly behind. The fireman's role is to come in and douse any late-inning fires that the opposition has managed to light. The stopper rarely pitches more than three innings and is thus known as a short reliever. There are middle and long relievers who enter the game earlier. One variety, the set-up man, came on the scene during this decade. Depth, even within the relief corps, is im-

Starting pitchers just love strong relievers.

portant. A club should have more than one closer, for instance.

Regardless of what role they play, relief pitchers must take a different approach to the game than starting pitchers. Late-inning relievers in particular know they can't make mistakes. A starter can have a bad game and still win. Trouble can come early, the pitcher can settle down, his team can have a big inning, and he's back on top. There's time to recover. With the reliever, it's now or never with small margin for error. He may even inherit a situation that gives him no wiggle room whatsoever. Most relievers tend to keep things simpler than starters do. They usually have fewer pitches. If a given pitch isn't working for a starter right away, he can work on it; a reliever can't, so he sticks to a couple of pitches he knows he can count on.

The reliever must be able to come in on short notice and start pitching effectively immediately. The starter has several days to prepare; the reliever may have only a few minutes. Instead of four days off between pitching assignments, the reliever may find himself pitching four days in a row. Depending on the frequency and duration of his last few outings, it may take the reliever varying amounts of time to warm up. Some pitchers like to take their twenty-five pitches or so and then sit down. Others like to keep throwing.

A WORD ON RELIEVERS
by Dave Righetti

Most relief pitchers are "different" to say the least, and short relievers are usually even stranger. There's a natural isolation to the position; you're not really one of the gang. There's so much pressure and, when you lose, guilt that you tend to keep to yourself.

I try to get to the park around 3:30 and relax. Often at that time I'll have to deal with the press, which is very seldom relaxing, particularly when I have a bad stretch and they ask ''Why aren't you starting?'' I'm not sure the writers (or the fans) have ever accepted my move from starter to reliever.

Although I usually stay away from the training room, I might take a whirlpool or a massage. I run my sprints, shag flies, play catch for ten or twenty minutes, usually long-toss with another reliever.

Some short men stay in the clubhouse for the first six innings. It's as if they know the nervous juices will start flowing as soon as they get to the bullpen and they want to delay that moment. I'm ready to step into my role anytime after the fifth inning. You usually can smell the situation. Most guys don't like to know in advance that they're getting the call.

You can be like Jell-O when you're sitting out in the bullpen. Or like a caged lion. Sitting is the worst—it's a relief to get the call. Once you get the call, you just try to get loose fast. You can't let the good things flow if you're tight. Your back and arms have to be as loose as possible as quickly as possible. I limber up my back, legs, and hamstrings by walking around. During the sixth or seventh inning, I'll rotate a weighted ball.

Going in is such an adrenaline rush—the game is always on the line. In close games, my butterflies start early in anticipation. I'm glad this is one sport where it's OK to be an oddball, a goofy left-hander. There's so much pressure it sometimes comes out in weird ways.

NOTE BY DAVE WINFIELD

Dave Righetti has as good athletic talents and instincts as I've seen. He's highly intelligent and versatile. He was one of the best starters in the American League and then was asked to become a relief pitcher. His five consecutive seasons with 20+ saves prove he can fill both roles effectively.

I like his demeanor, his combination of brains and craziness. Rags is a practical joker, prankster, kibitzer, and storyteller. He injects his peculiar form of levity throughout the clubhouse. He's really good at deflating whiners with something that sounds like a baby's bawl—''Waaaahhhh!'' As good friends as we are, I must confess we'd probably be a bit closer, but those relievers can get a little too wild and crazy for me.

Donnie congratulating Rags on another save.

RECOMMENDED RESOURCES

Tom House. *Pitching Absolutes: An Instructional Video.* (R. S. Productions, 1988). $39.95.

Tom House. *Pitching Mechanics: Problem Recognition & Solutions: An Instructional Video.* (R. S. Productions, 1989). $39.95 (or both House videos can be ordered for $75.00 by calling 800-937-7766).

Tom House. *The Winning Pitcher.* (Contemporary Books, 1988). $10.95.

Martin Quigley. *The Crooked Pitch.* (Algonquin Books, 1988). $9.95.

Tom Seaver with Lee Lowenfish. *The Art of Pitching.* (Hearst Books, 1984). $15.95.

Bob Shaw. *Pitching: The Basic Fundamentals and Mechanics of Successful Pitching.* (Contemporary Books, 1972). $9.95 (out of print).

John Thorn and John Holway. *The Pitcher.* (Prentice Hall, 1987). $19.95.

CHAPTER FIVE

Hitting

GETTING STARTED

Beating the Odds

I don't wish to discourage you at the very start, but I want you to recognize that hitting a baseball is an extremely difficult task. Many players and commentators have called it the hardest feat in sports, and I won't dispute that assessment. Think about it. Although the pitcher's mound is 60 feet, 6 inches away, by the time the pitcher releases the ball, it has only about 55 feet to travel. This sphere, 3 inches in diameter, is speeding toward you at up to 100 miles per hour, and very seldom is it traveling a straight path. You have about three-tenths of a second to watch the ball and decide whether to swing and a bit over a tenth of a second to complete that swing. Your tool is a 2-pound tapered cylinder averaging 35 inches in length and no more than 2¾ inches in diameter at its widest point.

Of course, the task is even more difficult because you not only are trying to strike the ball with your bat, you also want to hit the ball into fair territory. To do this, you must get the bat to the right place (within fifteen degrees of perpendicular to the path of the ball and in the same plane) at the right time (within the fifteen-thousandths of a second that it takes the ball to traverse the hitting zone). And even if you accomplish this, there are eight players in front of you and one behind you ready to make sure that you do not reach base safely. Good luck!

Studying the Pitcher

The act of hitting should begin long before you step into the batter's box. Within team sports, there is probably no more intense a competition or individual a contest than that between the pitcher and the hitter. Though the duel does not formally begin until the batter steps into the box, the batter should prepare for that moment by studying the pitcher beforehand. What is the book on this pitcher? If you've faced this pitcher before, what was your experience? If you haven't, what are the experiences of others? What should you be looking for? When the pitcher is in a hole, what pitch does he go for? If the pitcher lasts nine innings, he will typically throw around 130 pitches. As he warms up, as you sit on the bench or wait in the on-deck circle, or when you're on the base paths, you have continual opportunities to study the pitcher. Use them. What you learn will help you to anticipate the pitch you are going to get. If you're right, you may be on your way to a hit. If you're wrong, you try to adjust. This is where your study of the pitcher pays off.

Pitchers try to disguise the kind of ball they are set to deliver. They will also try to distract the batter with misleading arm and leg movements and other tricks. Your job is to penetrate the disguises and maintain your concentration. Look for visual clues that might tip you off as to what and where the pitch will be. Where does the pitcher focus his eyes before release? Does he favor a certain side of the mound or a particular stance on the rubber? Are there any telltale movements to the glove, or does he ever expose the grip? These are little giveaways that sometimes spell the difference between success and failure at the plate.

Watch the ball from the moment it leaves the pitcher's glove to the time it hits your bat. Follow the pitch intensely, particularly from the point of release. There is no way to exaggerate the importance of the classic adage, ''Keep your eye on the ball.'' Watch for tip-offs before the pitch, but when it comes to deciding where to swing, learn from the flight of the ball. Watch its rotation. Wait and learn. Wait as long as you can; learn as much as you can.

THE GRIP

Holding the Bat

Begin by placing the bat at the base of the fingers of both hands. If you hold the bat only with the fingers, you will lock your wrists and lose power and control. If the

The traditional way to grip the bat is so the knuckles of your hands line up, but your comfort is the key element in how you decide to hold the bat.

bat is held back in the fleshy palm of the hand, you limit hand action and flexibility and slow bat speed. Your hands should be touching with no space between or you will have difficulty releasing the swing and following through.

Another important aspect of holding the bat is how you align your knuckles. For maximum flexibility and wrist movement, I recommend that the middle knuckles of your top hand line up between the middle and lower knuckles of your bottom hand. With this grip you should be able to hit the ball at any part of the plate. If this grip is not comfortable for you, however, experiment with different alignments. Comfort is more important than conforming to the classic prescription.

You must also maintain the right hand pressure. The correct tension is like a watch spring—wound, but not too tightly. Some of the best batters in the game hold the bat so loosely that you can almost slide the bat out of their grasp. During the swing, your grip will tighten. Until then, stay loose. Tension is your enemy at the plate, and if you grip the bat tightly the tension will move up your arms and into the rest of your body.

Grasp the bat more firmly with your bottom hand than with your top one. Your lead or bottom hand and arm anchor the swing, helping to pull the bat through its path. Even though my bottom hand is tighter, I keep my index finger and thumb loose to gain fluidity in my swing and avoid pulling the ball. Your back or top hand is the support hand; it is closer to the point of impact and pushes the bat through its contact with the ball and into the follow-through. The looser grip allows you to better make split-second small adjustments until just before contact and then follow through.

I'm known, by the way, as the most prolific bat thrower in baseball. One television commentator observed that I could "throw to all fields." When the bat flies out of my hands, it's the result of a loose grip, a hard swing, and being fooled by the pitch.

The End Grip

As a power hitter, I use the end grip most of the time. This permits maximum arm and bat leverage. I actually grasp the bat about a quarter of an inch from the bottom. If your hand is flush against the knob of the bat, your movement will be restricted and your wrist will not turn over completely. For this reason, some players opt for no knob or for a very slight flare at the end of the bat. I advise young players to use bats with knobs. Smaller hands need assurance that the bat will not slip from their grasp. If you use the end grip, just give yourself a bit of room.

Oops! There it goes again. Two of the elements that contribute to flying bats—a loose grip and a hard swing—are positive traits.

The end grip is preferred by power hitters.

The Choke Grip

The other basic grip is the choke. Holding the bat four to six inches from the end produces a shorter swing and allows greater control of the bat through the hitting zone. Even power hitters shift to a modified version of this grip with two strikes or when there is a particular need to place the ball. The choke grip is also used by hitters who

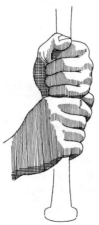

The choke grip gives the batter greater control.

want to give more jump to the ball through using a heavier bat. Regardless of which grip you use, keep your hands together.

THE STANCE

Batter Up!

Stance is the most individual and idiosyncratic option in hitting. Nevertheless, there are pointers that will help hitters no matter how or where they stand. A general rule for spreading the feet, for instance, is to keep them at least as far apart as the breadth of your shoulders. Your stance is the foundation of your swing, so you must be well balanced and able to react to a variety of pitches. Young players often keep their feet too close together—resulting in an early step, a long stride, and the tendency to pull the body away from the plate. When your feet are too far apart you will have difficulty striding forward and shifting your weight.

Many players do not dig in at the plate, perhaps fearing that if they dig a hole, the pitcher will bury them in it. I dig a very shallow trench in the dirt with my back foot, a toehold, a brace that allows me to push off as I step toward the ball and yet rise on the ball of my foot and turn. Some players simply make a line in the dirt where they put their back foot as a reference point. Though I don't think either practice is essential to successful batting, I recommend that players try them. Experiment with a variety of stances and refinements. If your experiment makes you feel more relaxed at the plate, it has succeeded.

Feet First

There are three basic ways to position your feet: closed, even (or parallel), and

Closed stance

Even stance

open. Most major leaguers use a closed stance, with the front foot nearer the plate than the back one. The next most common stance is the even, where the feet are equidistant from the plate. Only a few players regularly bat from the open position, where the back foot is nearer the plate than the front one, which is angled about forty-five degrees toward the field. Even these players close their stance when striding into the pitch.

Your stance will also vary according to where you want to place the ball or depending on what sort of pitcher you are facing. You may want to close your stance against outside pitches, balls that tail away from you, or when you want to hit to the opposite field (left field for left-handers, right field for right-handers). An open stance will help you against curves thrown from your side of the plate, inside pitches, and when you want to pull the ball to the field on the same side of the plate on which you stand.

I recommend that young players begin

with the even stance. It's easier to maintain good balance and to keep the weight evenly distributed and on the balls of the feet, and they seldom face the situations described in the preceding paragraph. Regardless of

Open stance

which stance you adopt, however, remember that your front foot should stride toward the pitcher.

Positioning Your Body

Once you have chosen where to plant your feet, you can then concentrate on what should be happening to the rest of your body until it becomes automatic. You're in a slight crouch. You've bent forward at the waist and then bent your knees a bit. It's easier to distribute your weight properly if you bend at the knees first. Your body is erect but compressed. Your hips and head are level, and your shoulders are almost level. I suggest you lower your front shoulder slightly, locking your head into place looking directly at the pitcher and preventing your back shoulder from dipping. There is more wasted motion in the shoulders than any other part of the hitter's body. Any steps you can take to reduce unnecessary movement should improve your hitting. Whatever you do, don't tuck your head behind your shoulder. This will tilt your head and limit your vision.

Comfort will help determine how far from the body you place your hands. If your hands are too close you reduce bat speed, and if they are too far you reduce leverage and force. I recommend that you keep them fairly close to your body, no more than four to eight inches away and approximately letter to shoulder high. I think you will find this gives you greater quickness, hand-eye coordination, and control over your bat. Your front arm is roughly parallel to the ground and your elbows are away from the body and about at the same level, although your front elbow can be lower.

The bat should be held between vertical and horizontal. I hold the bat fairly perpendicular to the ground. For one thing, the greater the angle at which you hold the bat, the heavier it will feel as its resistance increases. Other factors should be considered, however. You launch your swing with the bat at approximately forty-five degrees. You may wish to begin with your bat near to this angle. Wherever you hold the bat, as the pitcher begins his delivery, keep the bat as still as you can. Don't make the already difficult task of hitting the ball any harder. I have the habit of keeping my bat in motion, so in this case, do as I say, not as I do.

Position Within the Batter's Box

How far away you stand from the plate depends on such factors as your size, arm extension, bat choice, and where you plan to hit the ball. Batters should make sure that they can cover the outside of the plate, where pitchers consistently direct the ball, and minimize getting jammed by inside pitches. The traditional way of achieving this is to position yourself so that when you bend over slightly you can touch the outside edge of the plate with your bat. I do not advise using this method, which brings you too close to the plate. You don't want to be able to hit balls out of the strike zone; you want to ensure that from your normal stance you will be able to cover the full strike zone. Step into the box, rise to the balls of your feet, and extend your bat so that the meat of the bat can reach an outside pitch. You want to establish control over outside pitches and be able to react to inside pitches.

How far toward the front or back of the box you stand depends largely on what sort of pitcher you are facing. The farther back

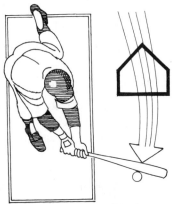

Even though you usually begin your swing deep in the batter's box, you always want to make contact with the ball well in front of the plate.

in the box you are the more time you have to react to the pitch, which is a benefit, particularly when you are facing a fast-baller. On the other hand, the deeper you are in the box the easier it is to foul off the pitch. If you are facing a "soft tosser," anticipate looking at sinkers, screwballs, and curves. You may wish to move up in the box and reduce the zone where these pitches break most sharply.

Experimenting with Stance and Swing

A common mistake young players make is to imitate the stance of a favorite hitter and stick with it. As I was growing up, I remember trying various poses in front of the mirror at home. You should experiment with your stance and position, but not copy anyone slavishly, and especially not during a game. Find out what works for *you*. You will probably make a range of adjustments over the course of a career or a season, and sometimes even a single contest. You want

to be comfortably balanced, relaxed but poised, ready to coil and spring into action the moment the ball leaves the pitcher's hand. Pick up tips from other batters. See how different bats alter your stance. Experiment on ways to adjust and adapt your stance to the needs of the game. Whatever stance you choose, practice it until you can go up to the plate and assume it naturally, automatically, and confidently.

Once you decide what kind of hitter you want to be and have read the section on swing, you should have a better idea of what stance is best for you. You can then visualize where you want to end the act of hitting the ball. Choose a stance that allows you to make an easy stride, swing, and follow-through. Efficiency of motion is essential to the hitter. Any motion that does not add to your ability to hit the ball detracts from it. Keep this in mind at the plate. Avoid needless motion. This does not mean that you eliminate the rhythm or motion that most batters find a necessary prelude to the swing. I sway my body as I await the pitch. It helps me to establish the timing and back-and-forth motion that brings me into the cocked position and soon becomes the stride and swing. You will also find that some rhythm reduces tension and places you "on your toes" or, more accurately, on the balls of your feet. Your body should be in a state of ready relaxation, in balance but moving.

THE STRIKE ZONE

Get a Good Ball

I'd like to begin this section with a piece of advice from Ted Williams and pay tribute to one of the game's finest hitters and best students. The first rule in Williams's

The legal strike zone. When you chase pitches the width of one ball outside the zone, you increase your vulnerability 40 percent.

gram showed what happens if you increase the strike zone by the width of the baseball. The pitcher's target increases 40 percent.

The Zones

The Official Baseball Rules define the strike zone as that area over the seventeen-inch-wide home plate between the top of the knees and a horizontal line midway between the top of the shoulders and the top of uniform pants as the batter prepares to swing at the ball. (This midpoint is close to the level of the armpits or the lettering on the uniform.) In addition, the pitcher and umpire both have their zones, and with two strikes against you, the zone expands. Good pitchers create and maintain their strike zones—which differ slightly from the legal strike zone—by consistently pitching to a particular part of the plate. The pitcher does this to be in control of the hard-to-hit borderline areas and to influence the umpire's decisions. If the pitcher discovers in this cat-and-mouse game that the umpire is accepting the pitch as a strike, you'll see more of it. If not, the pitcher will change. My experience in the subjectivity of strike calls is that veteran pitchers often get calls that young ones don't.

The Science of Hitting is: Get a good ball to hit. This means a strike! Yes, I know there are notoriously good bad-ball hitters, but don't pattern your hitting on the exception. All good balls to hit are strikes, though not all strikes are good balls to hit. Williams explains the distinction graphically.

I remember a photograph in *The Science of Hitting* that showed Ted awaiting a pitch, and over the strike zone was a diagram of his personal preference strike zone. It showed his batting average depending on the position of the pitch. Williams could hit down-the-middle pitches for .400; high and inside, his average fell to .320; low and outside pitches yielded the lowest average, .220. Most dramatically, the dia-

Having learned the legal, personal best, and pitcher's zone, the smart batter conforms to the ultimate strike zone: the umpire's. In moving between different levels of play and even different professional leagues, I've found that umpires have differing views of what constitutes a strike. When after eight years in the National League I became an American Leaguer, I was disappointed to learn that the AL strike zone was larger. Some of this difference may be explained by the different kind of chest protectors used by umpires. All NL umpires use an inside protector; AL umpires use both the inside and the outside (or balloon) protector, which restricts their view of low pitches because they must look over the catcher's head instead of his shoulder.

In the constant balancing act of maintaining equilibrium between hitters and pitchers, baseball officials sometimes reinterpret the strike zone. This happened recently in both leagues. A few years back, umpires would seldom call strikes much above the belt. Now letter-high pitches are often called strikes, although without the regularity that I observed when the change was first made.

The strike zone also alters depending on the count. With two strikes, for instance, you must guard against the corner-catching called third strike. Move closer to the plate, choke up, and aim for greater control and quickness. A major flaw of many sluggers is that they always go for broke. Two strikes is the time to rein in the fencebusters and make adjustments.

Remember, you will get what you ask for from the pitcher, for better or worse. By this I mean that if you stand firm and demand a strike, the smart pitcher will realize that he must either give you a ball you can hit or walk you. If, on the other hand, you chase after bad balls, that's what you'll get. Swing only at strikes and the pitcher will give you the benefit of the doubt. Maybe even the umpire will. Discipline yourself. The heart of batting is aggressiveness, but the brains of batting is patience.

The First at Bat

You can learn a lot from your first time up. I prefer looking at a few of the pitches my first at bat and am less inclined to swing. Personally, I hate to risk making an out on one of the first pitches. Waiting also increases the chances that the pitcher will make a mistake. If the first pitch is a ball, the pitcher is under immediate pressure to deliver a strike or fall behind 2 and 0. More than 80 percent of the walks given up start with a 1 and 0 count. More times than not, I let that first pitch go by. This allows me to see just what the pitcher has going for him that particular day.

With the first pitch of your first at bat, you usually see the pitcher in top form. How fast is his heater? How much movement does his breaking stuff have? You can also learn a bit about the umpire. Where's his strike zone on a close pitch? Later in the game this information may prove vital. Of course, this strategy may change with men on base and should change in subsequent at bats.

Ted Williams claimed that, in his effort to learn more, he swung at the first pitch only 5 percent of the time. This may have been carrying a good idea to an extreme, but it's hard to argue with a man who sports a .344 lifetime batting average. Nevertheless, my advice is that unless you're Ted Williams don't get into a rut that makes you too predictable. You are the pitcher's problem; avoid becoming part of the solution.

THE SWING

The "Meat" of Hitting

In taking up the swing, we are turning to the meatiest part of hitting. It is appropriate that we begin by discussing the "meat" of the bat. This six-to-eight-inch section of the bat, located at the head, a few inches from the end, is also called the "sweet part" or "joy spot." It certainly gives hitters joy to lay this part of the bat into the pitch; the best wood in the bat gives the best jump to the ball, and that is what successful hitting comes down to. Get the head of the bat out front and into the pitch.

You will probably not see many pitches down the middle, where it is easiest to connect with the meat of the bat. Despite what you might read or hear about swinging level or even down, your regular swing should be slightly upward at the moment of impact with the ball. This just makes common sense. The pitcher releases the ball about head high while standing on a mound ten inches high. He is generally aiming to deliver the pitch to the lower part of the strike zone, about two feet off the ground. Over the distance to the plate most balls travel downward at about seven degrees. For maximum effectiveness, the bat should be as completely within the plane of the ball as possible; this means matching the angle of the pitch with an upward swing of seven degrees. Any deviation from this path will reduce the zone of impact. Naturally, getting the bat behind a breaking pitch is even harder than hitting a ball that doesn't move much. You must develop a swing that allows you to make hard contact with lively balls consistently if you are to succeed at higher levels of play.

Having advised you to swing upward, let me emphasize how slight an angle we are talking about. You do not want to uppercut the ball and end up with a pop fly or weak grounder. You want to produce line drives; seven or eight out of ten will go for hits. Only one or two flies in ten and two or three grounders per ten result in hits. If you achieve a level swing, you'll be close to right-on. Let me also say that to get from where you hold the bat at ready to the point where you begin to swing up, you have to swing down.

There are occasions when you might want to vary your swing path. When I'm going for a sacrifice fly, I'll increase my upward angle slightly. If I want to hit a grounder, particularly when I'm playing on Astroturf, I swing downward a bit. Again, recognize that I am talking about slight adjustments. Avoid tomahawking or chopping the ball (although Matty Alou used to get an amazing number of hits this way).

Coordinating the Body

Let's move from where you swing the bat to how you swing it. There is no other action in baseball that requires as much coordination and timing. Let us review the stance from which you begin the swing. You are in a slight crouch with knees bent and your hands close to the body, approximately level with your upper chest. Your front arm is roughly parallel to the ground. Your head and hips are level and your front shoulder is lowered slightly, locking your head into a direct look at the pitcher. You are relaxed.

As the pitcher begins his windup, you begin yours; your body goes back as his arm goes back. Think of yourself as a pistol. The safety is off, you're pulling the hammer back and cocking the gun, and your finger is on the trigger. You're ready to explode.

Starter Mechanism and Stride

The explosion is initiated by the starter mechanism. As you begin your attack on the pitch, several actions occur simultaneously. As in cracking a whip, casting with a fishing rod, or teeing off at golf, backward motion precedes forward motion.

A good swing begins with a relaxed but ready stance. My weight is back on a firm right leg.

My bat goes back as my foot goes forward.

Your weight shifts back before you stride forward. This movement begins by turning your front knee inward as you lift your foot backward. Your shoulders and hips rotate to the rear, properly cocked.

You continue with a short, light-footed stride directly toward the pitcher. Strides longer than eight inches may throw your balance and timing off. The stride begins before the pitcher releases the ball and should be smooth. Be aggressive, but avoid lunging. You're not stomping a bug, you're landing on the ball of your foot and maintaining your balance, and your foot and leg are all that move forward. The rest of your body and about 70 percent of your weight stays back, ready to come forward at the moment of impact.

As my foot goes forward, my hands go

Don Mattingly shifting his weight back before striding forward.

backward. I have a long swing. Like a rubber band, the farther back I pull, the more forward force there is. My movement at this time is pronounced; other players have little or none. Rod Carew, for instance, was "back" to begin with, held his bat almost stationary until the ball was upon him, and then made a short, quick flick with his bat. A compact swing without a loop is what you're aiming for.

When you complete your stride, your foot should land in an even or, at most, slightly open position. To accomplish this you may have to try to land in a closed position. If you land in an open stance, you lose balance and power by prematurely opening up your hips and shoulders. It will also be harder to hit outside or off-speed pitches. While your leg is slightly bent as your foot touches down, it should be stiffened immediately to brace your swing.

With my stride completed and my bat launched forward, my swing begins to level off and my hips to pivot.

Using Your Head and Hips

With the stride completed and foot planted, the hips open up and lead the rest of the body through the rest of the swing. The midsection is your center of gravity, and it makes sense that it is the core of the swing's action, the place where you generate your power. Imagine a pole through the middle of your hips. Your hips pivot around this pole, pulling your shoulders and arms, which rotate around your hips.

At the beginning of your swing, your head was steady and level, looking directly at the pitcher. As the pitch hurtles toward you and your eyes follow the ball, your head will tilt progressively downward. Indeed, keeping your head down is the *only* way you keep your eye on the ball. You should watch the ball into your bat or the catcher's mitt; the lower the pitch, the lower your head. Your head should stay down at least through impact—and ideally through follow-through. When your head moves, your body follows, and if you raise your head too early your whole swing suffers. A steady head is a key part of the torque developed by your body as you swing. In conjunction with your feet, it provides the torsion as the hips and shoulders rotate.

Point of Contact

By this time, the bat has lessened its downward arc and has begun to flatten out and accelerate. Your hands and arms direct the bat. Keep them and your elbows close to your body, ensuring that your bat will make a tight circle and concentrating the energy of your swing. Your bottom hand pulls and anchors the bat while your top hand pushes and guides it. For maximum support, your top hand should be under-

My hands continue to lead the bat which begins to rise as I shift my weight forward and my back leg forms an "L."

The ideal moment of contact. My bat is well in front of the plate. I continue to drive forward forcefully, my back hand moving as if to deliver a karate blow. The "L" of my back leg deepens as my upper body continues to rotate around a straight and firm front leg.

neath the bat so that its back surface rests against your palm. Your bottom forearm will be almost perpendicular to the bat, and your top forearm will move as if delivering a forceful karate blow or swinging an ax straight into a tree.

As your hips open further, your shoulders begin to open. Your arms and hands are well in front of the plate while the bat trails slightly behind. Your wrists remain solid and firm as the bat moves into the ideal hitting zone in front of the plate.

To attack and propel the ball fully, you need a firm foundation, with your legs helping to provide the power to drive through the ball. Legs are the body's strongest part. The more you can bring them into play, the more power you can

deliver. With your front leg braced, your back leg bends and turns as your back foot pivots. If you have shifted your weight correctly as you swing, your back toe will be pointing directly downward.

This is the moment of truth for the hitter. I can get eager for the impact just thinking about it. Timing is all. The spring is sprung. The coil becomes uncoiled. If you have anticipated correctly or adjusted accordingly, the bat hits the ball. I can see that line drive into the alley now!

Follow-through

The last essential action of the swing, the follow-through, occurs after the ball leaves the bat. Without it, however, the ball you

My head stays down and my arms are fully extended as my bat swings through the ball.

My bat has made a full circle around me and my top hand releases it as I complete my follow-through and prepare to run.

Johnny Bench shows the torque he develops by the time he follows through.

Ken Griffey, Jr., rotates his upper body around a firmly planted front leg.

hit will not travel far. Only now does your bottom wrist break and roll as it must for the bat to swing through the ball. If you roll the top hand too early, you will lose power. You will not be able to hit outside pitches or hit to the opposite field. Some batters may choose to release their top hand from the bat at this time to facilitate their follow-through. Your arms should be fully extended. The bat makes an almost complete circle around your body, finishing high behind you. Your weight is on your front foot. A balanced swing and follow-through leave you poised for your next move. Push off, drop the bat, and run.

BUNTING

A Necessary Tool

A frequently neglected weapon in the hitter's arsenal is the bunt. Some observers have even called bunting a "lost art." There are various reasons for the bunt's being used less often today. More sophisticated bunt defenses, artificial surfaces that make it harder to bunt, speedier players who take that extra base under their own steam, and an emphasis on power hitting have all contributed to the decline. And statistics support this shift. It's easier to produce runs with a few long balls than by stringing together several hits and moving players ahead a base at a time. Still, there are situations that demand the bunt, and complete hitters will be good bunters. And the threat of the bunt keeps defensive players honest: they can't play deep and rob you of a hit. In addition, an infield drawn in creates holes for hits. In youth leagues, where mechanics are not highly developed, bunting should be used more often. With hurried, off-balance, sometimes long

throws and more frequent errors, young bunters often end up on second base. Particularly if teams lack power hitters, advancing the runners with bunts will win games.

Getting Ready

As with swinging away, your initial stance and your position when you hit the ball is essential to the success of what follows. Poor bunts are often the result of poor positioning, which is frequently due to completing the move to the bunting stance late or starting to run before the ball is hit. When you intend to bunt, move up in the box to reduce your chances of hitting the ball foul. Hit the ball in front of the plate. Because high pitches are the hardest to bunt, stand tall (although your knees must be bent). What you do after that depends on whether you are laying down a sacrifice bunt or bunting for a hit.

The Sacrifice Bunt

With a runner on first or runners on first and second, particularly with no outs, the sacrifice bunt is often called for. It advances the runners and reduces the possibility of a double play. The batter gives up his chances of making a hit to move the runner(s) along. There are two ways to get in position to accomplish this.

The most frequently used bunting stance in the major leagues is the pivot. The batter turns on the heel of his front foot and the toe of his back foot so that he can face the pitcher. This stance can be assumed quickly with a minimum of body movement so the element of surprise is retained. It is also easier to get back to a modified standard hitting stance if a fake bunt is in order.

With the square-around stance, the front foot is moved backward and toward the

The pivot stance

ward. There is no weight shift at the moment of impact. Your hands and arms are well in front of your body. If they are too close to you, there's no room to give and you'll tend to jab at the ball. Your grip on the bat is extremely loose.

As you assume the bunting position, slide your top hand up to the trademark of the bat. Pinch the bat between your thumb (on top) and your fingers. Some players use only the index finger or the index and middle fingers, curling the others beneath the bat or into their palm. This pinch grip serves two purposes: it prevents the ball from striking the fingers and it forms the hand into a cushioned U, allowing the bat to give on impact. Remember that you do not want the ball to travel far and end up as an easily handled grounder. You're trying to deaden the ball, so let it come to you and then give with the ball, "catching" it with the bat. As you progress as a

outside of the box or the back foot is moved forward to the inside line of the box. In either case, the feet are parallel to the plate and each other about shoulder-width apart. The square-around gives the batter a little better plate coverage, especially on outside pitches, and is probably easier to teach to young players. Because the sacrifice is rarely a surprise anyway, many players do not mind "tipping their hand." An added benefit of squaring around to bunt is that it often brings the infielders charging in and the hitter can sometimes coax the ball past them.

Try both methods and use the one that is most comfortable. Whichever one you adopt, make sure that your hips and shoulders are square to the pitcher and that you are in a slight crouch with your knees bent. If you must go down for a low pitch, your entire body will lower. You're on the balls of your feet and your weight is already for-

The square-around stance

hitter and a bunter, you may no longer need to move your top hand up the barrel of the bat, but until you advance, that top hand near the trademark will give you better bat control.

Hold the bat high—in fact, at the top of the strike zone. There are several reasons for this:

1. If the pitcher suspects you are about to bunt he will probably try to give you a high inside fastball, the hardest pitch to bunt.

2. You can take any pitch above your bat because you know it's a ball.

3. It's easier to put the bottom of the bat on the top of the ball, which is the ideal configuration for the bunt.

4. You'll have fewer pop-ups and fouls.

5. It's easier to bring the bat down than to raise it; simply bend at the knees and waist.

At the moment of impact your bat should be relatively level. There is conflicting advice, however, as to whether to hold the bat level or diagonally as the pitch comes toward you. I defer to the best bunter I ever saw play, Rod Carew. He believes that keeping the head of the bat higher than the handle is one of the most important elements of successful bunting, and even devised a little mechanism to ensure this positioning. As he awaited the pitch, Carew's bat head would make a small, circular, clockwise movement that left the barrel higher than the handle. Rod had observed that other batters who started with the bat held level frequently dropped the head before they hit the pitch, producing fouls and pop-ups. While you may not incorporate

Carew's stratagem into your bunting technique, take his advice on the angled bat. He was phenomenal! He practiced tirelessly and could stop his bunt with uncanny accuracy. In his prime he could count on twenty-five to thirty bunt hits a year, and when he was past his prime he still benefited, getting almost as many slap hits past drawn-in fielders who feared his bunting.

Where you bunt the ball depends on what bases are occupied. With a runner on first, hit between the mound and the baselines, preferably toward first. With a runner on second or first and second, hit toward third base to pull the fielder from the bag. Don't aim to have the ball roll down the foul line just fair. This leaves too small a margin for error. Remember, it's not important that you reach first safely; it is essential that you advance the runners. Bunts to a fairly large area of the infield will accomplish this. If you don't hit the ball too hard at a fielder or too soft for the catcher or directly at the pitcher, you will probably succeed. The direction of the bunt is controlled by the bottom hand, which serves as a rudder to angle the bat. Location of the pitch is also a factor; right-handers will find it easier to hit inside pitches toward third and outside pitches toward first (vice versa for lefties). Regardless of where the ball is, make sure the bat is in front of the plate, get a good pitch to hit, strike the ball with the end of the bat, and don't swing down.

Squeeze Plays

The squeeze play is a gambling sacrifice bunt with a runner on third. It is usually employed in the late innings of a tight game with no more than one out. With the safety squeeze, the batter waits for a good pitch to bunt and the runner doesn't take off for home until he sees that the ball has been successfully bunted. The suicide squeeze requires the runner to break for home the moment the ball leaves the pitcher's hand. Because the runner has already committed and must be protected, the batter must bunt any ball that can be caught by the catcher. This is the one time that you are not looking for a strike. It is essential that you put wood (or aluminum) on the ball or your runner is most likely a dead duck. I got lucky once on a suicide squeeze when the batter missed the sign and didn't swing and I still managed to escape the rundown and reach home. Keep in mind that with a suicide squeeze it almost doesn't matter where you bat the ball. Don't worry about placement; if the ball is on the ground and fair, you will score the run. The only way you can be defeated is if you miss the ball, pop it up, or if a pitchout is called and you can't reach the pitch.

One of the most exciting plays in baseball is the double squeeze. With runners on second and third, the runner takes a big lead off second. He rounds third at full speed and makes for home. The play's success depends on the batter's ability to hit the ball so that the fielder does not see the runner and goes for the putout at first base.

Bunting for a Hit

The biggest difference between bunting for a hit and sacrificing is surprise, and the other differences stem from that. I'm known as a slugger, but if the third baseman is playing me too deeply, I get a great deal of joy out of laying down a bunt in his direction. When the bunt is unexpected, it is more likely to succeed. That is why you must disguise your intentions until the last possible moment. The mechanics of bunting for a hit are different. With a sacrifice,

Squeeze plays are often the best way out of a tight spot.

you want to be set and stationary when the ball reaches you and there is no weight shift. When you're bunting for a hit, you're moving as you hit the ball and there is weight shift, sometimes complete. You should also have a firmer grip on the bat and your hands and arms will be closer to your body so that they can extend and push the ball.

Push Bunts

Also called the dump bunt, this tactic is particularly effective when basemen at the corners are playing deep. A right-hander begins by putting his weight on his left foot and moving his right foot backward. Once this foot is set and the weight is back, the hitter moves toward contact with the ball and the weight shifts quickly to the left foot as hitter prepares to become runner. Although the ball can be hit toward third, most righties aim for the hole between first and second, hoping to beat the pitcher to first base.

The left-hander executes the push bunt by taking his first step with his left foot toward the pitcher to avoid pulling away from the pitch prematurely and adding to the difficulty of hitting an outside pitch. The ball is lightly tapped down the third base line. The batter must make sure he hits the ball before turning to run.

Drag Bunts

A well-placed drag or pull bunt is one of the prettiest plays in baseball. Only left-handers can execute the true drag bunt, which gets its name because the ball appears to be dragged along the first base line by the runner. The bunt begins as the hitter steps toward first with his right foot. The weight is on this front foot as the bat head points to third base and contact is made. By this time the left foot has moved forward and begins to cross over the right leg and the batter is well into his second stride. These extra steps and the left-hander's closer proximity to first are often all that is needed to beat out the bunt. The batter must make sure that contact is made before the crossover is completed. Placing the bunt well is more important than gaining a half step.

Fake Bunts

There are several occasions when it makes sense for the batter to decoy the bunt. The batter can either pivot into the bunt stance and stay there or pivot back into the hitting position. If the ruse works and the infielders charge the plate, the batter can take a short, easy swing (a swinging bunt) and chop the ball over or slash it past the fielders. The fake bunt also helps a base runner trying to steal. It confuses the infielders and may get them moving in the wrong direction. Squaring around to bunt can rattle the catcher and make both his catch and throw more difficult. The fake bunt can also distract the pitcher and cause him to alter his delivery. Lastly, the swinging bunt can be used as part of a hit-and-run. If so employed, the hitter must protect the runner by hitting the ball regardless of where it is pitched. A true bunt-and-run is a bit different. The ball is actually bunted toward third, and if nobody covers the base, or if the throw is being made to first as the runner rounds second, he goes all the way from first to third.

Sequence showing how a left-handed batter lays a bunt down the first base line as he takes his first steps in that direction.

OTHER SITUATIONAL HITTING

The Sacrifice Fly

With a runner on third base and less than two outs, your job is to drive the man in, and the usual way of doing this is with the sacrifice fly. With a deep enough fly to the outfield the runner should be able to tag and score even if he's a leadfoot and the fielder throws a bullet. Many coaches recommend that you do not change your swing when trying to hit a sacrifice fly. I swing up a bit more than I usually do. In this situation, the pitcher is usually going to pitch you low (high balls are easier to hit in the air). If this is what happens, uppercut the ball, but not much. Focus on hitting the bottom half of the ball at a slight upward angle. You don't want to pop the ball up when you do hit it. The sharper your angle through the path of the ball, the less chance you have of hitting it.

In the late innings of a close game with a man on third, the infield is usually pulled in to guard against an infield grounder's scoring the run. It's a gamble. If the ball is hit directly at the infielders, they can stave off the score, but because their range is so limited, they are vulnerable to most hard-hit ground balls. Don't try too hard to aim the ball or hit it over the fielders. Just hit it *hard*. It will often have eyes of its own and get through for a hit.

Runner on Second with No Outs

Your job here is to get the runner to home or third and the usual way a team player does this is to hit to the right side of the diamond. Even though left-handers pull the ball naturally to right field, right-handers with good bat control can advance the man in this situation. Bring the hands forward as fast as possible while delaying slightly bringing the head of the bat forward. If you do this, the head of the bat will still be a bit behind your hands at the moment of impact. The ball follows the direction your knuckles are pointing and because of the angle of the bat you should be able to hit the ball to right if you master the maneuver. When the hands lead the bat into the hitting zone and the wrists whip the bat into the ball, it's called swinging "inside out" and is more of a push without the full extension of the arms. It requires a great deal of bat control, which takes practice. Young right-handers without this ability should consider pushing a bunt between the mound and the first base line.

The left-hander needs to get the bat head out in front of the plate early to execute this play. The pitcher will not be making your job any easier by giving you an easy ball to pull and will probably be pitching outside. Cheat in a little toward the plate and put a bit more emphasis on your top hand as you swing. If the pitch is inside, accelerate your hand movement. Don't get jammed into a pop-up or weak grounder.

Hitting Behind the Runner, Hit-and-Run, Run-and-Hit

A basic offensive tactic is hitting behind the runner. With first base occupied and one or no outs, the batter tries to hit a ground ball into the gap between first and second bases caused by the first baseman's having to hold the runner close to the bag. A well-hit ball will travel into right field, advancing the runner to third. Even a ball that is fielded is likely to be taken by the second baseman moving left. The play is at first and the runner advances to second.

If the runner breaks for second at the start of the pitch, the second baseman must protect against the steal and an even wider gap is opened up for the hitter; or the short-stop covers second, opening a different hole for the hitter. If the batter manages to hit into the hole vacated by the fielder, not only is the double play avoided but the runner can also take third. A good batsman is essential here. Even if he does not succeed in hitting into the hole, he must be able to get a piece of the ball. The runner has not begun with a base-stealing lead and would be an easy out if the batter misses the ball. A line drive is even more disastrous and results in an automatic double play, so the ball must be hit on the ground. This is why the play is not usually called unless the pitcher is behind in the count and there is reasonable expectation that the next pitch will be a strike. Even if the pitch is out of the strike zone or a pitchout has been called, lunge for the ball or throw your bat at it. Your prime responsibility is to protect the runner.

The run-and-hit has similarities to the hit-and-run (the runner breaks for second with the pitch and makes third when the play succeeds), but the differences are significant. The hitter is not obligated to swing at the pitch unless it is a strike, and he can put the ball into play anywhere instead of having to hit to the right side of the field. The hitter does not have to have as great bat control, but the runner should have better-than-average speed, because if the batter takes the pitch, the runner is on his own, in essence trying to steal second.

Hitting Behind the Runner Stealing Second

When you have a speedster on at first base, or even a slower runner when the steal sign is on, you may have to take a strike to increase the chances of a successful steal. There has to be some coordination and communication between batter and runner, either discussed beforehand or through a signal given from the plate. What you want to avoid is fouling off a pitch or hitting a fly when the runner has gotten a good jump and could have swiped the base. Even more embarrassing is a line drive that results in a double play.

Hitting to the Opposite Field

Most players can pull the ball (hit the ball early with the head of the bat out in front of the batter). The results are predictable: the right-handed batter hits to the left side of the field and the left-hander to the right. Because more power can be generated, pull hitters are often home run hitters but seldom hit for average. The defenses shift and overshift against them and there are fewer hits and more double plays. The complete player hits to *all* fields, and this means he can hit to the opposite field and away from the double play as the defense must spread out. About the only pull hitter I can think of who hit for power and average was Ted Williams. And he accomplished this against some of the most extreme shifts ever used. Frequently, there was only one fielder on the left half of the diamond.

I'm tall with long arms and great reach and need to stand back off the plate, which helps me get good extension and go to right field. But players without my physique can develop their ability to hit to all fields. Being able to wait longer with confidence and then take a quick stroke helps. Also important is where you aim the ball. Take Charley Lau's advice: practice driving the ball right back through the pitcher's box. If you succeed, you've got a hit up the middle. If your swing is a bit late, you have a drive to the opposite field. If your swing is

early, you might pull the ball for extra bases. Just don't get into the all-or-nothing pull syndrome.

SWITCH-HITTING

Ultimate Versatility

Few other single factors can improve your batting average, your value to the team, and your versatility as much as the ability to hit from both sides of the plate. The benefits are several. You can see the ball longer if it comes at you from an opposite-side pitcher. You don't have the tendency to back off or bail out from a same-side inside pitch. You can benefit from your dominant eye at least part of the time. Your dominant eye, like your dominant hand, is your body's natural inclination. Ideally, it is this eye that should be closest to the pitcher. Usually, right-handers have a dominant right eye and vice versa. If you are serious about hitting, you will make an effort to learn which way your body "leans." A quick and usually reliable way to find which eye you favor is to pretend to pick up a camera and focus it. The eye you use is dominant.

There are more of both right-handed batters and right-handed pitchers in baseball, reflecting the division within the general population. Batting lefty allows you to take advantage of this imbalance. You'll face three times as many right-handers as southpaws, and their curves and sliders will break toward you rather than away. In fact, the only pitch a switch-hitter has greater mechanical difficulty with is the screwball. You also gain an edge by standing several feet closer to first base than your right-handed counterpart, and when you've finished your swing you're facing first base and with a good follow-through are on your way to the bag, a tremendous advantage in legging out hits. All this shows up in the averages. Lefties usually hit about twenty points higher than righties do.

A switch-hitter also often saves the team from having to go to a pinch hitter, doesn't give a relief pitcher coming in an immediate righty-versus-lefty edge, and can play different parks to full advantage. In short, switch-hitting adds dramatically to the hitter's versatility and is a skill worth striving for. Young players just developing their hitting are at the ideal stage to learn switch-hitting, and a smart coach or parent will help them practice, because this is what it takes. Even if you are past the age where learning to switch-hit seems feasible (although some players learn as adults), it pays to take regular practice swings from both sides of the plate. The exercise helps to keep you in balance.

The Great Switchers

I came into baseball too late to see some of the modern era's best switch hitters, such as Maury Wills, who retired the year before I entered the majors, and Mickey Mantle, who preceded me to Yankee Stadium. I've been lucky enough (or unlucky enough, because they were opponents except in All-Star games) to personally watch two great ones and another who just might blossom into greatness. And when I was a San Diego Padre, I played with a fourth talented switch hitter.

My first year in the majors, 1973, Pete Rose set several switch-hitting records. He stroked 230 hits that year and hit 181 singles. He also won the batting title and the MVP that year. Pete believes that becoming a switch hitter was the most important thing in his entire baseball career. With his father's encouragement, he began at the age of nine, but he kept up practicing for more than three decades. Since he batted lefty three times as often as righty (his natural side), switch-hitting was the key ingredient in Pete's becoming the all-time leader in hits.

Eddie Murray may just be the best clutch switch hitter I've played against. He's got power, and hits for average. Maybe some younger players will overtake him, but over the last decade, no one has had more home runs or RBIs. He was the first player in history to hit both lefty and righty home runs in two consecutive games. In 1989, he moved from the cellar-dwelling Orioles to the World Champion Dodgers. I wish him luck and several more productive years.

From 1979 to 1980, I played with Ozzie Smith at San Diego. While there he was known primarily as a defensive whiz. Nobody I've played with was as slick a fielder and could so effortlessly "pick it." Since then he has come into his own as a hitter, and I think this is largely due to his development as a switch hitter.

The young switch hitter who just seems to be getting better and better is Harold Reynolds of the Seattle Mariners. A two-time All-Star second baseman, Harold didn't first switch-hit until 1980. He describes himself as two different players from the two sides of the plate with different stances, swings, and bats. He states what separates the switch hitter from his one-sided brethren succinctly: "We work harder."

BATTING FLAWS AND HOW TO CORRECT THEM

Lunging and Overstriding

Although these two faults are separate, they occur at the same time and often together. The overstrider takes too long a step into the pitch. The lunger steps into the pitch too early and too heavily. Loss of control, power, and timing result. The wrong "first step" throws everything that follows off.

Correction Widen your stance to limit your stride, step softly, and concentrate on achieving correct distribution of weight—60 to 70 percent on the back foot until moment of impact. Let the ball come to you. In practice, place an object near your front foot and do not stride beyond it.

Hitting Off the Heels

Shifting your weight to your heels as you swing makes the body and bat move away from the plate. You lose a great deal of power and have difficulty with outside or off-speed pitches.

Correction Keep your weight on the balls of your feet and stride toward the pitcher.

Stepping in the Bucket

Striding away from the pitch causes a loss of power and an inability to hit an outside pitch. Sometimes, particularly in younger players, the fault originates in a fear of being hit by the pitch.

Correction Overcome your fear of the ball, close your stance, concentrate on the hip cock, and extend your rear arm back.

Step in the bucket too often and you might end up with a regular seat near the water cooler.

Locked Front Hip

Failure to unlock the hip during the swing reduces your power considerably. Your follow-through suffers and pulling the ball is virtually impossible.

Correction Open your stance slightly and step toward the pitcher. During practice and warm-up swings, rotate your hips fully and get into the swing of things.

Hitching

Dropping the hands leads to a rushed, late, upward swing likely to produce fly balls or complete misses. High inside pitches are particularly hard to hit.

Correction Lower your hands and keep them still and raise the rear elbow. Many "hitchers" do not realize their error. If the bat is held against the shoulder, the hitter should feel and recognize the hitch.

Lazy Wrists

Failure to bring the bat around quickly enough results in a loss of power, diminished follow-through, and weak sliced balls to the opposite field.

Correction Weak wrists are often the source of the problem. Exercise the wrists, hands, and fingers; develop your strength. Squeeze a rubber ball, lift weights, and do wrist curls, or swing at a medicine ball and knock it off its perch.

Uppercutting

When the batter dips his rear shoulder, drops his back knee, and swings up at the pitch, his front shoulder rises, hindering his view of inside pitches and making it more difficult to hit high pitches. Weak fly balls or complete misses often result.

Correction Raise your back elbow, lower your front shoulder and aim it at the pitch, and begin your swing with a downstroke.

Uppercutting is a good way to knock yourself out of the lineup.

Unless you're one of those chop-and-run speedsters, save swings like this for the woodpile.

Chopping

Swinging down on pitches reduces your hitting area and makes it particularly hard to hit low balls for anything but grounders.

Correction Keep your weight back, drop your rear shoulder slightly, and concentrate on your basic form and level swing.

Turning and Bobbing the Head

Up and down movement or moving the head too far forward during the stride or turning the head when swinging impair vision and the control of the rest of your body.

Correction Keep your head down and still, focus on the ball all the way, and shorten and soften your stride.

Fear of the Pitch

Some players, especially young ones, have an inordinate fear of the pitched ball that limits their ability to hit. Though players should have a healthy respect for the ball, very few injuries result from being hit by a pitch—and even fewer are serious. Batting helmets should, of course, always be worn. Players should also learn to roll away from the pitch. It's a simple move. Turn your upper body quickly a quarter turn toward the rear to protect your head and upper body. Practice rolling until it is a reflex. A drill that will help you is to have someone pitch to you as if in regular batting practice. The pitcher should use a tennis ball and occasionally throw directly at you, giving you the opportunity to practice your roll.

Periods of Adjustment: Surviving the Slump

The individual batting faults sketched on the preceding pages mostly result from or in your timing's being off. They generally affect only your ability to hit a certain kind of pitch. When you can't hit any pitch, when your timing is gone and your faults seem more collective than individual, you are in a slump, or what I call a "period of adjustment."

Slumps are inevitable; they happen to all hitters. Leveling off from a period of top

In the midst of a slump, it's hard not to feel down and out.

form or suffering through a prolonged period of below-par play is distressing and can have many causes. As the season gets longer, fatigue and staleness may set in. Players may be physically or mentally tired, distracted by personal concerns, temporarily overmatched by the pitchers, or injured. Once they lose confidence, they can be overly zealous and desperate to get out of the slump and even more inclined to get into bad habits. They can even be hitting the ball solidly but not safely. There are several ways to go 1 for 30.

My most memorable slump (and the one I'd most like to forget) occurred during my only appearance in the World Series. It was 1981, my first year with the New York Yankees, and we were playing the Los Angeles Dodgers. During the regular season, I'd led the team in RBIs and was second in hitting and home runs. I batted .350 against Milwaukee in the division series and then fell off to only two hits in three games against Oakland in the league championship series. It was against the Dodgers, however, that I just couldn't buy a hit. Several times I hit hard shots, but they always were right at a fielder. Finally, in Game Four, I dumped a little shot to left that fell in front of Dusty Baker. I called time and in jest asked for the ball to be thrown in, a gesture usually reserved for milestones in a player's career. I thought if I lightened up and broke the ice, the whole team might benefit. Everybody on the field got a good laugh, but that was my last hit and we lost the Series in six.

Getting through a period of adjustment is no easy task, and there is no one way. Begin by analysis. Review the basics. What are the pitchers doing to you or what are you doing to yourself? A coach, manager, teammate, or relative may be able to spot a flaw. In altering your style, if this is nec-

Don Mattingly practices hitting as much as anyone I know. Young players who think batting off a tee is beneath them should follow Donnie's example. He uses the tee regularly.

essary, go for intelligent adjustments, not dramatic changes. If you can isolate the cause, practice can help; if not, maybe you've been analyzing and practicing enough. Analysis can produce paralysis. Extra practice can also result in increased tiredness and decreased concentration. Try taking a few days off. Relax, regain your perspective, and come back for a fresh start. If you are fortunate enough to have film or videotape of your performance when you were in good form, replay and study it. There are lots of ways to go wrong, but only a few ways to go right. What were you doing then that you are not doing now?

When I'm in a period of adjustment, I'm like a car misfiring. I need a tune-up; my timing must be adjusted. (At this point in my career, since I know the fundamentals, it's nothing major.) Some players attempt

to achieve this by extended batting practice during which they take an easy, level swing, trying to drive the ball directly back through the middle of the box, gradually increasing their power. Don't try to kill the ball; just make contact to begin with. Don't be overanxious. Practice waiting on the ball and hitting to the opposite field. Increase your concentration on the pitch by practicing your bunting. Try bunting during a regular game. A bunt might just be the hit that breaks your slump. If you're missing balls that are strikes, you may be taking your eye off the ball. With its emphasis on watching the ball and quick response, play more pepper. Review and reestablish your basic mechanics by working off a batting tee.

Whatever it takes, maintain or regain your confidence. Just remember: you'll get back into the swing of things. It's just a matter of time and timing.

RECOMMENDED RESOURCES

Rod Carew with Frank Pace and Armen Keteyian. *Rod Carew's Art and Science of Hitting.* (Penguin Books, 1986). $9.95.

Walt Hriniak with Henry Horenstein and Mark Starr. *A Hitting Clinic: The Walt Hriniak Way.* (Harper & Row, 1988). $9.95.

Charley Lau with Alfred Glossbrenner. *The Art of Hitting .300.* (Elsevier-Dutton, 1980). $9.25.

Jim Lefebvre with Ben Lefebvre. *The Making of a Hitter.* (Lefebvre Training Aids, Inc., P.O. Box 2326, Mission Viejo, CA 92690; 1979). $7.95.

Ted Williams and John Underwood. *The Science of Hitting.* Revised Edition. (Simon & Schuster, 1986). $9.95.

CHAPTER SIX

Baserunning

BEFORE YOU START

The Ideal Runner

Some guides to the game tell you that baserunning starts with the crack of the bat, but for the smart base runner it starts long before he even steps into the batter's box. The ideal runner is well prepared. He knows the condition of the turf he will be running and sliding on. From the dugout and on-deck circle, he studies the pitcher's moves, the fielders' responses, the catcher's arm. When he steps to the plate he checks out the defense and knows where the fielders are playing. Watching the other team take infield practice can teach a runner a lot about his opponents.

All this helps the runner anticipate, which is one of the keys to success on the base paths. You not only have to be speedy with your feet, you must also have speed above the neck. You need to be on top of the game situation, know who's coming up, how many outs there are, and other details. You don't want to end an inning or nip a rally by getting caught taking the extra base. At the same time, in a close or low-scoring game, aggressive baserunning can

Don't miss any signals, but at the higher levels of play, once you get running, it's best to make your own decisions.

mean victory. Turning a single into a double, stealing a base, advancing without sacrificing the batter, all these can mean a run and spell the difference between winning and losing.

Although speed is an essential element for the ideal base runner, its importance should not be overestimated. I've known

101

Thunder on the base paths. Harold Reynolds shows good running form, staying low, keeping his arms close to his body, and driving hard with arms and legs.

GETTING TO FIRST BASE

The Quick Start

Whether you are getting out of the box after you have hit the ball, starting a steal, or moving to field a ball, the first few steps are absolutely crucial. When you are batting, you must make sure you complete your first task, hitting, before you begin your second, running. It helps if you have a smooth swing so that you don't need to work to recover your balance. Don't neglect your follow-through in your hurry to hustle down the baseline. For left-handed hitters, a good follow-through will actually start you on your way to first. Regardless of which side of the plate you bat from, take your first step with your rear foot. Drop the bat with your bottom hand. Don't overstride and don't watch the ball unless you can do so while focusing your attention and energies on getting out of the box. Stay low and build up your acceleration through the first half dozen steps, and then rise to your regular running posture.

Contrary to the advice of some coaches, once you're on your way you should try to pick up the ball. You should be able to do this without slowing down. Don't turn your upper body at all and turn your head only slightly and only if you must. A quick glance will suffice. You should be able to spot most balls with your peripheral vision. If you can't connect with the ball out of the corner of your eye, then tilt your head a bit toward the infield and return your focus to first base as soon as you can. If you just can't pick up the ball, then, of course, you must rely entirely on the first base coach, who will tell you whether to run through

fast runners who weren't good base runners because they lacked the other qualities, and slower runners who did well on the bases because they brought other skills beside raw speed to the effort. Quickness and agility count for a great deal. Good reflexes, split-second reactions, and acceleration are part of what you need. You also need to be deceptive and aggressive. Good base runners must take chances. They are confident, but not foolhardy. They use judgment and have honed their instincts to the point where they can trust them. Indeed, instinct seems to be more a part of baserunning than any other aspect of the game. The best runners don't use the coaches much at all, and even sometimes ignore them and make good on their daring and their judgment. Lastly, the ideal base runner has practiced different kinds of slides and is sure about using them.

the bag or take a turn. It is desirable for a runner to take full responsibility for himself because there is no delay or chance of miscommunication. Younger players, naturally, will depend more on coaching until they develop their skills and begin to trust them.

No matter what kind of ball you have hit, run as fast as you can. There is no such thing as a routine grounder until the putout has been made. The fielder can bobble the catch, he may have a hard time getting the ball out of his glove, his throw may be off the mark, or there can be an error on the part of the first baseman. The faster you run, the faster the fielder must make the play and the greater the chance that an error will occur. Run in a straight line, but to the outside of the foul line, so that if a fielder's throw hits you, you will not be called out for obstruction. Never lengthen your stride or lunge or jump to reach first, these moves are counterproductive and actually slow you down. They also increase your chance of a leg or foot injury.

Slide into the base only if the first base-

Ken Griffey, Jr., pivots on his front foot, takes his first step with his back foot, and stays low as he bolts from the box.

man is pulled off the bag and you are trying to avoid the tag. On all other plays, aim to touch the front half of the bag with either foot. Any time there is a chance of a play at first, you want to run through the bag at full speed. It is common practice to turn into foul territory, but you can also continue down the baseline—just don't make a move toward second base. Slow down quickly and look over your right shoulder for the ball so that if there is a chance of advancing to second on an error you can do it safely.

Rounding the Bag

A good turn at first base is based on the theory that there is no such thing as a single until the defense proves it can hold the runner to one bag. The batter wants to come around the bag, and if the fielder is having any difficulty coming up with the ball (or if he's napping, or if you can hurry him into a miscue), continue right on to second. One key is to not take too wide a turn rounding the bag. Obviously, the more ground you have to cover the longer it will take, and when you consider how close many plays are, you realize the importance three or four feet can make. Where you begin to angle out to make your turn is largely a matter of field conditions and personal preference. Some players run straight down the baseline and wait until they are within fifteen feet or so of the bag, then veer to the right; others begin their move to foul territory about halfway to first; still others pick a spot several feet off the bag and aim for it right out of the box. I recommend running entirely in foul territory in a gradual curve that allows you to take approximately a twelve-foot arc into first base and run straight to second.

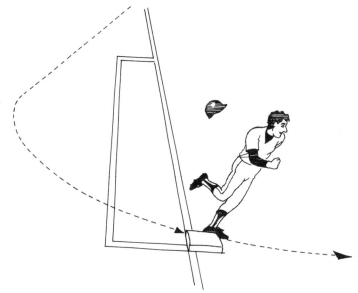

A smooth turn that allows you to head straight to second is the correct way to round first.

Whatever suits you, make your turn smooth and tight. Ideally, you touch the inside of the bag with your inside (left) foot and pivot toward second. Using the left foot helps your body get a balanced lean toward the infield and allows you to push off the ground, control the turn, and accelerate with the right foot. But whatever foot gets to the bag first is the one you use to plant and push off the base. You don't want to break your stride even if it means that you will touch the base first with your right foot. Once you have turned, you should be able to go a considerable distance down toward second before you have to decide to advance or retreat. The distance you go depends on where the ball was hit. Go farthest on balls to left, less on balls to center, and not far at all on balls to right. Your speed, the opponent's fielding ability, and the game situation are other factors. Run in a straight line. If you're more than a yard off a direct line between bases, your turn was too wide. If the ball is fielded cleanly, return to first. One possible exception is if you have taken an aggressive turn on a ball hit to left and the fielder misses the cutoff man or throws behind you, in which case you may decide to try for second.

The principles of rounding the bag at first can be applied to other bases when you are going for extra bases or have been advanced by a following batter. There is one important difference: the mechanics of accelerating and getting out of the box may require you to slow down as you approach first and make your turn. Under no circumstances should you be running at anything less than 80 percent of top speed as you round first. If you make the turn correctly at other bases, you shouldn't have to slow down this much. Retaining balance and control is essential, but if you practice baserunning, rounding the bag at sprint speed will come easier.

TAKING A LEAD

Types and Stance

Once you are *on* first, you want to get into a state of readiness to get *off* first. This begins with leading off the base. First check the fielders and look for signs from the third base coach (young players might review the game situation with their first base coach). All this is done with your left foot against the bag. As the pitcher takes his sign, you take your lead. You don't want to be moving while the pitcher is in his stretch; you might be moving in the wrong direction. Once you're a step or two away from the bag, you move with a shuffle step, first your right foot then your left, sliding along sideways, constantly concentrating on the pitcher. Whatever you do, don't cross your left foot over your right and make yourself a sitting duck for a pickoff.

The length of your lead is determined by whether the pitcher is a righty or a lefty and how good his moves are, the condition of the running surface, the game situation, your reflexes and skills as a base stealer, and the type of lead you are taking. Try not to vary the length of your lead when you are stealing and when you are not. An observant pitcher or catcher will pick this up and plan accordingly. The goal is to get as far away from first as you can and still get back on a pickoff attempt. Most runners gauge this to be a step (or two) and a dive. Some of the best in the business start from four and a half steps out, although Rickey Henderson prefers three and a half. If you can get back standing up, touch base with your left foot and wheel backward with the right foot so that you can lean away from the first baseman. If you dive (and this should be the norm if you have a long enough lead), reach for the base with one hand only (because you can reach farther and quicker that way than if you extended two hands). Keep low and absorb the brunt of hitting the ground with your chest.

Against a right-handed pitcher, once you are twelve or fifteen feet off base, you have reached the position of your *primary lead*. Your eyes are focused intently on the pitcher, watching for the pickoff or a tip-off that will allow you to steal. You should be comfortably crouched, leaning forward at the waist with knees bent. Pointed at the pitcher, your feet are at least shoulder-width apart and parallel to each other (your right foot can be opened slightly toward second). Keep your arms hanging loosely in front of you and do not rest your hands on your knees. Your weight is evenly distributed on the balls of your feet, enabling you to go in either direction. This is called a *two-way lead*.

If you extend your lead a bit and lean toward first, intending to draw a throw and return to the bag, you have taken a *one-way lead*. This is a tactic used to determine just how long a lead you can assume with this pitcher and what kind of moves he has. The information will benefit you and all your teammates who subsequently try to run on this pitcher. A variation on the one-way lead occurs with a lefty on the mound and runners on first and third. You try to draw the throw at first while the runner at third breaks for the plate.

After the pitcher breaks from his set position, you can move farther toward second base and assume your *secondary lead*. At this time your attention is directed at the plate. Your body will be facing a point midway between second and third, and your right leg should be descending from a step as the pitch crosses the plate. If the catcher handles the ball cleanly or if the batter hits a catchable line drive, you will pivot on the right foot and return to first. If the batter hits the ball on the ground, in the air for an apparent hit, or if the ball is in the dirt, you bring your right foot down, push off, and accelerate to second base. Timing is of the essence here, and a misstep almost always results in an unnecessary out.

One last kind of lead is called the *walking lead* because the runner ambles off first and begins shuffling toward second as the pitcher assumes the set position. It is used mostly against right-handed pitchers who are not paying attention to the runner. A left-hander or alert right-hander will see the movement toward second and make the runner stop or pick him off. Lou Brock was a master of this maneuver. John Wathan, the Kansas City Royals manager, used this move to steal 36 bases in 1982 and set the stolen base record for catchers. You don't see it used much in the majors because it is so easily thwarted.

Leading Off Second and Third Base

Even slow runners can afford to take a longer lead off second base than they did at first base. It's harder for the pitcher to keep tabs on you, and if he tries the pickoff, he's got to wheel and turn before he throws. In addition, there is no fielder holding you close to the bag. If a fielder tries to keep you honest, you have succeeded in dis-

rupting the opponent's defensive alignment, giving the hitter an edge.

A primary lead of twenty feet in a straight line toward third base is about right. If the fielders are playing you loosely, your lead can be even longer. You develop momentum and advance even farther as the pitcher delivers the pitch. When the ball crosses the plate, you can be more than a third of the way down to third base.

With two outs, you take a lead about fifteen feet from second and twelve feet behind the bag. You have less than one chance in three of scoring from second with two outs. In a close game, you'll be going on anything. With the lead behind the bag, you're already into your arc and can round third and head straight for home on a single.

The lead from third base is shorter. You will sometime be picked off with a stealing lead off first or second and a pitcher with a good move. It's embarrassing, but part of the game. Getting picked off third is inexcusable. Your secondary lead is far more important than your primary lead. To begin, you should not be much farther from the bag than the third baseman is, but as the pitcher begins his movement to the plate, so can you begin with a walking lead. By the time the ball crosses the plate you should be fully turned to home, with your weight on your front foot, ready to return to third or break for home. This will allow you to score on a wild pitch, a passed ball, or just about any ground ball.

Be sure you take your lead in foul territory to avoid being called for obstruction on a batted ball. Return to the base along the foul line, but in fair territory. This will make it harder for the catcher to see the third baseman and harder for the third baseman to handle the throw if one comes.

With two outs, take a lead off second that puts you into position to round third and head for home. In other situations, running to third in a straight line is usually called for.

Tagging Up

While most people associate tagging up on a fly out with a runner on third base, runners can advance from any base. The mechanics are the same. Depending on which one will give you the clearest view of the baseball, place your right or left foot on the bag. Crouch and keep your weight on your front foot which is 18 to 24 inches from the bag. As soon as the ball touches the fielder's glove, push off the inside edge of the base, and take a full stride with your contact foot. Some coaches recommend another technique in which you do not crouch until the last moment before the catch, gaining momentum as you move into your stride.

When tagging at a base, brace your foot hard against the bag until the catch has been made and then push off.

Baserunning blues. Too many Yankees for one base. If you get into a rundown, look for the chance to run into a fielder in the base path and draw an obstruction call.

Look how intently Rickey Henderson scrutinizes the pitcher, looking for any little sign that says, "Go!"

GETTING THE JUMP

Reading the Pitcher

It is an axiom of the game that bases are stolen "on the pitcher." This is not to say that the catcher or fielder is never an accessory to the theft, but merely places the primary blame for most thefts on the broad shoulders of the hurler. The most successful base runners can detect the small signs that reveal which direction the pitcher will throw. The best runners operate on a subconscious, instinctive level that can't be taught, but even mere mortals can watch for the giveaways that help a runner make the right decision.

If the pitcher is left-handed, he will be facing you and easier to read. Even so, two of the best pickoff artists I ever encountered

One key to reading southpaws is to watch their striding foot. If it breaks the rear plane of the rubber, the pitcher must deliver the ball to the plate.

in my career were Steve Carlton and Jerry Koosman. Watch the southpaw's eyes and his head. The basic move that most left-handers use is to look toward first before throwing home and vice versa. Once the pitcher is set, watch his left foot. If it moves off the rubber, the ball is coming your way. If he gets his striding foot into the air, look how high he lifts his leg. High kicks usually result in a pitch and low ones in a pick-off attempt, but some pitchers are just the opposite. If the pitcher's striding foot breaks the rear plane of the rubber, he must pitch to the plate. If his rear leg is bent, he is probably preparing to push off and go to the plate. If his leg stays straight, watch out for the pickoff. The shoulders and trunk can also reveal intention. A tilt back with the whole upper body often precedes a throw to first, whereas a rotation of the shoulders to the left is used most frequently to deliver the ball to the plate. There are no hard and fast rules here; some pitchers are very creative.

The two key spots to watch on right-handers are the right foot and left shoulder. The pitcher must have his pivot foot in contact with the rubber to pitch and can only throw to first if he pivots, so watch his right heel. If it comes up, scurry back to base. The pitcher also needs a closed left shoulder to begin a proper delivery to the plate and an open right shoulder to be able to throw to first. Some pitchers will duck their head a bit to check the runner and then raise their head before going to the plate. If this happens consistently, watch for the bill of the cap to come up and then take off.

Much of this advice depends upon the pitcher's being a creature of habit. It is true that pitchers like to establish a tempo, a rhythm, and then stay in the groove. Do a cadence count on the pitcher's delivery and see if he falls into a set pattern. A pitcher may also give the same number of looks to first before going to the plate. Other little telltale signs crop up, a twitch here, a move there. The savvy pitcher breaks out of his rhythm with runners on base, but many remain predictable, so study the pitcher, watch the keys, and, when you get the chance, run!

One-Two-Three-Go

After you have taken your lead, assumed your stance, and watched the pitcher for any tip-offs, you're ready to go. As soon as you see that the pitcher is committed to throwing home, you can take off. You break for second by digging in with the ball of your foot, lifting your heel, and pivoting on your right foot and pushing off and crossing over with your left foot. Your left arm will cross over your body as your right arm drives back, setting up the pumping action that will help you accelerate and establish momentum. As with getting out of the box, the first few steps are crucial. Don't overstride and lose balance or understride and lose steps. Staying low will help you keep your balance as you lean and drive toward second. Once you have completed your first half dozen steps you can rise up and get into your regular stride. While some coaches tell you never to look back, to just concentrate on reaching second, I recommend that you glance back quickly toward home to see what's happening. If you time your glance correctly and don't turn your head, you'll be able to pick up the ball without losing any speed and have more time to respond to the play as it develops. I call the way I get from base to base, "nine strides and a slide," but unless your legs are as long as mine you will probably take more steps.

SLIDING

Headfirst

The headfirst slide is the fastest way to make it to a base. Less area is in contact with the ground for a shorter period of time, and instead of easing your center of gravity backward (as with a leg-first slide), you are instead propelling it forward and taking advantage of your body's natural lean as you run. While it may look more dangerous, it is actually safer if you know how to do it.

The foremost practitioner of the headfirst slide in recent times, Pete Rose, was never injured while sliding in more than twenty years of hard-charging, hustling, aggressive play. The hands are the most vulnerable to injury, but with care and the use of batting gloves you can lessen the chances. With a headfirst slide it is also easier to see the ball, to reach for the base, and to avoid the tag—and the fielder has less of a target.

You're better able to see if and where the ball has gotten away from the fielder, but it will take you longer to get up and proceed to the next base if this is in order.

You begin the slide about ten feet from the bag. You have moved your upper body progressively lower as you approach the base. You launch yourself from one leg with your body in a single plane parallel to the ground. The move is smooth. If properly executed, you are not leaping or diving, but gliding into the base. Extend both your arms. Keep your body straight but not rigid. You want to be relaxed as your thighs, chest, and forearms hit the ground at the same time. Keep your head and hands up. Don't use the headfirst slide going into home or when you break up the double play. If you know there is going to be hard contact on the slide, go feet first.

As with all slides, but perhaps most so when you go headfirst, he who hesitates is lost (and maybe injured). The cardinal rule of base stealing is not to be timid, hesitant, indecisive. Whether you take the headlong plunge or the feetfirst option, go for it!

Bent-Leg Slide

This is the most popular slide in baseball—in part, I think, because people have an innate fear of throwing themselves headfirst into anything, particularly if a hard ball, the hard ground, and a hard-nosed infielder are involved. The bent-leg slide is also easy to teach and allows for a quick recovery in case the fielder doesn't come up with the ball. It is a versatile slide and can be used to approach the bag directly from the front or from the side.

Start the slide ten feet from the bag. As with the headfirst slide, think "glide." Control is important here. You don't just collapse or throw yourself to the ground. You fall in stages. Push off with either leg and then tuck it underneath you so that your bent leg and your top leg together form a figure 4. After your bottom leg touches down, you sit back on your backside and ride the rest of the way. Throw your hands into the air and restrain the impulse to use them to help break your fall. An old trick is to pick up a handful of dirt in each hand as you take your lead. This is a prime time for hand injuries. You will be conscious of your closed fists and less inclined to lower them to the ground. Even though your torso is arched back, your chin should be close to your chest to give you the best view of the base and ball. Your top leg is bent slightly at the knee to allow your leg to flex when you touch the base. You make contact with the heel of your foot, which is

Your hands may touch down first, but if you are sliding correctly, your arms, chest, and legs will reach the ground at roughly the same time and distribute the blow evenly.

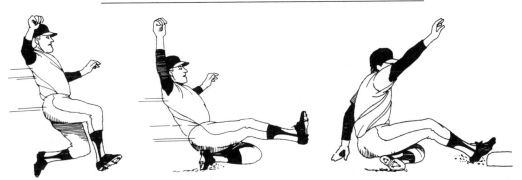

Launch! Hit the dirt! Touch the base! The three stages of the basic slide. Fold your bottom leg under your top leg so that together they form a "4." Keep your hands high.

Ole! Ken Griffey, Jr., after liftoff. Practice sliding until you feel confident about hitting the dirt.

about six inches off the ground to avoid catching your cleats.

A variation on this slide, called the pop-up slide, enables the runner to stand up quickly and dash off to the next base. You start the slide a bit closer to the bag and do not lean back. As the instep of the foot on your extended leg touches the base, you should be sitting up in a fairly erect position. You straighten your top leg as you make contact and brace against the bag, and begin to rise up on your bottom foot. With your center of gravity more forward, your momentum should bring you to your feet, ready to push off to the next base. The pop-up slide is the one most commonly seen in the majors. It is simple to master, relatively safe, and you can stay fully aware of the action.

Hook Slide

The hook slide is basically a desperation maneuver to avoid a probable tag. It is the slowest and most dangerous of the slides, but the most creative and evasive. Because the runner slides past the bag before making contact, it is sometimes referred to as the "ninety-three-foot slide." The runner also runs a higher risk of leaving the baseline, oversliding, or missing the base entirely. There is no exact way to execute this slide. You essentially design it and do it in the same instant. One advantage to the slide is that as you move past the bag you have more than one option how to touch it. You can use the trailing foot or either hand. You can even pull a "bait and switch" on the fielder by first extending one hand and pulling it back as he goes for the putout, then reaching out to touch the base with your other hand. Tricky? Yes. Desperate? Yes. Remember, you're trying to evade an otherwise certain putout. The ball has beaten you to the base and your only hope is that the throw pulls the fielder to one side of the bag. You then slide to the opposite side.

To slide to the right, take off on your left foot and drop to your right side. The outside of your calf and thigh and your hip bear the brunt of the slide. Your right leg is relatively straight as it slides to the right of the bag. Your left or top leg is bent only enough to allow it to touch the bag. The bigger the bend, the longer it will take to reach the base. Touch the corner of the bag with your toes. Your two legs together should resemble slightly opened scissors. As your body goes past the bag and you make contact, the scissors will open wider. To slide to the left, simply reverse the directions of these instructions. Even good and elusive base runners have a natural tendency to slide on only one side. The versatile, complete player can be confident, comfortable, and safe sliding on both sides.

Regardless of which slide you use, good timing is essential. If you start too early,

To pop up quickly from the bent-leg slide, keep your torso more erect and use your braced front leg and momentum to stand up.

Bait and switch slide on Jim Presley. Do you see why they call it the ninety-three-foot slide?

Another improvised hook slide. In a game of inches, a long reach can be a big advantage.

you are slower to the base and may in fact not reach it. Sliding late increases your chance of injury. Two keys to sliding are: when in doubt, do it; and don't hesitate or, worse yet, change your mind. Get down! You can't be afraid to slide, and the best way to gain confidence is through regular practice. It is a skill you will not use in every game, but when you need it, you have to be ready, willing, and able.

VARIATIONS ON THE THEME OF LARCENCY

Thou Shalt Steal

The combination of necessity and opportunity and changing times has brought about an increased emphasis on speed and base stealing since I entered the pros. Oh, sure, Ty Cobb set his records a generation before I was born, and Maury Wills became the first major leaguer to steal 100 bases in 1962, but these players stand out because none of their contemporaries came anywhere close to their accomplishments. Now there are speedsters all over the place. I think this happened because artificial turf required faster defensive players and this defensive speed translated into offensive speed, and because players are better conditioned today than previously. The new stadiums, such as the "Homer Dome" in my hometown, Minneapolis–Saint Paul, may yield some cheap home runs. By and large, however, they are roomier, and the days of bandbox stadiums like the Polo Grounds or Ebbets Field are long past. The offense has had to develop additional ways to score runs.

We've also gotten more scientific about base stealing. Lou Brock started us in that direction. My first full year in the majors,

1974, Brock (at age 36!) broke Wills's record and stole 118 bases. He not only was fast and quick; he was also smart and did his homework. He could probably tell you how many inches he was off base in his various leads, he calculated his speed to second from various spots, and he knew how long it took the pitcher to get the ball to the plate and the catcher to get it to second. The pitcher–catcher–second baseman connection in the majors takes about 3.3 seconds. The fastest runners make it to second in about two-tenths of a second less than that. Some major league coaches bring their stopwatches right into the coaching box with them and relay times to the dugout, where the steal sign is signaled when appropriate.

Despite the analytical approach, stealing is one of the most exciting parts of the game and still involves risk, however calculated. Most analysts and strategists think that for the reward to outweigh the risk the base stealer needs to succeed 70 to 80 percent of the time. Some of the advantages of having a threat on the bases do not show up statistically, however. Defenses have to tighten up, the batter sees more fastballs because the pitcher wants to get to the plate quickly, and there is a general apprehensiveness afield. The defense is edgy and has one more thing to interfere with their concentration. If I had to choose between a team with power and one with speed, I'd go for power, because one swing can win the game. But speed can win a lot of games for you also. I sure know that if the team lacks both, the season can get long real fast.

Making Second Base

Second is the base most frequently stolen. To begin with, more runners get to first than to second. The catcher has his longest throw to that base, and once the runner is there, he is in scoring position. Many clubs are reluctant to jeopardize the chance for a run by having the runner try for third. The best time to attempt the steal of second, all other elements being equal, is when a left-handed batter is at the plate. He will block the catcher's view of the runner and alter the release point of the throw. The catcher has to count on his teammates to tell him when the runner is going, and the split second lost is often the difference between safe and out.

Taking Third Base

Third is the easiest base to steal. The runner gets his longest lead off second. The pickoff is mechanically the most difficult to make and requires the most precise timing. Alert coaches help the runner stay abreast of sneaky fielders. With the preponderance of right-handed batters in the game, the catcher is forced to throw over or around the hitter to get the ball to third. There are nine more ways a runner can score from third than from second, so depending on situation and personnel, this can be a good gamble. More than once, I've seen the Yankees go up a run in the first inning without the benefit of a hit. Henderson worked the pitcher for a walk, stole second and third, and all we needed was a grounder to the middle of the field or an outfield fly ball to score.

Reaching Home

Stealing home is the ultimate in baseball larceny and probably the most exciting single play in the game. You just don't see it very often. Ty Cobb's career total of 36 is as unbreakable a record as there is in baseball. When I consider that on two occasions he did it twice in the same game, I just have to shake my head in amazement. A right-handed batter at the plate is advantageous in stealing home because he obstructs the catcher's view of the runner. The hitter can further help the runner by swinging late at the pitch (and missing, of course) and by staying in the box until just before the slide, preventing the catcher from moving quickly into position. This base is stolen entirely on the pitcher. If he is really concentrating on the batter, has a lapse of alertness, or an unusually long windup and slow delivery, you have an opening. Don't tip off your intentions.

Stealing home is a low-percentage play and is generally attempted only late in the game when a run is really needed and there is a weak hitter at the plate. To add to the air of desperation, there are usually two outs.

I've played seventeen years in the major leagues and have managed to steal home just once, and that was unintended. The first time I ever attempted it, I was a young and foolish buck in San Diego. I tried it just to see if I could do it and was out by a mile as a surprised Willie McCovey took ball four and Johnny Bench slapped that big tag of his on me. My "successful" steal came in Yankee Stadium against Oakland. I charged home on a suicide squeeze. The batter missed the sign and I was hung out to dry. I managed to slip out of the rundown and score. I suppose I shouldn't look down my nose at the accomplishment; it tied me with Lou Brock for career steals of home, and that's nice company to be keeping regardless of how I got there.

Delayed Steal

The delayed steal is seldom attempted at advanced levels of play and, like the steal of home, depends upon special circumstances. This is a steal on the catcher. If his throws back to the pitcher are nonchalant and the second baseman and shortshop are not close to the bag, the delayed steal is possible, especially with a left-handed hitter at bat. As the catcher starts his throw back to the mound, you break for second. You may have already faked a return to first to lull the defense into complacency. Your dash to second forces the catcher to try to change his release, velocity, and target in mid-throw. Indeed, the catcher doesn't know exactly where or to whom he is throwing the ball and is faced with the choice of throwing to a bag that no one is covering, delaying his throw, or not throwing at all.

Double Steal

The double steal is possible when any two bases are occupied, although it is most commonly seen with runners on first and third. There are several ways to execute the play. Usually the runner on first breaks on the pitch and the man on third breaks on the throw from the catcher. Sometimes the runner on first breaks while the pitcher is in his set position. Occasionally a flustered pitcher will balk and both runners advance without cost. More often the move forces a rundown, with the runner on first holding up and avoiding the tag long enough to allow the runner on third to score. The man on first can also initiate the play by drawing a pickoff throw or going on a delayed steal.

In a sense the play is a kind of sacrifice.

You assume you are going to lose the man on first but gain the run. Sometimes you advance both runners, particularly if the player covering second charges into the diamond to take the throw early and fires home to no avail. Sometimes the player at third can cause the fielder to attempt this play by faking the dash home. In that case his team will have runners on second and third and there will no longer be any possibility of a conventional double play.

Good timing and positioning on the part of the runner at third make this play. As the pitcher prepares to deliver the ball, the runner advances down the line, but is usually stationary at the time the catcher receives the ball, so the catcher will not know whether the double steal is on or not. If the runner is right on the line, the catcher will not be able to see the base directly behind the runner and thus will have a harder time gauging the length of his lead. If the catcher takes the bait and throws to second, the runner breaks for home, making certain that the throw is all the way to second and not back to the pitcher.

Fake Steal

Another piece of trickery on the base paths is the fake steal. Like the long one-way lead used to draw the pickoff, it is employed primarily to gain information about the defense. The runner at first bluffs the steal of second by taking three quick strides from his primary lead. Actually the third step is a half stride that helps to slow the runner down and leaves him at the end of his secondary lead, ready to move accordingly as the ball crosses the plate. The runner's movement should cause the fielders to reveal their susceptibility to the hit-and-run. If it draws them out of position,

it might open up a hole for the hitter. In any case, it gives the defense one more thing to think about.

RUNNING AS A CONTACT SPORT

The Takeout at Second Base

In addition to evading the tag and reaching base at full speed without going beyond it, sliding is also used to break up the double play. This is one of the few occasions on the diamond when you deliberately make contact with another player. Your aim is not to cause injury but to prevent or disrupt the pivot man's throw to first. Discard any thoughts you might have of sharpened spikes flying high or a rolling block. There is a legal, effective, and relatively safe way to take out the fielder. At many levels of play, *all* attempts to break up the double play are outlawed, so make sure that your league allows the maneuver.

The takeout begins as a standard bent-leg slide with two wrinkles. With the top of the foot on your extended leg, you are going to try to hook the fielder's striding foot and knock it out from under him. To increase your chances of doing this, bend your extended leg so that it is "cocked" and put more of your weight on your bottom leg side so that it's easier to bring your top leg into action. Keep in mind that your primary objective is to reach the fielder. Depending on which side of the bag he pivots from, you may have to slide to the right or left of the bag. It helps if you have observed infield practice before the game and noted how the shortstop and second baseman pivot.

There are rules dictating how and where contact with the fielder can be made. You cannot slide more than three feet out of the baseline. You must be on the ground when you touch the fielder, and you have to be able to reach the base with some part of your body. Other than that, the man is fair game. You are entitled to the base and it is your responsibility to see that the throw is never made or is off target. This is a move the team can appreciate because it can allow the run to score or give your side another out to work with.

There's No Place Like Home

There can sometimes be a major obstacle between you and the plate. He's called the catcher. If he is blocking the plate and doesn't have the ball, he is guilty of obstruction, and after contact is made the umpire should award you home plate. If the catcher has the ball, however, you are going to have to earn the base. The wages are high and the work is hard. Catchers are often burly types, and with all their equipment, they are padded and protected. Nevertheless, it's your job to score. If there is a gap or some daylight so that you can see the base and touch it with a slide, go for it. If the catcher is doing *his* job, though, and the plate is indeed blocked, you must barrel into him and hope to dislodge the ball. I must emphasize that this is no time for a cutesy slide. You've got to make something happen.

There have been some spectacular collisons at home plate over the years. Two of the most famous occurred in All-Star games, and I was involved in one of them. The first was between Ray Fosse of Cleveland, catching for the American League, and Pete Rose, trying to score from second on a single. It happened in the tenth inning of the 1970 game. There were two outs with Pete on second when Jim Hickman singled. Pete knew that if he stopped at third it would take another hit to score him. He also knew the outfielder's arm and knew it would take a perfect throw to nail him. The perfect throw came, but Rose beat it by a fraction of a second and won the game.

The play I was involved in occurred in the ninth inning of the 1987 game. I was on second when Hubie Brooks threw wide of first on a double play attempt. I was rounding third when I saw that pitcher Steve Bedrosian, who was covering the base, had to dive for the throw. I figured he'd have to come up with the ball cleanly, know I was going, and throw accurately to the plate. And even if all that happened there would still be a collision, so I went for it. I sure did try to jar the ball loose from Ozzie Virgil, but he was a rock and held on to the ball to keep the game scoreless. While I didn't succeed on that play, I'd try it again. It was our best scoring opportunity in a game we went on to lose in the thirteenth inning. Sometimes you make it; sometimes you don't. But don't let anybody be able to say you didn't try.

RECOMMENDED RESOURCES

Maury Wills on Baserunning. (Athletic Institute, 200 Castlewood Drive, North Palm Beach, Florida, 33408). Video Tape. $120.00.

I didn't win this dance at home plate; Rick Dempsey did.

But *this* was a score. Note how my front foot has dislodged both ball and glove from catcher.

CHAPTER SEVEN

Fielding

THE BASICS

Positioning

One might think fielding begins with the act of catching the batted ball, but for the thinking player it really begins with anticipating where the ball is likely to be hit. Winning baseball frequently comes down to having the right people in the right place at the right time. You don't always achieve that ideal combination, but try to station your available personnel appropriately. Planning, preparation, and practice are necessary to correct positioning.

Even casual fans are aware of positioning at some level. They see the infield playing at "double play depth" or moving in to cut off the run at the plate, but few people recognize the extent to which conscientious professional players try to gain the edge through anticipation. Approximately 150 times or so in every game, the ideal fielder will compute the situation based on what he knows about the hitter, pitcher, count, inning, and a host of other details. On the ideal team, every player is involved on every play. The changes in position might be subtle, but if the player is really

No, that's not Seattle Mariner coach Rusty Koontz waving to a fan. He's positioning an outfielder according to the "book" on the hitter.

in the game, he is making them. If he doesn't, a coach should get his attention and move him. The best players anticipate and make the plays in their mind before making them on the field. Visualization precedes execution.

The whole process of positioning has gotten more systematized and sophisticated as baseball has become more scientific. To be sure, "keeping book" on your opponents goes back decades. The most famous defensive alignment ever used in baseball was designed by Lou Boudreau to counter Ted Williams more than forty years ago. The most extreme shift I ever witnessed was used regularly against Willie McCovey. Until recently, the pitcher might direct fielders from the mound based on where and what he was going to throw. With the advent of computers, however, the practice has reached new levels.

Even those teams that do not rely heavily upon the microchip must ratchet up whatever method of recording and analyzing they use just to stay competitive. Baseball is a game of percentages, and those who ignore them do so at their own peril. Extensive charting and pre-game briefings are now a way of life in major league baseball.

Teams record every pitch that is made to every hitter they face, and the result. They show where in or out of the strike zone the pitch was delivered, the count, and the location and kind of hit made. This way they can discern patterns. They throw out the bloops or check-swing hits and determine a hitter's true strengths and weaknesses. Where will he hurt you? What's his "out pitch"?

Most teams supplement this historical record of the player with the most current information. You know what he has done in the past. What has he done in the last three days? An advance scout is on the road all the time. He watches the team's next opponent and sends his charts and reports to the team. The Texas Rangers use a different system. Using a satellite dish, they record their opponent's last seven games and then excerpt the relevant footage. Their hitters can see what kind of pitches they will be facing and their pitchers can study the other hitters in action.

Naturally, this degree of preparation and approach to positioning is beyond most teams except at the highest level of play. This is not to say that any team can't initiate a less formal and exhaustive analysis of the opposition. And the complete player should be thinking along these lines. Think! Anticipate! Position! Execute! If you fail to prepare, prepare to fail.

Running

Unless the ball is hit to or near you, running must precede catching. Outfielders will run more forward and backward and infielders more side to side as a general rule. Whichever direction you run, go on the balls of your feet. The ride will be smoother and faster. You usually will have your eye on the ball as you run. If you run flat-footed, hitting on your hard heels, you will jar your upper body and may interfere with your view of the ball.

To help improve your speed, review and practice sound running mechanics. Eliminate any wasted motion. You want to achieve a smooth and easy stride. Your arm swing should be relaxed, with rotation at the shoulder, not the elbow. Don't cross your body with your arms. Swing your arms straight ahead. Make sure your hands go no higher than your forehead on the foreswing, and your elbows go no higher than your shoulders on the backswing. Your elbows should almost be grazing your hips. Short, quick, regular, powerful arm pumps will help you to drive your legs. You should be pushing as you run, getting good leg extension with your rear leg driving you. Run on the balls of your feet with your weight forward. Keep the force you gen-

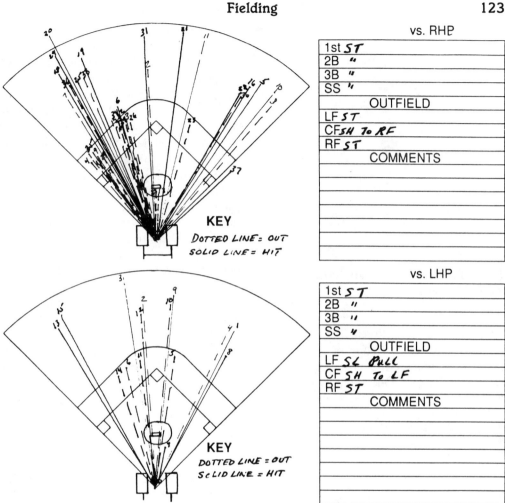

vs. RHP		
1st *ST*		
2B "		
3B "		
SS "		
OUTFIELD		
LF *ST*		
CF *SH To RF*		
RF *ST*		
COMMENTS		

KEY

DOTTED LINE = OUT
SOLID LINE = HIT

vs. LHP		
1st *ST*		
2B "		
3B "		
SS "		
OUTFIELD		
LF *SL Pull*		
CF *SH To LF*		
RF *ST*		
COMMENTS		

KEY

DOTTED LINE = OUT
SOLID LINE = HIT

These charts show how Cal Ripken, Jr., has hit Seattle Mariner pitchers and are used to determine the best way to play him.

erate going forward, not laterally or vertically.

Naturally, you must adapt this technique when running backward or to the side. Stay as balanced as you can within the lean that is necessary to reach the ball. The faster you run, the more energy you must put into slowing down, getting into position, and throwing the ball if required. Shorter, more chopped steps and a conscious effort to lower your center of gravity will help bring you to a controlled stop.

Catching

To make sure everyone understands the importance of catching the ball *with two hands*, let me say at the very beginning

Catch the ball with two hands whenever you can.

that, with few exceptions, this is the way it ought to be done. Young players in particular (and their coaches) need to stress the two-handed catch. One obvious benefit is the insurance factor. Less experienced fielders drop more balls, and having the throwing hand near to cover the catch will save the team grief and the player embarrassment.

Another important reason for the two-handed catch is that your throwing arm is brought into position early. As you cover the ball and make the exchange from glove to hand, no extra motion is needed and time is saved. You move naturally from catching to throwing. If you do this all the time, then you don't have to think about it on those occasions when a quick throw is essential. This reason for the two-handed catch becomes more important the higher the level that you play because you will face speedier, more aggressive, smarter runners.

When I emphasize the importance of two-handed catches, some young players

ask why more professional players don't catch this way. Many of the best, like Kirby Puckett, do. Others, more nonchalant, stylize their catch—like Rickey Henderson's infamous "snatch." Pros should probably set a better example of good form for the kids, but I'll tell you, pros handle a lot of routine flies out there and it takes discipline sometimes not to be a bit blasé.

For some players, the catcher and first baseman, for instance, the one-handed catch is how you receive the pitch or that long throw from short. Look the ball all the way into your glove. Young players especially will sometimes close their mitt prematurely, perhaps overeager in their anticipation.

The higher you catch the ball, the closer your arm will be to its throwing position if a throw is needed. So that you can move smoothly into the throw, make the catch on your throwing side with your opposite shoulder angled toward your intended target.

Throwing

Every player should master the mechanics of good throwing. For the good of individual players and the strength of the team, injuries must be minimized, and the arm is one of the more vulnerable parts of the athlete's body. The other reason for making throws that are mechanically correct is to increase their strength, accuracy, and quickness.

A good throw begins with a good grip. Your index and middle fingers should be a half to one inch apart, crossing one of the long seams of the ball. Your thumb will be directly below your middle finger, gripping the ball. A firm but relaxed grip is ideal. You inhibit your throwing ability by grasp-

Learn to grab the ball or rotate it in your grasp quickly so that you throw with this grip.

ing the ball too tightly. Your other two fingers should be comfortably off to the side of the ball. Their main function in the throw is to stay out of the way.

This grip allows the ball to "bite" the air with four seams, maximizing accuracy and lift. Practice grabbing the ball in your mitt and, if necessary, rotating it to achieve the correct grip. Do this through touch only, no peeking. This grip must become automatic for you.

Unless you are throwing out of position or must hurry, throw with the three-quarters overhand motion. This gives you the greatest accuracy and strength. Square to your target. Swing your arm back in a long arc and complete, closing your upper torso preparatory to opening it up and uncorking your throw. Then come forward. Keep your eyes on the target and aim all action to that point. Your fingers should be behind and on top of the ball. Shoulders level, lead the way with your elbow. Keep it up, even with or higher than the shoulder of your throwing arm. If you drop your arm, you will throw from the wrong angle. Your wrist is fully cocked through this stage.

The arm precedes the leg on the way back, but the leg leads on the way forward. To get the best zip to your throw you must

Outfielders usually and infielders sometimes can make a full stride, three-quarters, overhanded throw.

thrust forward and plant your striding foot. Push off explosively with your pivot foot, which is planted perpendicular to your target. Stride to a point beyond an imaginary line between your pivot foot and your target. This helps open up your body as you move to release. Longer throws require longer strides.

Release the ball with a whipping action of the arm and good snap to the wrist. This is the famous motion known as "pulling down the shade." You pull your fingers down and impart that last rotation to the ball. Your arm should continue across your body and into the follow-through, which, like the batter's follow-through, helps to power the ball.

Follow-through is as important for you as it is for a pitcher. You have just forced one of the most delicate and complex parts of your body to explode. Now you must slow your body down and regain control and position. Your throwing arm continues its sweep in front of and then to the side of your body. Your glove hand is fully behind you and, like a pendulum, swings back and helps reestablish your balance. Your lower body follows the momentum of your upper body. Your pivot foot comes forward to parallel your striding foot in a comfortable spread, facing the action.

Fighting the Elements

Even if you have mastered all the elements of fielding sketched above, don't think you've got it made. There are elements beyond your control that will also be a factor in how well you play the game. Balls get "lost" in the sun, or in lights at night, or in the roof of a dome, and all of a sudden a routine pop-up turns into a double.

The sun will be a powerful enemy of yours in the field. Those bright and beautiful dream days that fans love can be a nightmare for fielders. Minimize the sun's effects with flipdown sunglasses, your throwing hand, or your glove. If you use the sunglasses, make sure you have plenty of practice so you are not getting used to them or fumbling with the flip when you need to be concentrating on the ball. If you use your bare hand, hold it close to your face or you won't shield out much sun. It's better to use your glove hand. You will block more of the sun, and if you position yourself correctly, your glove should be close to the right position for catching a fly. You can also have problems with stadium lighting.

If you catch the full glare of the sun or the stadium lights in your eyes, all is not lost. You may be able to recover your vision in time to make the catch. Some coaches recommend that you look down to the ground momentarily in the attempt to regain your full vision. Another way is to keep your head in position and close your eyes for a moment. I just try to wait it out and hope the ball will emerge from the lights and I can see where the devil it is again.

If you have truly lost the ball, you have two options. You can call out and inform your teammates "I lost it!" and hope that one of them can reach it on the fly or at least pick it up quickly. With runners on base, you might try to decoy them instead of giving them the immediate advantage of knowing that you're probably not going to catch the ball. Stay in your flycatching position and pretend that it's a can of corn.

Winds are fickle, but they blow fair and foul to friend and foe alike.

Hope that the ball lands near you, preferably in front of you (but not on you). Lou Piniella pulled this fake in the 1978 playoff against Boston to help the Yanks win the game.

The wind also plays havoc with balls. A windblown pop-up can land in the darnedest destinations. Heavy and even moderate winds can move the ball farther than you might think. The spin the hitter puts on the ball combines with any movement of the air to make the ball do funny things. You can't always judge what the currents are like near you by looking at which way the wind might be blowing a flag at another part of the field. Swirls and crosscurrents are fairly common.

The wind can also be your ally. Even balls stroked smartly into a wind can hang up and be blown back instead of making it over the wall. San Francisco is notorious for the strong winds that buffet its Candlestick Park. The wind giveth and the wind taketh away. Pop-ups can go for extra bases and powerful clouts can run into a headwind and hang up, slow, or die there, dropping harmlessly to a grinning fielder below.

Perhaps the most dangerous playing conditions to face are those resulting from rain. A wet field is easy to slip on, and serious injury can result. An unexpected slide can take you out of a lot more than the play. Depending upon the situation, you may decide to approach the ball with shorter, more controlled strides. Rain is even worse when it's also cold out. In 1989 in Baltimore, the fog even rolled in. The Orioles lost a game when a routine fly to the outfield descended through a fog bank and went for extra bases.

ON THE MOUND

The Fifth Infielder

Teams love to have a pitcher who cannot only pitch a whale of a game but can also field his position well. Once you release the ball to the plate, you become a full-fledged member of the infield. You are literally the center of the infield. Beyond the skill with which you deliver the ball to the batter, you can win ball games with your defense. Learn to pivot, tag, backup, cover, and all the other elements of fielding.

Think of how important it is for a team to be strong up the middle. The pitcher can't afford to be the weak link. Teams win and lose games, but only the pitcher gets his name next to the W's and L's. A good arm is even better when it's connected to a good glove. If you can be counted on to handle balls up the middle, your ball-hawking middle infielders can spread their wings and fly a little farther into the hole, tightening the team defense.

The pitcher has to cover or play backup on just about every ball hit. No player on the field will go as frequently to as many different destinations. The mound is rarely where you should be. In fact, if you do not move in the correct direction after your pitch, you'll probably be in someone's way. You must become familiar with and regularly practice the plays you are expected to make so that they are like second nature to you when you need them in a game.

You've got enough to think about when you are on the mound. Learn your plays and positions so that they are conditioned responses, automatic reactions. You need to be quick on the mound. Just calculate how quickly the ball gets to the "hot corner" and divide by half. It gets hotter faster on the mound.

Follow-through and Fielding Position

Most guides to the game stress the importance of completing your follow-through in such a manner that you are ready to field the ball. Very few pitchers can do this naturally. Tom Seaver was one, and indeed he was known for his fielding. The two smoothest fielding pitchers that I ever faced were Jim Kaat and Ron Guidry. Not so smooth was Bob Gibson, whose hard follow-through left him on one leg off to the side of the mound like a stranded stork (and still *he* was also known for his fielding). It might be easier if the pitcher considers the completion of the follow-through and the move into fielding position as two separate actions.

Ideal fielding position for the pitcher is feet parallel, squared to the plate, weight evenly distributed on the balls of the feet, glove high, ready for anything off the bat of the enemy. In reality, few pitchers ever reach this position regularly because they have a more important task: completing their follow-through (and before that, finding the strike zone and getting the batter out).

At the end of your follow-through, you should have completed a weight shift in front of and then behind your striding leg. You move from full arm extension and pronation (rotation of the palm away from the body, thumb down and out) to deceleration. This is a critical part of your deliv-

Once you have finished your follow-through try to assume a ready fielding position as quickly as possible.

ery. Slowing down your arm puts strain on your body and is indeed a shock to your system. Most hurt shoulders result from bad mechanics during follow-through. The better you extend and balance on your rear leg, the farther you can extend your upper body and absorb the shock.

As you can tell from this description, your position at this point is not very close to the ideal fielding position. In actuality, few pitchers finish their follow-through as well as they should. Many cut it short, perhaps to better get into fielding position. Fear might be a factor here. You sure don't want to be out of position and off balance with a ball coming back to you faster than you threw it (clocked at up to 150 miles per hour). Like most other actions in baseball, you strike a balance between extremes of position and conflicting needs.

Fielding Bunts and Grounders

Fielding the grounder or bunt is the play that you will be called upon to make most frequently. Like a batter moving out of the box or a fielder getting a jump on the ball,

your first two or three steps are the most important. Move fast and at the same time keep your rump low. Take shorter steps to slow down as you approach the ball and don't get too close. You want to reach straight down or in front of your body toward your throwing side for the ball, not between your legs. You want to be in a position to plant or pivot and make a good throw.

In the rush to pick up the ball, fire to the base, and nip the runner, some pitchers fail to complete the first step. You must control the ball! And remember, picking up the ball bare-handed is harder to do than most people think. Limit your attempts to balls that have stopped rolling. Even with those, exercise caution. Look the ball right into your hand or glove. Focus on the ball, not the runner. Make sure of your grip before you turn your attention to the base and your throw.

Footwork on your throws is important. You may have to crow-hop to allow your fielder to get into position. Keep moving and step as you throw. Avoid flat-footed tosses. Follow your glove to your target. Put some mustard on the ball. Throw through the base and not just to the base. Your throws to fielders are simple and direct with no movement, unlike anything that you want to be serving up to the plate.

The hardest ground ball to field is probably the high bouncer. Another hard play is the ground ball between you and the first baseman. You should try to reach every ball you think you can, because you want your first sacker at the bag if possible. Call quickly and loudly for balls you can field. You must do the same with your third baseman, although unless there is a runner on second, you won't be pulling him from the bag with a runner approaching.

Covering Bases

Another common play that the pitcher must master is covering first base. Every time the ball is hit to the right side of the field, the pitcher must immediately start toward first. Run to a spot ten feet or so from the bag, then turn slightly, hold your glove chest high, and parallel the baseline for your last few steps. This will give your fielder a better target to aim for and lessen your chance of injury through contact with the runner. Make sure you take the throw before you look to the bag. Immediately after you touch the base, pivot and be ready to cut off any other runners. This is good practice even when there aren't runners. You'll also cover first as the last leg of the 3–6–1 double play. The sooner you arrive at the bag, the sooner the fielder can throw and you can accept his offering.

The pitcher covers second base on all balls that the second sacker and shortstop chase into the outfield. If another baseman covers second, the pitcher covers the vacated base. Likewise, when the third baseman and shortstop both go after a fly and there is a runner on second, the pitcher covers third. The pitcher will cover for any fielder who precedes him to third. With runners on, the pitcher must also cover the base on any ground ball that draws the third baseman in.

Covering home is a job you must be ready to do every time the catcher is drawn away. It is particularly important with runners in scoring position. The passed ball or wild pitch with a player on third requires you to dash to the plate and take a position in front of it, but not blocking it. Give the runner the outside of the plate and hope for a timely, accurate throw from your catcher that will allow you to wheel to your right and tag the runner with the back of your

Give your fielder a good target and avoid contact with the runner when you cover the bag.

glove. Some pitchers make this play after dropping to one knee. Don't forget that runners can advance on foul balls. If your catcher goes back for a foul pop-up when there is a runner on third, you must cover the plate immediately.

Backing Up Bases

Balls to the outfield generally require you to backup a base. Backup second base on all singles and free your first baseman to stay at the bag. Man on first, backup third. Man in scoring position, backup home. Stay a base ahead of the lead runner, a base ahead on all extra-base hits. Position yourself deep behind the appropriate base in a direct line with the (anticipated) throw. Give yourself plenty of room to corral a maverick throw. If the batter hits a gapper and you do not know whether you should backup third or home, go to the midpoint to see how the play develops.

BEHIND THE PLATE

The Ideal Catcher

More than any other player, the catcher must be a multifaceted individual. He must be a take-charge kind of fellow, because he needs to be in charge of so very much. He calls the pitches. He directs the team's defense. He's the only player facing the entire field of play. His position has been compared to that of the quarterback on a football team, and I think the comparison is apt. He is the on-field strategist, the team leader calling the game. There's no room for shyness or mental slowness here.

Although pre-game meetings will help determine how to pitch certain players, it helps if the catcher is a bit of a historian who can remember how the batter has reacted before in similar situations. And he must be alert to subtle changes that the batter might make even in between pitches. He needs to be a student of the game. The ideal catcher must also be a good psychologist, skilled at handling hitters and pitchers (and umpires). He must know which pitchers will respond to a kick in the pants and which ones need a pat on the fanny. He's a cheerleader not only for his pitcher but also for the entire team. His encouragement, endurance, enthusiasm, and example go a long way toward setting the tone for the team. He's the energy in the battery that juices the team.

The catcher must be strong and durable. Think of the number of deep knee bends the constantly squatting catcher covered with hot and heavy equipment must perform in an inning, a game, a season, a career! How many foul tips, broken bats, wild pitches, and full-steam collisions must he survive? No position is tougher on the body or the mind. A catcher who cannot play hurt or injured will not play for long. For that throw down to second, the catcher should have the strongest arm on the team. Seldom will he be able to put his full body behind the throw as other players routinely do.

Lastly, the catcher must be able to live up to his name and catch. He needs a good pair of hands because he'll be handling all kinds of pitches and throws—hard breaking balls, balls in the dirt, and those high-pressure throws meant to nail the runner at the plate. As the receiver of the pitcher's offerings, the catcher will be a large factor in how the umpire calls the pitch.

Except for my catcher, every position player on my all-star team is playing today. The exception is Johnny Bench, and the reason is that he is so exceptional. He is hands down the best catcher I ever played against and with (in five All-Star games). He revolutionized the game. How the position is played, the equipment that is used, and even how the catcher is perceived—all this changed because of Johnny. You can legitimately refer to pre- and post-Bench eras in the history of catching.

Always big for his age and coached by his dad, a onetime minor league catcher, Bench acquired a proficiency and maturity way beyond his years. At fourteen he was playing with adults. His maturity was apparent as soon as he hit the bigs, and it went far beyond his ability to handle pitchers. Johnny Bench controlled the game more than any other player I ever saw. It took him just two years to go from Rookie of the Year to his first MVP.

He could beat you with his bat, his brains, his arm, and his glove. The calls behind the plate, the play at the plate, the rifle throw to cut down a runner, the clutch hit, the late-inning three-run dinger when his team was down by two—these were his specialties. I don't want to take anything away from the rest of his team, but Bench had a knack for making his pitchers look good and his manager look smart.

Bench exuded power. He held the bat at the very end, getting every bit of torque as

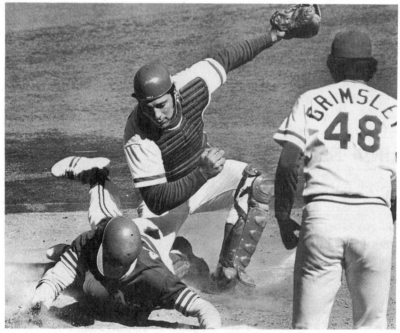

Sure tag at home. Johnny Bench in World Series action. Nobody I ever played against let you know so definitely that you were OUT!

he pulled, lifted, and drove the ball. He had meathooks for hands and incredible wrists. Johnny was built like a backstop. He was a rock blocking the plate. A runner who beat the throw and tried a cutesy slide found it was like trying to slide around a large tree trunk. I saw players bounce off his leg, then he'd catch the ball and bang them with it. On top of everything else, Bench was quick. Catchers are traditionally (and some, notoriously) slow. Not Johnny. If anybody was faster at getting out of the box and pouncing on a bunt or a runner, they played before my time. It's no wonder that Johnny is my all-time all-star catcher or that he was elected for the Hall of Fame in his first year of eligibility.

Position

The catcher is the only player on the team allowed to position himself in foul territory. How deep the catcher sets up is determined by where the hitter positions himself. You want to be underneath the hitter and as close as you can without risking being struck by the bat. This is probably closer than might first appear. Most hitters stride forward as they swing, so the path of the bat will not be as close to you as the hitter's initial stance suggests. If the batter is up in the box, move forward. If he's deep in the box, move back, but keep the same distance from every batter.

The other factor determining where you position yourself is what kind of pitch you call for. You have to give the pitcher a good target, and you must be ready for balls that are farther inside or outside than you wanted. If you signaled for an inside pitch, line up as square with the inside corner as you safely can. On outside pitches, you will not have to worry about the proximity of the batter. Never set up with the midline of your body outside the strike zone, however. Make this shift at the last moment to avoid tipping off the opponents. Some catchers make this move before they flash the signal so that there is no detectable movement after the sign. We're not talking great distances here. Six inches in either direction is usually sufficient.

Giving the Sign

The catcher's initial stance allows him to call for a pitch so that the pitcher and middle infielders can see the sign but the opponents can't. Squat comfortably directly behind the plate. Although different players with different physiques may vary the stance somewhat, start with your feet a foot or so apart. You should almost be able to click your heels together. Most catchers keep their feet even, but some drop one foot a little behind the other to help maintain balance. Your weight is evenly distributed on the balls of your feet. Your knees are spread far enough apart to balance you but not so far as to reveal your signs to either base coach. A little less than shoulder width seems to work best. If your right knee is pointing at the pitcher, you won't have to worry about the first base coach stealing your signs, and your glove, extended in front of your left knee, will hide your signs from the third base coach.

Keep your rump low, below the level of your knees and just above your heels. Your upper torso is fairly erect and you are looking straight at the pitcher. Rest your glove on the front of your left knee facing in to further shield your signs. Your right hand extends down from your thighs and is deep against your crotch. You must not extend your fingers below your thighs or an ob-

The key to giving the sign is to make sure the pitcher knows what you have called for but that none of your opponents do.

servant opponent will pick up your signs. Be careful not to move your arm or elbow on certain signals. You wouldn't want an opponent to detect that you wiggle your elbow for a change-up but not a fastball, for instance. It helps to keep your elbow tight against your body.

To minimize the chance of exposing your signals, run through them in practice. Position teammates or coaches at first and third and in the on-deck circle and the dugout. See if they can detect your signs and if so, make the necessary adjustments. During the game, your outside infielders can make sure you are not tipping pitches.

The Basic Signals

Even though there are different ways to give signals and variations on the signs themselves, the practice is remarkably standardized. The usual way to give the sign is by extending one or more fingers. Most hurlers have three good pitches, some have four, and a few, mostly relievers, get by with two. A very few pitchers have only one. You can also flash signals with the whole hand or by touching certain parts of your body or gear. Use these methods only under adverse conditions (deep shadows, a poorly lit field during a night game, or a pitcher with baaad vision) or at lower levels of play.

The universal signs are one finger for a fastball, two fingers for a curve (this is why it is sometimes called "the deuce"), three for a slider (or the change-up if the pitcher doesn't throw the slider), and four for the change-up. Spread your fingers as far apart as possible to give the pitcher the best chance of reading the sign. To further eliminate the possibility that three fingers will be confused with four fingers, you may choose to wiggle your digits when you flash four.

Some catchers use the flash or pump system, whereby the pitcher counts not the number of fingers but the number of times a sign is given. The location of the pitch is usually given after the type of pitch has been indicated. By holding his palm up or down, the catcher can signal whether he wants the pitch high or low. By touching his thigh or pointing his hand toward or away from the batter, the catcher indicates whether he wants the pitch inside or outside.

With a runner on second base, you no longer can use these simple signals. They must be disguised. The common way is to give several signs in sequence, having decided beforehand which sign is the true one. Using this method, your pitcher knows that no matter how many signs you flash, the second or, say, the third one is the one you want.

Other systems are based on reassigning the numbers, combining two signs (add the first and the third one given to get the true one) or restarting the sequence at a certain number. If you are using a four-pitch sequence and flash five times, you are really calling for a one, the fastball. Signs can also be switched by giving a prearranged signal. If this is the case, the pitcher must respond with his own signal to indicate that he knows the switch is on.

The key here is to complicate the procedure sufficiently to mystify your opponent without doing the same to your pitcher. You have to avoid cross ups. If you call for a heater and you get a curve that gets away from you and advances the runner, you've defeated your purpose. If there's any doubt in your mind as to whether the pitcher understands you, ask the ump for time and go to the mound.

Other Signs

In addition to calling the type and location of the pitch, the catcher originates other signs. He often uses a thumbs-up closed fist to call for the brushback or knockdown. He establishes a shakeoff sign in case he changes his mind and a false shakeoff sign to play with the hitter's mind. He'll indicate a pitchout with a simple fist. The catcher should also signal the fielder that a pitchout is coming in his direction. He can do this through a movement of the glove or some other motion that is distinctive but will not arouse the opponent's suspicion. The fielder then signals back that the play is on by a simple action such as touching his cap. One other time the catcher alerts his teammates is when there is a chance of a double steal. The catcher indicates to whom he intends to throw.

The Receiving Stance

The receiving stance is distinctly different from the one you use to call for the pitch. Again, however, comfort should be one of your goals. You should be able to move quickly into and, even more importantly, out of the receiving mode.

Once you have given the signal, move directly into the proper posture to catch the ball. If you've given the sign from the correct position, you shouldn't have to alter your depth behind the plate. You will be as far forward as safety permits. The closer you are to the plate, the better your position to handle bad pitches, get to bunts, and throw out the runner. Another advantage of playing up is that you have a better chance of catching foul tips. This is important when there are already two strikes on the batter.

Rise up (your rump should be about knee-level and your thighs parallel to the ground), bend at the waist, and lean forward. About 60 percent of your weight should be forward, with your heels just lightly touching the ground. Your feet are shoulder-width or farther apart, and your right foot will be a few inches behind your left foot. (If you are one of those rare left-handed catchers, lead with your right foot.) Your feet and your knees should be at least slightly turned out.

Don't crouch too low or go down on one knee or you will lose mobility. At the same time, if you are too high off your haunches, you will limit the movement of your arms and head and strain your neck looking at the pitcher. Hold your head up and keep your gaze level. With no one on base you can afford to squat lower and present your pitcher with a good low target.

Bend your elbows with the forearm of

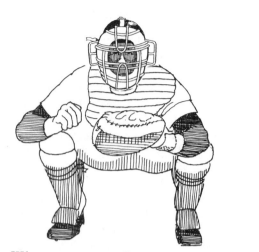

When you move from giving the sign to setting the target, you rise higher on your haunches but still stay low.

your catching hand at about a forty-five-degree angle to your body. Relax your arms. If you extend your catching arm too far, you run the risk of locking your elbow. Keep your elbows outside your knees. The fingers of your glove should point upward and the heel downward. Keep your hand relaxed and bent upward at approximately forty-five degrees.

Keep your throwing hand out of harm's way. Fold your fingers lightly around your thumb. If you make a loose rather than a clenched fist, your hand will have some cushion and give when it gets hit. With no runners on, you can hold your hand behind your back or to the side of your knee. With runners on, you must bring your hand up to the glove. Keep your relaxed fist with the thumb safely tucked in directly behind the glove's webbing. Cover the ball as soon as the ball hits the mitt so that you can speed the exchange and throw if this proves necessary.

Setting the Target and Catching the Pitch

Give your pitcher the best target possible. He should be able to look right into your mitt. With your wrist at a forty-five-degree angle, he won't have a full view of the pocket, but if you hold the glove at the center of your body, the pitcher will actually have a target within a target. As discussed earlier, you will have to move laterally for pitches that you want delivered inside or outside. Once you have set the target, keep it still until the ball has left the pitcher's hand.

The act of catching the ball well requires a certain delicate touch. If you are going to help your pitcher "paint in the black" (catch the corners of the plate), you'll have to be a bit of an artist yourself. Indeed, as will be discussed shortly, once the pitcher has delivered the ball to you, even if it's not picture perfect, you may have to "frame" it.

Receiving requires you to strike a balance, to find the happy medium between aggressiveness and softness. You must play the ball and not let it play you. At the same time, you cannot extend your glove with any rigidity or stab at the ball. Soft hands and letting the ball come to you are part of the equation, but you want to catch strikes in the strike zone. If you wait until the ball has passed through the zone, the force of the pitch will move your glove and make some strikes appear to be balls. You also may have difficulty receiving the ball in the pocket if you pull the glove back and give with the pitch.

Your arm, wrist, and hand must be as loose, relaxed, and flexible as you can make them. Make sure your elbow is outside your leg and your arms and hands are well away from your body. In general, pitches above your knees should be caught with the fingers up and the glove upright. For pitches below the knees, the palm should be facing up. If you are balanced on the balls of your feet or leaning a bit in the direction of the pitch, you should be able to sway slightly with the pitch and catch borderline pitches in such a manner that they will be called strikes more times than not. You must avoid any extra movement or pushing close pitches out of the strike zone.

The practice of funneling the ball fluidly toward the strike zone is called "framing the pitch." Don't try to take balls clearly out of the zone and pull them toward you in a hopeful representation of a strike. Umpires resent this charade and it will backfire on you. Your aim is to give the benefit of the doubt to the pitcher, not the hitter. Framing is a subtle, easing move that depends on the right glove angle and good wrist control. You roll your hands and rotate the glove. Curl your fingers and frame corner pitches inward. High pitches get framed down and low pitches up.

Pitches out of the Strike Zone

A good catcher has to be able to handle bad pitches. There's more involved here than simply stopping the ball so that runners cannot advance. If you can handle all kinds of pitches, you give your battery mate the necessary confidence to throw them. Although a pitcher with good control can lull you into complacency, you are better off if you anticipate a bad pitch every time.

Pitches that will not go into the dirt or force you to rise up can be handled by different methods of staying in your crouch and shifting your body. On pitches that are not far out of the strike zone, keep your feet in place and sway your legs, hips, and arms in the direction of the ball. For balls that are farther out of the zone, take a single step in the direction of the ball. Shift your weight to your other leg and push off. If the ball is so far outside of the strike zone that the single step or sway method will not suffice to catch the ball, begin with the step maneuver but follow by shifting your weight fully to the stepping leg and lifting your other leg so that you will be able to shuffle farther in the direction of the ball if needed.

The most surprising bad pitches are the ones that sail high. Seldom will you call for a high pitch, so when you get them they are the least expected. Don't push for the ball with your mitt. The best way to handle a high pitch is to raise the glove higher than the ball and angle it downward. That way if you miss the catch, the ball will not glance off and go behind you but should bounce down in front of you.

Balls in the dirt are a common part of the catcher's turf. If you cannot master stopping them, consider another position. You want your pitcher to be delivering balls low in the strike zone, and a large number of these balls will be lower than either you or he wanted. With runners on, you must forget about catching the ball and focus on blocking it. If you manage to catch the ball, fine, but this shouldn't be your primary aim. Just keep the ball in front of you. In the majors, unless there is a runner at third, some players go for the catch, ready to drop to their knees if necessary. Others will drop to one knee and lower the other if they have to.

The easiest dirt ball to handle comes straight at you. Kick your heels out and drop to your knees immediately, giving yourself as wide a base as possible. Face the ball squarely so that if it deflects off your body it will not tend to do so at an angle but in front of you, where it is most easily played. Move both hands to the center of your body and low so that the ball cannot get under you. Jam your chin into your chest, lowering your head and protecting your throat. Your upper torso should be pushed forward, your shoulders hunched. If you attack the ball at this angle, you should be able to smother high bounces and keep balls from running up and over your body. On high bounces keep your arms down and against your body.

On balls in the dirt to your right or left, you can use the blocking method described above if the ball is not far off the plate and you remember to twist your upper torso and square yourself to the ball. For balls farther away, you cannot use the immediate drop

to both knees. You first must step toward the ball. Do not raise up, as this will hinder your move to the side and require you to expend additional time and energy getting low. Step with the foot nearest the ball, drop the knee of your other leg to the ground, and move both hands to the space between your foot and knee. Make sure both arms are inside your legs and close to your body.

The Wild Pitch/Passed Ball

Whether the scorer rings it up as a WP or a PB is immaterial. The result is the same. The ball has gotten by you and must be retrieved. This is strictly a move to limit damage. You have already given the runner one extra base; you don't want to give him two. Be quick about it. Get out of your stance and turn, drop your mask, and run to the ball. Set your right foot behind the ball so that you will not lose your balance when you bend to pick it up. You will also be set to throw, although this is often not necessary.

Runners safely at second usually don't risk going to third unless you are unusually slow getting the ball in hand or they are unusually smart, aggressive, or fast, or some combination of the above. Then don't be surprised what they do behind your back and in your face. Your teammates will let you know if the runner is going to challenge you. If he doesn't, walk the ball back to the plate, call time, pick up your mask, and get back into your receiving position.

Throwing the Ball

Not counting the necessary footwork, the act of throwing begins when you take the ball from the glove. It helps if you have caught the pitch in the pocket and not the webbing, where it is harder to retrieve. While playing catch, in practice, and during games, even if you're just throwing back to the pitcher, get the ball out as quickly as possible until you are certain that you can consistently remove the ball rapidly when you need to. With repetition and practice, you should be able to improve your speed. The sooner you get the ball, the sooner you can grip and throw.

Proper grip is important. You want to be catching balls with movement, not throwing them. Leave the sinkers and sliders to your battery mate. Grip the ball across the seams where they are widest. With the right release, this grip will rotate the ball with backspin and give you the straightest throw. Reach into your glove with your full hand to grab the ball and feel for the seams. If you do not immediately grab the ball with the correct grip, rotate it as you bring the glove and ball back and cock your arm to throw.

You are looking to establish a continuous motion and a direct route back to the throwing position. Your glove hand will go back as far as your right shoulder, closing your left shoulder and helping to "cock the gun" for your throw. Bring your right arm above and past your ear. You seldom have time to bring the arm back to full extension as an outfielder might. The emphasis is on a quick release, so neither will you be able to stand up fully and lean back. The best catchers have learned to throw while still low with their knees bent.

Some guides to the game and coaches will tell you to "throw from the ear." Ignore them. Their advice is half-cocked; your arm shouldn't be. Your arm must go farther back than this or you will short arm the throw with a subsequent loss of power and accuracy.

As your right arm starts forward, keep your elbow up and your glove arm parallel to the ground. Your left shoulder should be aimed at the target. For greatest accuracy, throw overhand. Snap your wrist straight down as you release the ball. Make sure that your grip on the ball is firm but not so tight as to interfere with or delay the release.

The fewer steps you take in making your throw, the quicker will be your release. While still in your crouch, you should be up on the balls of your feet and moving. Basic footwork consists of pivoting and pushing off with your right foot as you stride with your left foot, but there are three principal variations on the theme of throwing to a base.

The *rock and throw* method is the quickest because it entails the least motion, but, for that reason, it requires the strongest arm. As you catch the ball, rock back onto your right foot, which will essentially stay in place. As you rise up and cock your arm to throw, shift your weight to your striding left foot and fire. Avoid a premature weight shift as this will diminish both the strength and accuracy of your throw. Efficiency is the big advantage with the rock and throw, and the lack of momentum is its biggest drawback.

The *jab step* or *step and throw* involves more footwork but gets more of your body behind the throw, allowing a catcher with an average arm a better chance of nabbing the runner. Just before you catch the ball, step forward six or eight inches with your right foot and plant it perpendicular to second base. You now can pivot, turn your hips, draw back your arm, stride with your left foot, and fire. If the pitch is to the left of the plate, a step with the left foot followed by a jump pivot is needed to make the throw. This is the best method to use, however, with pitches that require you to move sideways in either direction. One advantage to this technique is that you get the body in motion before you even receive the pitch. One disadvantage is that the play requires considerable timing and an accurate assessment of where the ball is going before you begin your step.

The *jump pivot* or *jump shift* method is probably the one used most frequently at all levels of play. As soon as you catch the ball, jump up, lift your feet, and make a ninety-degree turn to your right. Your right foot should land almost directly below where you were crouched and your left foot beneath where you set the target. With your body already cocked, take a short stride toward second and throw. You will need good balance and quick feet to perform this maneuver properly, but you gain a lot of momentum quickly for your throw.

As you may be able to discern, a good throw starts with the feet. A diligent catcher moves them constantly, shifting and shuffling as necessary. It's tempting to just stay in one place and reach for pitches. Don't be lazy and get into bad habits. Use footwork to stay in front of the pitch. And don't be lazy on the throw you will make more often than any other, the toss back to the pitcher. Put a little extra effort into your throw so that your battery mate doesn't have to put any extra effort into his catch. Aim the ball between his waist and his chest and deliver the ball to your target.

Catchers cannot extend their throwing arm as far back as other fielders but must get it far enough back to put zip on the ball.

Steals and Pickoffs

While you can go through several games without succeeding at the pickoff, you should continue to practice and attempt it. The pickoff is one of the most demoralizing plays that you can inflict upon your opponent. It's worse than being erased on a steal attempt where you at least made a run for your money. Getting caught stealing is an occupational hazard. Getting picked off is just downright embarrassing. At the same time, a pickoff throw that goes awry and allows the runner to advance swings momentum in the other direction.

The length of the secondary lead and how the runner's weight is distributed (and, of course, the individual talents of the base runner) determine the advisability of attempting the pickoff. How the runner is leaning at the moment the catcher receives the ball is key. The catcher also needs to observe the base runner's footwork, his degree of concentration, and any other tendencies that might contribute to a successful attempt.

The pickoff at first base is the most common and the easiest. You do not have to alert the fielder that it is coming because he should already be holding the runner on. Conventional wisdom has it that the pickoff to first is more difficult with a left-hander at bat. Another view is that it's best to try this play with a left-hander at bat because he will shield you from the view of the runner. You should set up a bit deeper than usual and call for an inside pitch, which will facilitate throwing behind the hitter. Pivot on your right foot and shift your left foot as you rise and face the base squarely. You should be able to make this throw without taking actual steps. If you find this

difficult, or the pitch forces you to move, or the batter's position hinders your throw, you should naturally perform whatever footwork allows you to make the play.

The catcher can initiate several kinds of pickoffs at second. If he sees the fielder get a jump on the runner, he should signal the pitcher to wheel and throw. The catcher can also signal the fielder that on the next pitch, or on the next missed swing, he will be throwing to the base. Make sure that you get a signal back from the fielder who will be covering. One play that really makes a team look foolish is when a perfect throw sails past an unattended bag to the center fielder or down a baseline while the runner is presented with an extra base or free run.

Remember also that just because you called for the pickoff doesn't mean you have to throw. The runner may have stayed close to the bag or the pitch was tough to handle. When in doubt, don't risk a throw. With the pitcher in a direct line between you and the base, you may find that the best way to aim your throw is to pick a spot on the pitcher and let fly. Don't worry about the hurler. It's his job to be observant and get out of the way. Your throw should reach the fielder about knee high.

The throw to third is similar to the throw to first except that you pivot and push off on the left foot. Third base is stolen most often with right-handed batters at the plate. Generally, you will throw from in front of them or over them. Depending on the location of the pitch and where the batter is in the box, however, you may even throw from behind him. Since he is not on the bag, the third baseman cannot serve as your target. Use the base itself, but aim two feet above it. Accuracy is important here. You don't want a throw that will hit the runner or, worse yet, elude the fielder. A mistake here will almost always give the other team a run.

Countering the double steal is probably the hardest single play the catcher is called upon to make. In part, this is because there are so many options and unless the runner breaks for second while the pitcher is still in the stretch, how the play unfolds is up to the catcher. In the double steal with runners on first and second, it may prove wise to gun the runner down at second. He probably got less of a lead than the runner going to third and he might not think you're throwing to second. With runners on first and third, the obvious need is to keep the run from scoring.

If you see the play developing, you can fire the ball back to the pitcher at cap level and take position for the tag or rundown. The pitcher will decide to throw based on the actions of the runner at third. Or you can arm fake a throw to second or third followed by a throw to third or a run up the line. You can also look the runner back at third and throw to second and get ready for a return throw. Lastly, you can throw to the shortstop or second baseman breaking toward the plate, hoping to spur the runner homeward, where you will be waiting for him.

Pitchouts and Intentional Walks

If you suspect the steal, hit-and-run, or suicide squeeze has been called for the next pitch, call for a pitchout or a ball up and in around the chin and try to nip the play. Ideally you will be getting a pitch that the hitter falls away from or otherwise finds next to impossible to hit but that you will be able to handle with ease. The pitchout is delivered to you about a foot off the plate and chest high. A ball at this level is well on its way to where you need to throw it from. Remember, you cannot leave the catcher's box until the ball has left the pitcher's hand.

Set up on the outside of the plate. As soon as the pitcher releases the ball, rise up partially, slide your inside foot to your outside foot, and take a step away from the plate with your outside foot. You don't want to straighten your knees and come completely out of your crouch in case the ball is delivered low. It is easier to go up for a high throw than to go down for a low one. As you catch the ball, you will either take a drop step back with your right foot, then stride with the left foot and throw (left-handed hitter); or you will simply stride with the left foot and throw (right-handed hitter).

An important consideration affecting whether to call the pitchout is the count and how much control your pitcher has. Runners, for instance, like to go on a 2–1 count. The pitchout will give the batter a favorable 3–1 count. You may have to choose between evils and hope that you don't put yourself in a hole.

With an intentional walk there is no element of surprise. You, therefore, can stand up to receive the pitch. You are still prohibited from stepping outside the catcher's box until the ball has left the pitcher's hand. You must therefore extend your arm in the direction you want the pitch and thus offer either your glove or your throwing hand to the pitcher as a target. Stand as close as you can to the edge of the box and move out of the box with the same slide step employed for the pitchout. While the intentional walk seems the most automatic of plays, some pitchers who seldom have been called upon to use it are capable of screwing up. It's just not where they are used to throwing or the right speed. Be alert to pitches wide of the mark.

Bunts

Batters who are bunting for a hit will try to lay the ball down beyond your reach, so the bunt you are generally called upon to field is the sacrifice. The chances of making the play on a bunted ball are increased if you can get a quick start. When the sacrifice is in order, you should be a bit higher in your receiving stance and drop your right foot back slightly so that you can move out faster. Don't move out too fast. You'll take quite a blow if you move out to field an anticipated bunt that doesn't get made. Talk about smashed expectations!

As you start, flip off your mask away from the direction of the ball and move quickly until you are almost upon the ball. Shorten your strides and lower your center of gravity to slow down and come to a controlled stop. Your chest should be directly over the ball when you field it. Be sure you bend at the knees and not just the waist. Use both hands to pick up the ball even if it has stopped rolling unless the situation is so desperate that a bare-handed grab is absolutely the only way of making the play. If you do grab the ball bare-handed, palm it to ensure the pickup and then grip it properly as you prepare to throw.

Balls down the first base line are the easiest to handle, particularly if you are throwing to first. Keep the ball to your right or run straight at it if the throw is to second or third. Place your glove in front of the ball and use it to sweep the ball into your throwing hand. Rise up, stride toward the bag, and throw. If the ball is close to the line and you have time, you may move into the infield to lessen the possibility of hitting the runner.

Whenever you can, you should throw overhand. This is particularly important when going to first. A sidearm throw may hit the runner. If he's in fair territory, he will be called out, but if he is not, you've just botched the play. If the fielder is not yet in position when you are ready to throw, you may have to crow-hop before releasing the ball.

Balls in front of the plate are handled similarly to balls down the first base line. Approach them from the left if the throw is to first so that your momentum will be carrying you in the right direction. Again, use the glove to scoop the ball into your throwing hand.

The toughest bunts for the catcher to handle are those down the third base line. Run to the right of the ball with your back to first. If the ball is rolling, place your left foot close to it to give you some space as it moves to your right. If the ball has stopped, place your right foot close to the ball. In either case, crouch and use your bare hand to sweep the ball into your mitt. Now you must pivot on your right foot and whirl around to your left. Pick up your target at first base, complete your step with your left foot, and throw. If, before you started your pivot, your right foot was closer to the foul line than your left, you will have less of an arc to turn. No matter how you cut it, however, this is a tough play.

Some catchers, especially in lower levels of play, use another method to field bunts down the third base line. They come at the ball from the left, in essence circling the ball. This play is also used if you think there might be a play at second or third,

Stand over the ball as you field a bunt. Bring glove and hand together in a sweeping/scooping motion that increases your chances of picking the ball up cleanly.

although in that case you do not circle as far. The advantage to this play is that everything is in front of you and you might make a more accurate throw. The disadvantage is that it is slower.

On balls close to either baseline, when it appears the runner cannot be put out, the best strategy is to let the ball roll and hope it goes foul. If there are other runners on, you must make sure they do not advance an extra base as you wait for the ball to go foul, because it might stay fair. Other than that situation, however, you have nothing to lose. If the ball does go foul, touch it immediately or brush it farther foul so that it will not come back into play. The catcher is also in the best position to help his team-

mates decide how to handle this kind of bunt. Tell your teammates to field the ball, let it go, or hit it farther foul.

Pop-ups and Foul Balls

A staple of baseball blooper films shows the catcher going for a pop-up, circling frantically, and then watching haplessly as the ball glances off his mitt or drops without his laying a glove on it. With rare exception, this doesn't have to happen to you if you can do one thing: get into the proper position promptly. Knowing how the ball is likely to travel will help you do that. To begin with, balls hit behind you tend to travel toward the stands on their upward flight and back toward the field on their downward flight. This is known as infield drift and is caused by the rotation of the ball. The higher the ball, the greater the drift. To catch some balls, all you have to do is turn around and, like a boomerang, the ball will return to you. Always keep the ball in front of you. It is more likely that you will underestimate rather than overestimate the degree of drift, and it is easier to move forward than backward.

As soon as you determine that a foul pop has been hit, remove your mask and hold it while you locate the ball. Scan the sky with your back to the field until you find the ball. Do this slowly; herky-jerky motions make the task harder. Only after you have spotted the ball and know in which direction you are going to move should you toss the mask aside where it will not be in your way. It may help you to know that right-handed batters generally foul inside pitches to the right side of the diamond and outside pitches to the left. Reverse these directions for lefties. If you know which way the ball went, make your turn in that direction.

Move to the ball quickly, but do not overrun. In addition to infield drift, you must take the wind into account. Take your position quickly, particularly if you must make the play near an obstacle such as the dugout. This allows you to get your bearings early and avoid having to look on the run or check for obstacles at the last moment, taking your eyes off the ball. If you are approaching the screen, wall, or dugout just as you are about to catch the ball and want to avoid a crash that might jar the ball loose, go into a feet-first slide. Your equipment should protect you from injury, and you can keep your eyes on the ball and your glove up. The sun can also be an impedi-

Keep your back to the mound, catch with two hands, look the ball right into the glove, make the out.

ment to making the catch. Shield your eyes with your bare hand or, better yet, your glove.

Make the catch with two hands at about eye level. The fingers of the glove should be pointing up. You should not reach for the ball but rather allow it to come to you. Some catchers prefer to hold their glove open-faced at the chin or the waist. If this works for you, do it, but the eye-level method allows you to better look the ball all the way into the glove.

Pop-ups in front of the plate may be handled better by the infielders. They usually have the superior angle. Naturally, if you are in the best position, call for it and go for it. If the first or third baseman also call for the ball, yield. They have priority. The pitcher may even get into the act by calling out the name of the teammate he thinks has the best shot. If you end up taking the ball, go toward the mound, turn, and come back in for the ball.

Practice catching pop-ups. You can't do it off a throw or a tilted pitching machine or fly ball cannon. Only a bat can impart the spin that you must master lest it master you.

Force Plays and Double Plays

With the bases loaded and a ground ball hit, expect a quick throw home from the infielder and remember that you need not tag the runner. Simply touching the plate is sufficient. This may seem to go without saying, but in the heat of the game a player can forget, and turning a force-out into a tag play may cost you the second out.

You will essentially be performing more as a first baseman on this play than as a catcher, even sometimes making the stretch to reach the ball. But you have two disadvantages. To begin with, you must get rid of your mask. Then you do not have a solid bag to snuggle your foot against. You must make sure that your right foot is in contact with the plate. Make good and sure! Plant your right foot right in the middle. This will also allow you to move in any direction to take a bad throw and maximize your chances of staying on the plate. (Fancier footwork may be called for if the throw draws you off the plate.) Your left foot should be in front of the plate. After you have done this, take the throw with both hands up and ensure the first out.

Then turn your attention to your throw. If an errant throw hasn't forced you to already take steps, make a jump pivot to your right, face first, and throw. While this move should take you out of the path of a sliding runner, you may wish to step farther down

the line and eliminate the temptation for some aggressive runner to try to take you out. Facing first as you are, you are particularly vulnerable to knee injuries if the runner does slide into you.

Blocking the Plate and Tagging the Runner

The play at the plate is usually one of the most exciting moments in the game. It is, after all, the ultimate putout. The game often comes down to this one play. Make it, you win; muff it, you lose. Strictly speaking, when the catcher blocks the plate before he has the ball, he is guilty of obstruction, and if the rules were enforced absolutely, the runner would be declared safe and the ball dead. In actual practice, this is almost never the ruling. Umpires give the catcher leeway on this play just as they allow phantom forces at second with a runner sliding into the base. More often than not, the runner and the ball seem to reach the catcher at the same time, so timing is the key.

At the risk of stating the obvious, you have to catch the ball before you can tag the runner. Balls from the infield should come in on the fly. Balls from the outfield tend to reach you on one or two bounces. The in-between hops are the hardest to handle. Try to get the ball on the fly or the short hop. You need to catch the ball and not just block it. By the time you retrieve a blocked ball, the runner will be on his way to the dugout.

To keep the runner from reaching home, position yourself just in front of the plate up the third base line on the infield side. Plant your left leg firmly on the base path or in foul territory, cutting off the direct route to the plate. Or you may stay off the line until the last moment; once the runner thinks he can slide clear, you put your foot down. You have protection; he doesn't. Nevertheless, point your foot up the third base line to protect the side of your knee and lessen your chance of a leg injury. Some players actually straddle the line, daring the runner to try to bowl them over. None are more famous for this play than "Iron Mike" Scioscia. Another gutsy (or crazy) catcher who craves contact is Rick Dempsey. He even took on Bo Jackson in a home plate collision and lived to tell about it, albeit from the disabled list.

If blocking the plate in this fashion is the *only* way you can keep the run from scoring, then do your job, stand your ground, get low, and try to absorb the blow with your entire body. If you have the time, make the tag and then spin, wheel, roll with and away from the impact. Most impor-

tantly, hold on to the ball. Grip it tightly and protect it in the pocket of the glove. Avoid the swipe tag. Make a two-handed tag from the waist to the neck, avoiding the runner's arms and legs, which he might try to use to knock the ball from your grasp. As soon as you have made the tag, pull your bare hand and the ball away. The one-handed tag should be used only when absolutely necessary. You may have to leave the plate to take the throw and then dive back to get the runner, for instance.

If possible, avoid the collision. You may be lucky and win the battle, or you might just lose the ball, the game, or your consciousness. If you're unlucky, you may lose a couple of months, the season, or even your career. It's best if you can get in, make the tag, and get out. If you can draw the slide, all the better. You force the runner to commit while staying in control of the

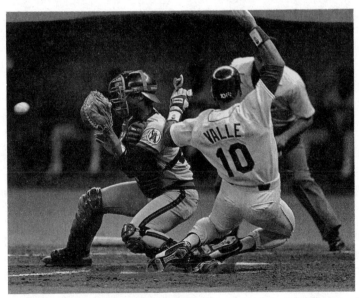

Catcher *vs.* catcher. Notice how Darrell Miller puts his weight on his left foot and takes the plate away from Dave Valle.

If you must block the plate, block it any way you can; but unless you hold on to the ball, nothing else counts.

Backing Up, Covering, and Cutting Off

The catcher's sole job when there are runners in scoring position is protecting the plate. At other times, the catcher is responsible for backing up fielders, covering bases, and assisting the cutoff man. One of the most thankless tasks in professional baseball is backing up first base. It's a long distance to run several times a game and more than a thousand times a season for a play where you'll only see action a few times a month. But part of the job is to be there on those rare occasions when you need to be. At lower levels of play, where erratic throws are more common, the backup at first becomes more important.

The catcher must back up first base on balls hit to the infield and sometimes on those hit to center and left. As soon as you read the hit, run as hard as you can parallel to the first base line, but several feet in foul territory. (Some coaches recommend that you be as much as forty feet off the line, but this is too far away to back up effectively.) You will not be able to get directly in the line of fire on balls hit far to the left. The important thing is to be in the area and moving. On balls hit to the second baseman, you won't have to run as far and should be able to have pretty good position, particularly if he fields the ball in the hole. If you can catch the overthrow, well and good. For balls on the ground, scoop them up with your glove, even if the ball has stopped rolling.

You may have to cover first base on short flies that the first baseman chases. On singles to right, the first baseman might move toward the outfield hoping to draw a wide turn from the runner. You should trail the

plate. When the runner tries to slide around you, push the ball and the back of the glove toward the runner and tag him on the foot or low on the leg. If you aim higher, there is a chance that the runner will touch the plate with his toe before you can apply the tag. You should not have to reach out far to make the tag if you stay correctly positioned. The runner will have to come to you. If you make the tag in this fashion, you should be able to follow through by swinging your arm to your throwing side, ready to catch other runners if they try to advance.

runner and cover the bag if your team uses this play. The runner will also sometimes take a wide turn when a ball in the hole takes the first baseman far from the bag. On all these plays you need to be alert and quick.

The catcher must cover third when the third sacker comes in to field a bunt or a slow roller. By moving in front of the plate, you can back up the second baseman on a single to center when there's a runner at first. You should also back up the pitcher when he is backing up third on balls hit to left. In addition, you will help the pitcher and other fielders get into the correct cutoff position on throws from the outfield and then direct them by telling them to "let it go," "cut," or "relay." The most important cutoff play you will direct is when there is a play at the plate. If the play is going to be close and the throw will take you more than two steps away from the plate, call for the cut.

Working with the Ump

No one will be closer to you throughout the game than the umpire behind you. Indeed, many umps put an arm on you or lean on you in some way to better peer over you and observe the pitch. Not to worry. He's just trying to do his job. If, however, you find your motions constrained by a big black shoe behind you, it is proper to ask the ump to move his foot. You, on the other hand, should make sure that none of your movements interfere with the umpire. Don't block his view of the pitch by rising up to catch it, for instance.

The critical element in your relationship with the umpire is how you disagree with him. It should be a question of "how" and not "whether." The umpire is bound to make calls that you disagree with, and if you do not indicate this in some way you will give the impression that there was nothing wrong with the call or that you don't care. This is not to suggest that you should dispute every call. But one of your many jobs as catcher is to keep the umpire on his toes and ensure as best you can that the game is called consistently.

When you disagree with a call, do it agreeably. Never turn around and challenge the ump. Face forward and ask why the pitch was called a ball. If a pitch you think is a strike continues to be called a ball, you might continue your inquiry, but don't press too hard. Your object should be to plant a doubt in the ump's mind or get a favorable call the next pitch around. If all you do is antagonize the man in blue, you have accomplished neither.

Calling the Game

To be able to call a smart game, you need to know baseball, the abilities of the opposing hitters, and your pitchers. The most important of these elements is knowing your battery mates—not just the kind of pitches they throw, but what makes them tick. One pitcher may respond best to sympathy and calming down, another to a chewing out or a challenge. Whatever route you take, you must be able to instill confidence. Once the pitcher believes in *you* and feels good about himself, calling the game becomes easier.

Each pitcher has a different repertoire of pitches and unique strengths and weaknesses. The only way to learn them is to catch those pitchers as often as possible. Then your general knowledge of each

The relationship between battery mates is the closest on the field. No two players work more together. A good catcher establishes a good rapport with all his pitchers.

pitcher must be adjusted by the specifics of the game you are calling. Your pitcher might have a great curveball that just isn't working that day. Or your pitcher might have a strong pitch that he wants to use too often. Rein him in. Young pitchers in particular frequently strive for the strike out when they should simply be looking for the out. Sandy Koufax said he didn't become a good pitcher until he stopped trying to

make the hitters miss the ball and started to make them hit it. Your pitcher may not always like what you call, but if the result is an out, he will be happy with the result.

Selection involves not only the type of pitch but also its location, in-out, up-down. Changing both the placement and speed of the ball is essential to limiting the hitter's ability to anticipate. Generally up and in or low and away is where you want the fastball. Low and away works well for most curveballs. The key is to not get into a rut; keep the hitter guessing. There are many different ways to get the batter out depending on how you set him up.

Your knowledge of the hitter must go beyond whatever the "book" and pre-game briefings might tell you. Of course, that information must be fully absorbed. Does this hitter like to go for the first pitch? Does that hitter have trouble with low breaking balls? Will a recent hand injury make the batter vulnerable to inside pitches? Beyond that knowledge, however, is what a given hitter is doing during a given at bat. Smart hitters adjust. Has the batter changed his stance in anticipation of a certain pitch? Always be looking for cues for what the batter expects and then dash those expectations.

A final factor to be considered in what pitch you call is the game situation. With a five run lead you may call a much different game than if the score was tied. The pitches you select may be based not only on who is in the batter's box but also by what hitters will follow him to the plate. Is the hit and run or sacrifice bunt a possibility? With a runner on third and less than two outs, what pitch will get you a pop-up or strikeout? The pitch you call is also influenced strongly by the count. When you are way behind the hitter, you obviously need a strike. When you're ahead in the count you have flexibility.

Calling a good game and handling the pitching staff adroitly are the most important contributions a catcher can make to his team. If he also is a steady fielder or regularly delivers timely base hits, these are bonuses, but other teammates can fill in here. No one else on the team can fill the role of field general, setting up the hitters,

working with the pitchers, establishing the tempo of the game. Focus your primary attention on this aspect of your position and you will have your priorities right.

INFIELDERS

The Second Line of Defense

After the battery has had its opportunity to retire the batter without his hitting a fair ball, the infield is the next line of defense. The infield is where the team must mount a consistent defense if it is to be a winner. Letting the ball get through, missing the double play by a stride, dropping the ball, allowing the runner to escape the rundown—these are the plays that will kill you, because more balls are hit to the infield than to the outfield and you will have more opportunities for a miscue. While everybody loves those highlight film defensive gems that leave you with your mouth open, the strength of an infield is determined by how well it turns the routine plays—assists, putouts, double plays, rundowns, cutoffs, relays, backups—these are the bread-and-butter plays that make or break a team.

Position and Stance

Infielders play at varying depths according to the game situation. With no runners on and no other reason not to, most infielders play as deep as they can. With runner(s) on and less than two outs, the infield moves in to double play depth. With a runner on third and the need to keep the run from scoring, the infield moves in again. You will further position yourself according to the inning, the count, the pitch, the type of hitter, your own strengths and weaknesses, and those of the other infielders.

The infielder's preliminary stance is one of relaxed readiness. Spread your feet approximately shoulder-width apart, feet opened outwardly. Distribute your weight evenly on the balls of your feet, poised to move, but comfortable. Your hands can be on your knees until the pitcher begins to release the ball. By that time you should have dropped your glove low to the ground. A low glove is the foundation of good fielding. It is easier to bring your glove up than to lower it.

As the pitch moves toward the plate, so should you. Step with your left foot and shuffle with your right foot. Break the inertia and move in anticipation of the batted ball on every pitch. This is your defensive starter mechanism.

Ground Balls

About 50 percent of all balls hit are on the ground. To become more adept at fielding grounders, keep your head down and your eyes on the ball. Look into your glove every ground ball you can. Your first decision is whether to stand your ground or move in to field it. For all except the hard-hit ones, charge. Different kinds of grounders require different approaches and speeds. In essence, you need to identify the kind of grounder coming in your direction and judge the best way to play it instead of letting the ball play you. Get in front of ball. Keep your glove low to the ground, even on the ground. It is easier to move the glove up than down, and some of the big hops you anticipate may never develop.

Your glove and throwing hand should be well in front of your body, allowing you to see the ball into the glove better and giving you the freedom to adapt quickly to bad hops. You will also have more room to give with the ball. Be sure your glove is angled correctly and open to the ball. Give yourself a good base to work from. Spread your feet comfortably. The width of stance should increase with the length of your legs or the difficulty of the play. Keep your knees, wrists, and elbows bent. Rigidity is the opposite of what you want to achieve. If you are flexed, your soft hands can bring

Ready!

Set!

Go!

When you can, use your body to funnel the ball into your glove.

tions than outfielders, they will use a greater variety of tosses and more of their throws will require finesse. Whenever possible, use the three-quarters overhand throw with the proper stride. This just can't be done for many balls that the infielder will be called upon to handle, however. You might use an overhand snap throw that allows you to put something on the ball even when you cannot stride. Because you will not be able to get your whole body behind many of your throws, they must be delivered sharply, with as much shoulder and arm motion as you can muster and a frisky snap to the wrist.

the ball into your body, cushion it, and prepare to throw it. Even if you do not make a clean catch, knock the ball down with your glove or body. If you can keep the ball in front of you, more times than not you will recover and make the play.

After fielding a ball on the run to either side or in front of you, you might decide that you have time for only a sidearm throw. Most infield throws are, in fact, sidearmers. Part of getting the ball off quickly is to field the ball so that you are close to where you need to start your throw or at least moving in the right direction. A continuous motion is what you should aim for. Generally, you will release the ball below your belt and above your knees. You may

Underhand and Sidearm Throws

Because infielders must make shorter, quicker throws from more different posi-

Going either to your left or your right, you begin and frequently end with a crossover step.

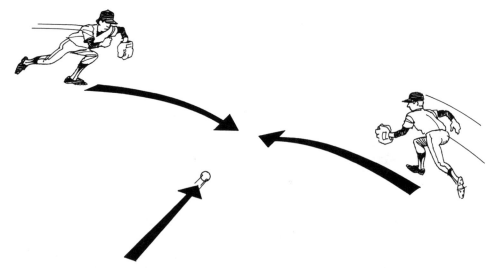

If possible, take a gently curved route to the ball and direct your momentum to get off a better throw (often called the "banana route").

The sidearm throw is used more by the second baseman than any other player, but all infielders and the battery must master the toss.

have to throw from a squatting or bent-over position or on your knees. Infielders benefit by practicing throws from the full variety of unusual poses that they might find themselves in during a game. (Some of the best throws I've seen were from behind the back.)

The underhand throw is used when the fielder is close to the target, has fielded the ball low, and needs a quick toss. It is even more important than usual to get the ball out of the glove quickly to give the fielder the maximum chance to see the ball. The movement is similar to that of a bowler. You do not want a ball with high arc. You want it to go directly to the fielder's chest, so put lots of wrist into the toss and follow through, but not above your waist.

The hardest infield throw to master is the backhand flip. This is not a throw for long distances. It is made with a stiff wrist and

Two keys to the underarm throw are to get the ball out of the glove quickly and to throw it with a low arc.

a motion similar to that of a basketball player passing to his right. Again, the ball may prove difficult for the second fielder to see. Throw it to him at chest level. A less accurate backhand flip (and underhand toss) is made directly from the glove. Because there is less control throwing from the glove hand, this play should be attempted only when it is absolutely necessary to catch the runner.

Communications

One of the keys to getting an infield to work well together is frequent and clear communication. The average fan would probably be amazed at how much chatter goes on and how little of it is idle in a well-oiled infield. Compared to the roomy expanses of the outfield, the infield operates in cramped quarters. There are more alter-

Make the backhand flip with a motion similar to passing a basketball.

"I got it!" "Mine!" "I have it!" However you say it, make sure your teammates know the ball is YOURS. Harold Reynolds calls for the ball.

natives to consider and communicate, and infielders must communicate faster than outfielders.

One of the most obvious ways infielders talk is by calling for the ball on pop-ups. Other communications relate to who is covering which base, the kind of pitch coming, whether a pitchout is coming, and other details that affect the way you play. Generally, shortstop and second base communicate with silent signals to each other and with verbal signals to the first and third basemen. During infield practice, before the game, and on the bench, infielders will frequently talk and go over plays so that on-field communication during the game can be kept to a minimum.

FIRST BASE

The Ideal First Baseman

First base is sometimes thought of as a position where you can hide a player with defensive weaknesses or the place where old ballplayers retire when they can no longer range the outfield or cover third. And indeed first base is where Dr. Strangeglove (the nickname given to Dick Stuart) and Marvelous Marv Throneberry exhibited their legendary, but all too real, ineptitude. While it is true that the first baseman doesn't have to have the arm of other fielders, he certainly should be a good gloveman.

No one except the pitcher and the catcher will handle the ball more in the course of a typical game. The first baseman must catch the greatest variety of throws. If he is tall and rangy, the theory goes, he'll present a bigger target and be able to reach farther, so some coaches look for this kind of player. (First basemen get a lot more low throws than high ones, however.)

While height is an asset, my all-star first baseman doesn't fit this mold. At 5'11", Don Mattingly is probably the shortest first sacker in the major leagues, but he doesn't give an inch to any other player. He's the best in the business. While he lacks speed, a quality he shares with many of the big men who play this position, he is plenty quick, which is far more important. Mattingly moves easily in all directions. His quick (soft and smooth) hands and feet allow him to compensate for bad throws. He seems to be able to take a ball out of the dirt without effort. Our infielders feel that if Don can touch the ball he'll make the putout. His recent streak of almost 1,400 chances without an error proves their faith to be well founded.

The ideal first baseman is left-handed, as is Donnie. As a lefty, his glove is on the side where he has the most territory to cover. He doesn't have to pivot on the throw to second or third. Lastly, his glove

Don Mattingly is as good with his glove as he is with his bat, and that's saying a lot.

is already on the right side of the bag on pickoff attempts. Don's quickness and agility give him great range, and he starts the 3–6–3 double play as well as anyone I've seen.

In addition to physical quickness, the ideal first baseman is mentally quick, and here is another category where Mattingly excels. More split-second decisions are probably made by the first baseman than any other position. Whether to handle and where to throw on the bunt. Making the cutoff or not. Throwing to the pitcher or making the putout unassisted. These are just a few of the snap judgments a first baseman is responsible for.

Traditionally, the first baseman is a solid hitter, even a slugger: Lou Gehrig, Hank Greenberg, Dick Allen, Orlando Cepeda, Johnny Mize, Gil Hodges, Willie McCovey, Frank Howard, and now Don Mattingly. Quite a tradition, and what a way to carry it on. Every year Donnie sets a Yankee, American League, or major league record. Home runs in eight consecutive games. Six grand slams in one season; 238 hits, including 53 doubles, in 1986. A lifetime .327 batting average.

I play behind Donnie in the field and bat behind him in the lineup, so I have plenty of time to study him. He is proof positive of how you can change your style and your impact through hard work. In high school and the minors, Mattingly hit for solid average but with little power. Then in his first full year in the majors, he homered twenty-three times and followed with three straight thirty-plus seasons. I saw that transformation. He studied and worked and learned how to get down behind the ball and drive it. Lou Piniella helped him with his weight shift and how to pull the long ball into the short porch at Yankee Stadium, and Donnie is now proving to be one of the game's most feared power hitters.

Picking my all-star team involved some tough decisions, but not at first base.

Positioning and Footwork

The first baseman commonly positions himself four different ways depending upon the situation he faces: holding the runner, playing deep, halfway, and playing in.

With a runner at first, you have to hold the man on. You face the pitcher squarely and give him a good waist-high target. Your feet are about shoulder-width apart. Any farther and you will cut down on the speed with which you can change position. The back of your right foot is nestled against the front inside corner of the bag and your left foot is in foul territory. From this position you should be able to handle just about anything the pitcher throws your way and also be able to cover all parts of the bag or runner's body when applying the tag. If the pitcher goes to the plate, cross over with your left foot and move quickly

Mattingly about to snare one out of the stands. One of the realities of major league baseball today is that your opponents include not only the other team but also some fans.

down toward second. Before the ball crosses the plate, you should be facing the batter, crouched and ready, with your glove low and open.

Taking the Throw

No player on the field takes as wide a variety of throws as the first baseman, and I've seen some pretty wide ones. Always anticipate a bad throw. Here's where a good stretch and long reach might shave a bit of time on a close play. Don't stretch too soon, because if the ball is off target you will have to recover, and if you're already committed you probably won't make the play.

Your large glove allows you to make one-handed catches, but if you must throw or if you are inexperienced, catch with two

hands. Follow the flight of the ball all the way into your mitt. You may have to cushion the ball on low throws. "Give to get," as they say.

Taking the low throw or digging the ball out of the dirt is one of the toughest plays a first baseman must make—and he has to make it often. A ball right in front of you, "the short hop," is relatively easy to catch. Either stretch and try to get the ball before it bounces or catch it soon after it hits the ground so that even if it takes a bad bounce it doesn't have far to go. A ball a yard or so in front of you should be caught on a high bounce. It's the "in between hop," the ball that hits five or ten feet or so in front of you and whose bounce is unpredictable, that is always hard to play.

You have three options on the high

Give your pitcher a good waist-high target while holding the runner on and be ready to slap your glove on the runner or between the runner's reach and the bag the moment you control the ball.

Stretch as far as you can to nip the runner, but don't commit prematurely; once you're in your stretch, it's hard to correct your position to adjust for the throw.

throw. You can stay on the bag and reach as high as you can, you can leap up from the bag and descend upon it, or you can move into foul territory. Move off the bag to save the ball. If this is required, how to play the runner must be your next decision. Remember that he can run you down in the baseline, evade you, or slide into first base to duck under your tag. You may end up leaping, twisting, or diving toward the runner or the bag.

Two other throws that the first baseman regularly takes are the pickoff attempt and an underhanded toss from the pitcher or second baseman. If you're holding the runner on, you should be in position to take the throw in front of the bag and drop the glove to complete the tag. If you are playing behind the runner, you and your pitcher must work out a system of signs. On the short, sometimes soft, tosses from fielders playing near the bag, set a big target with your glove as soon as you can.

Bunts

One key to handling bunts is making the right guess or having quick reactions. You charge the ball hard and make a decision in midstride. You and the pitcher must determine who can best take the bunt. If he calls early for the ball, you can just "stay at home." If you end up taking the bunt either the pitcher or the second baseman will cover first base. Take the banana route to balls down the baseline so that your momentum will carry you into your throw to second or third or into your pivot to first.

In the majors the roar of the crowd makes it very difficult to hear other players. At other levels of play the catcher often calls out to the fielder which base he should throw to. This is one of those split-second timing plays where it is best if you can come up with the correct play by yourself and not have to depend on outside direction.

Backing Up, Covering, and Cutting Off

With runners in scoring position, the first baseman is responsible for cutoffs on all balls hit to right or center field. If he can get into position on a ball hit to left center he should even cover that. On most balls hit solidly to left field, the third sacker will handle the cutoff. If for any reason he can't take position, it's your responsibility. Move to a spot between home and the mound in line with the throw. Watch the runner so you can correctly anticipate the play. Hold your hands high and give the outfielder the best possible target. If you keep your hands high you will also be in a good position to turn and throw. Even when you intend to let the ball go through you might consider faking the catch to decoy or confuse the runner.

With no one on, back up second base on all throws from the left side of the field. You should cover second base or home plate anytime these bases are left unoccupied.

SECOND BASE AND SHORTSTOP

The Ideal Middle Infielders

A team that is strong up the middle can overcome weaknesses elsewhere. It is no wonder that the second baseman and shortstop are known as the keystone combination. They are the team within the team and the heart of the defense. No club will be able to regularly turn the double play, nail the base stealer, hold off the run, and win the tight ones without consistent performers at these positions.

Quick as a cat! The middle infielders must be able to pounce on, nab, toss, flip, and snap the ball with speed, dexterity, and accuracy. The great ones do it with a grace and fluidity and flash that make the whole effort seem effortless. The shortstop and especially the second baseman are called upon to make more different kinds of throws than any other fielder. Overhand, underhand, backhand, sidearm, moving to the left or right, even upside down. Strength and quickness are the essential elements here—quick hands and strong arms and, because you need a base to throw from, quick feet.

Up-the-middle plays frequently demand dazzlingly deft displays of ball handling and split-second timing. Indeed, the entire body must be under the control of these acrobats of the diamond as they leap, bound, and dive. Making the throw from second while evading a hard-charging runner, they more closely resemble matadors. Small players excel here if they are quick and strong. They should be lithe and wiry, sinewy, and most of all strong.

My all-star selections fit the physical ideals of the positions to a tee. No one will be surprised with my choice at shortstop. To say that Ozzie Smith is the best defensive shortstop that I've ever played with or against just begins to do justice to his level of play. He may be the best person *ever* to have played shortstop. It's probably better to just think of Oz as beyond compare and let it go at that.

My choice at second base may surprise some. I went with youth and with a player who continues to improve dramatically each year. He plays in a media black hole of sports, Seattle, and doesn't get the credit he deserves, but professionals know Mariner Harold Reynolds to be a bona fide all-star who will blossom even more in the 1990s.

Reynolds has already made the AL All-Star team twice, took the American League base-stealing championship the only year in the past decade that Rickey Henderson didn't, and won a Gold Glove. And he's just beginning to achieve his full potential. He's capable of stealing more than the 60 bases he swiped in 1987. Despite that total, Harold depends more on speed than a good jump. Once he begins to read pitchers better, watch out. Right now, on some plays such as peeling back to snare a quail, nobody's better. With Reynolds's work ethic, as he accomplishes more he just keeps setting his sights higher and moving to the next level.

I have been watching Harold for a long time and I've seen him progress. At San Diego, I played with his brother Donnie. (Another brother, Larry, played for the Rangers.) Donnie used to bring Harold into the clubhouse when he was just a little squirt, and even then you could see his capacity for learning. He'd ask questions and then listen and learn. He's still doing it, on the field and off.

Ozzie and I first played together in 1978 in San Diego. I was amazed even then at his confidence and ability. Here was this kid who jumped up from one year in A League ball in Walla Walla, Washington, and he was so sure-handed. His minor league management felt certain that he could cut it in the bigs, and they sure were right.

That first year he made a play so spectacular that it is seared forever into my

Ozzie taking off and landing. He ought to be required to file a flight plan with the FAA.

Here Harold Reynolds avoids the runner and gets his throw off. His range and quickness make him one of the best second basemen around.

memory. I never saw a more fantastic play. Jeff Burroughs hit a bullet up the middle. Ozzie dove for the ball and while he was completely stretched out, I mean body straight and glove hand fully extended, the ball took a wicked bad bounce, an in-between one-hopper with topspin that hit the meat of the infield and shot back toward Smith's face. Ozzie reached back, caught the ball with his throwing hand, hit the dirt, came up throwing, and caught Burroughs. It is no wonder that he's called the Wizard of Aaahhs. Describing the plays he makes reveals the inadequacy of language. Even when you see him in action or on videotape, it's hard to believe your eyes.

A few stories from Ozzie's youth help delineate the man. To begin with, he grew up in poverty in Los Angeles. His first baseball "glove" was a brown paper bag. He practiced constantly. He knew even then that there was a lot more to the game than what you can see. Literally. He used to throw the ball in the air, close his eyes, and catch the ball. Feeling is as much a part of Ozzie's game as seeing. Another exercise of his as a kid was to throw the ball up on the peaked roof of a house and then run around to the other side and try to catch it before it fell to the ground. He did it hundreds of times without ever making the catch. Now that's determination!

Determination is a key to understanding Ozzie. As good as he is, he's still reaching, trying to discover how good he can be. When he broke in, he was a weak hitter, a wannabe slugger. I saw him study hitting, come to recognize his strengths, change his style, and constantly raise his average to the point where he is now a bona fide offensive threat. Indeed, in the last few years, he took up weight lifting, put on twenty-five pounds of muscle, and now has a lot more pop to his bat. Kids, especially small ones, could find no better role model than Ozzie Smith.

Position and Stance

With no one on, the middle infielders play as deeply as possible, approximately thirty feet from the bag and twenty-five feet behind the line. At double play depth, they move four or so steps closer to home and two steps closer to the bag. To cut off a run at the plate, they move all the way onto the grass. Right-handed and left-handed pull hitters are shaded appropriately.

When circumstances allow, the middle infielders like to "cheat" closer to the bag; there are more balls up the middle than into the hole. Keep in mind, however, that generally it is easier to go to the left than to the right. It's also a matter of who is playing on each side of you. If your shortstop can move and your first baseman has less range, the second baseman may decide (or be directed) to play well over toward first.

Both of these positions move on every pitch. Their stance is low, but light on their feet. There's more movement more frequently for the middle infielders than for their teammates. They must be prepared to explode with the jab step or crossover and move in all directions. Concentration is essential. You can't just be looking at the hitter. You must focus on the ball coming off the bat from the instant it is hit. With experience, you will learn to read its spin and count the hops off the bat.

The Pivot

The three keys to what kind of pivot works best are: where the pivot man is coming from, where the ball is coming from, and which direction the sliding runner is coming from. If the first two variables beat the third variable to the bag, you will probably execute a successful play. Unless the middle infielders know several different ways to pivot and can do the instant vector analysis that the quick pivot requires, they will not be playing at full speed.

When preparing to make the pivot, first spot the ball. Anticipate a bad throw. You may find that touching the base with the same foot each time is more your style or that using either foot gives you greater mobility. The safest, easiest pivot is to straddle the bag and drag your right foot over the base. On a bad throw to your right you can drag your left foot over the bag. This is a timing play; you want to get to the bag just before the play and use your momentum to go right into your throw.

One of the quickest pivots comes off the planted right foot. As you take the throw step back on your right foot, then forward with your left to complete your throw. Another fast pivot that is a little harder to execute requires the pivot man to touch the base, take the throw, and as he relays to first, leap into the air to avoid the runner.

Accomplished middle infielders can execute the following pivots:

- Straddle and drag with right foot.
- Step into the infield from the mound side of the bag.
- Back off.
- Step with the right foot and throw.
- Straddle the base and kick with the left foot.
- Leap from either foot and flip.

The Double Play

The reason the pivot is so important is that most double plays require a pivot to succeed. There are many other elements that go into the DP. While it is axiomatic, the first step bears repeating: get the first

Step! Catch! Pivot! Throw! Harold Reynolds as the middleman on another double play.

One of the easiest pivots begins when you straddle the bag and trail your back foot across the base as you pivot and throw.

out. Throw the ball to second chest high and don't lead the pivot man by more than a tad. If you make him reach, it will usually complicate both his catch and his throw. He must be able to see the ball clearly, so get it out of the glove and into throwing position quickly regardless of what kind of throw you are going to make. Speed is even more important for shovel throws and backhand flips.

If you are the pivot man, you must go straight for the bag as quickly as possible and slow down about five feet from it. Square to the throw and don't expect a good one. Catch the ball with two hands near the heel of the glove to facilitate the transfer to your throwing hand. If your chest is in front of the throw, your feet and body are likely to be in the correct position to shift to either side should this be necessary. Focus on the ball, not the runner. You sometimes have to know where the runner is sliding, but on many plays you've completed the pivot before he gets within sliding distance. The best middle infielders seem to sense rather than see the runner.

Shortstops usually have an easier time making the pivot and turning the double play because they can always see the runner coming.

Lastly, touch the bag, or at least make the effort and come close. In the major leagues, there is sometimes outrageous latitude given to the fielder in how close he needs to actually be to the bag. This very loose approach to proximity is seldom as extravagant at other levels of play.

Cutoffs, Covering, and Backing Up

When making the cutoff, catch the ball on your glove (pivot) side. The shortstop relays on all extra-base hits to left or center. The second baseman is responsible for balls hit to right center and over. The double cutoff is sometimes used in larger parks. Both middle infielders go out and fall into a line between the target base and the outfielder, prepared to handle a bad throw. The shortstop covers second on all bunts and grounders and most flies to the right side of the diamond. The second baseman does the same for balls to the left of the diamond.

The second baseman and shortstop share the responsibility for covering second on a steal. Unless they switch, the second baseman covers when a right-handed hitter is at the plate and the shortstop covers with a lefty at bat. Depending on where the throw comes from, the middle infielders back each other up at second. With a man on third, the second baseman must back up the mound. The shortstop backs up third when the catcher throws there. He must cover third whenever the third baseman moves to his cutoff position or covers home.

THIRD BASE

The Ideal Third Baseman

I've enjoyed competing against some of the best third basemen in the business, including Mike Schmidt, George Brett, Graig Nettles, Paul Molitor, and Wade Boggs. As you might be able to tell from that lineup, a lot of good hitters seem to hang out at third. You can't beat Boggs for consistency (six straight 200-hit seasons, career .356 average); Brett's no slouch with ten .300 seasons (.390 in 1980); and, for power, how about Schmidt's 548 home runs and 1,595 RBIs?

With this kind of competition, if I had announced my choice of all-star third baseman a few years ago, people would have either said "Who?" or, if they knew who Gary Gaetti was, "Why?" He played a solid if undistinguished game for the Minnesota Twins with a career batting average around .250.

Since then, Gaetti has established himself as the premier third sacker in the major leagues defensively and offensively. In the last three years, he has hit almost 100 home runs, averaged over 100 RBIs per season, won two of his three Gold Gloves, and last year batted .301. Few players in recent times have improved as much and as fast. If you need to produce a run, give the job to Gary. He fields his position in a workmanlike manner. There's nothing flashy or fancy about him. He makes plays look easy because he's so often at the right place at the right time.

Gaetti is as tough as they get in playing through injuries. He's a gutty and determined gamer who hangs in there. This is a key factor in why I picked him for the Avon All-Stars. Except for catcher, no position on the diamond is tougher on the body. At the hot corner you take a large number of balls off your chest, throat, head, or other portions of your anatomy. Some third basemen may have better numbers than Gary in certain categories, but none can touch him for endurance. Another way in which Gaetti

Gary Gaetti is one of those players with an instinct for where the ball will be or how the play will develop.

goes the distance is powerhitting. With Mike Schmidt retired from the position and now from baseball, Gary has little competition among third basemen in driving the long ball.

An all-star third sacker must have quick reactions or extremely good insurance. The ball gets down the line to him soooo fast and often skips or skids erratically—hard-hit grounders with wicked hops, caroms, bounders, vicious line drives that seemingly could decapitate a player. Then there are the balls that are sliced, dinked, and slapped, and all the varieties of bunts. They spin, and dance, and roll, sometimes in slow motion. It's nice to have a third baseman who has both speed and quickness; the range of the position is wide and deep. But quickness is more important.

Because a hard-hit ball reaches him so fast, the third baseman frequently has lots of time to throw the ball. On plenty of other plays, however, he must, like all infielders, be able to make a quick throw, often off balance. A strong, accurate arm is another quality of an all-star at third. Particularly when he is playing deep, the player must be able to execute a long throw across the diamond to nip the runner.

Stance and Position

The third baseman is a player of many positions. He ranges all over the left side of the diamond. The game situation dictates that he place himself from hard on the line to over toward second base, from deep in the hole to most of the way to the plate. He is more affected by who's winning, the kind of hitter, the inning, and the count than any of his teammates. The third sacker must not only be always ready to change positions; he often also fakes a move or tries to decoy the hitter into a play. One key to making this work is to make sure that you don't trick both the hitter and the pitcher.

If a bunt is in order you must play on the grass. When you are not expecting a bunt, play four yards behind the bag and five yards off the line. Some players prefer to be even with the bag and not as far off the line. Facing a right-handed pull hitter or guarding against a late-inning extra-base hit, move toward the line. Most balls will be hit between you and the shortstop. The more you can shade in his direction, the better he can cover the middle and be protected from his hardest play, the ball to his right.

Your stance is wider and lower than that of other fielders. A lower center of gravity increases your stability. You will bend a bit more at the waist, ready to catch or block everything that comes your way and to propel yourself in any direction.

Ground Balls and Bunts

Playing the topped or slow roller or the bunt is the third baseman's hardest single task. It is complicated when there is a runner on second base. Knowing your capabilities and those of your pitcher and shortstop is essential to making this play. Can the pitcher field the bunt? Can the shortstop cover the bag for you? Can you reach the ball in time to make a play? Where should you throw? Dare you risk a bare-handed pickup?

Get off to a fast start and charge the ball hard. Take the banana route to direct your momentum. If your pitcher or catcher can call for the ball early, you are free to cover the base. Don't make the mistake, however, of assuming someone else will go for the ball. Once you get the ball, get an out. If you catch the ball with your left foot forward, you can go directly into your throw.

Grounders to your left allow you to look back a runner at third or second and then make the throw to second or first. If a runner at third breaks for the plate, you must throw home immediately. If he doesn't break, you may go for the putout at another base. The throw to second is shorter and it is to your advantage to keep the opponents from placing another man in scoring position, but the important thing is to get the out.

All infielders must be able to make the dive play to the right. If the third baseman doesn't stop the ball, it usually means extra bases.

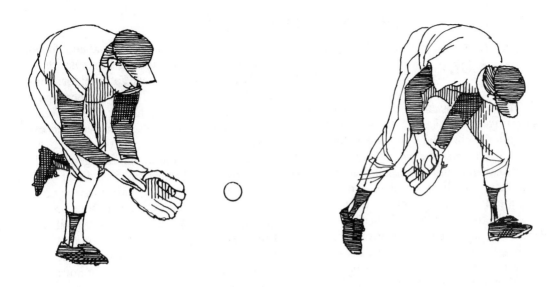

How to charge a bunt or slow roller and throw on the run.

Covering, Backing Up, and Cutting Off

The third baseman is responsible for covering second base with no one on and the middle infielders chasing a fly. If no one else covers home when the catcher goes for a ball, the third baseman must move to the plate. On all other plays, with runners on, the third baseman must cover his own bag. He backs up second on throws from right and the pitcher on throws from first. With a runner on second and a hard-hit ball to left field he will take up a deep cutoff position fifteen to twenty yards from the plate. From this position he can move forward to take the throw in the most advantageous manner. He also sets up in this approximate location on flies and hits to left.

OUTFIELDERS

The Ideal Outfielder

Outfielders often make the team largely on the basis of their hitting. Check out the statistics. Year after year, the home run, RBI, slugging, and batting champions come from the outfield ranks: Ruth, Aaron, Williams, Cobb, Mays, Mantle, Snyder, DiMaggio, Canseco, Gwynn. To be sure, Boggs, Brett, Mattingly, and a few other interlopers from the infield will not be denied and take their share of titles, but an outfielder is expected to be a solid hitter.

The ideal outfielder, however, is not only going to win games with his bat but also with his defense. An outfielder who is not a good gloveman may prove to be a great liability. Although he handles fewer chances than an infielder, his mistakes generally are more costly. If an infielder boots a ball, the usual result is a runner being called safe or gaining an extra base. When an outfielder makes an error, you almost always can count on two or more extra bases. The ideal outfielder can judge balls well and get a good jump on them.

An all-star outfielder must have good speed. This has become even more important since the introduction of artificial turf because balls move a lot faster on that surface. The outfielder should be on the run on almost every ball hit. If he is not moving quickly to catch a fly or charging a grounder, he's running even farther to back up his teammates. Outfield play requires a great deal of discipline and concentration. The ball will not be hit to the outfielder often, but he has to be ready constantly and anticipate. He must be not only alert but also quick thinking. Once he gets the ball, he must know where to throw it.

Lastly, the ideal outfielder has a good arm. He'll be making the longest throws on the diamond. They have to be strong and accurate. A quick release helps to keep base runners honest.

Left Field

Dodger Mickey Hatcher, who has been known to play a bit of left field, once said: "The center fielder has to be able to run. The right fielder has to be able to throw. And the left fielder has to be able to hit." Although left field is not as demanding defensively as the other two outfield positions, the position presents its own special problems. To be sure, this is the place for your weakest arm. The left fielder will not have to make the long throws that go with

Stealing third base is increasingly popular. The key to tagging the runner out is to get the glove down, let the runner come to you and then get the ball and glove out of danger.

the territory in center or right. He will be challenged by the runner going home more frequently than the other fielders, however. He'll also have a tougher time gauging where the runner going from third to home is, and his throw to the plate is more likely to strike the runner.

Because there are many more right-handed than left-handed hitters, and because left-handed batters hit to the opposite field more often than right-handers, left fielders see a lot more action than right fielders. The drives to left tend to hook and slice more than those to other fields. Being able to judge those curving line drives is

one key to playing the position well. The most difficult balls will be hit to the left fielder's right side, so coaches have traditionally sought to maximize the advantage by putting right-handed throwers in this position. A right-hander can also throw to second more easily than a left-hander. To keep runners from taking the extra base, the left fielder should be able to play shallow. To be able to go back fast and also guard the line against extra-base hits, the ideal man in this position will have speed.

My all-star selection in left may be the fastest man in the game. Nobody gets down the line to first faster, not even Bo! And

A lot of hits go down the line to left and the fielder must be able to reach these balls.

undeniably, Vince Coleman stole 400 bases faster than any other major league player and is on a pace to steal more bases than anyone else in the bigs. In 1989, he shattered major league records by swiping 50 consecutive bases. He's so fast he can play shallow enough to almost be another infielder. While his baserunning got him to the majors, Vince is earning his spurs as a "complete player."

He is becoming savvier at the plate, discovering the value of patience and increasing his number of walks (and on-base average), as a good leadoff man should. He's a switch hitter who uses the bunt to near perfection and can hardly be beat on the chop-and-run hit. He hits to all fields. Coleman is a tough gamer who provides

stability at his position. Despite the beating he takes on the base paths, he plays more than 150 games a year.

Center Field

In keeping with the need to be strong up the middle, center field is where you generally put your best outfielder. He'll handle 20 to 25 percent more chances than the other outfielders. He is the "captain" of the outfield squad and has the most territory to cover. (When Gary Pettis played for the Angels in a Gold Glove year, the head groundskeeper calculated that he covered 35,000 square feet!) He must be able to start quickly and run far in all directions. In addition to speed, he'll need stamina. He has *two* outfielders to back up. The main advantage that the center fielder has over his cohorts is that he seldom has to handle balls that hook or slice. Center is the one outfield position where you can sacrifice some offense to ensure that you are solid defensively. Put your best flycatcher where there's the most territory.

With the center fielder on my all-star team, I don't have to sacrifice an iota, offensively or defensively. Kirby Puckett is a three-time Gold Glover who is famous for his "rob jobs," stealing hits, especially home runs, away from his opponents. He's victimized me more times than I would care to count. He snatches homers and gappers from everyone. Maybe the best tribute that I can pay him defensively is that he's held me at third on fly balls that would have brought me home with another fielder play-ing the ball. He doesn't have one of the strongest arms in the game, but he does have one of the quickest releases and uses his momentun well.

At bat, he is as tough as they get. There probably isn't a better clutch hitter in the majors. Kirby thrives on pressure. It's uncanny! When the game is on the line, he always seems to be at bat. He's one of the few players in the game to gather 1,000 hits in his first five seasons. To his consistency at the plate, he's added power. He's like a Boggs or a Rose with punch. As if all this weren't enough, Puckett has charisma. To fans, teammates, umpires, and even opponents, he's lovable. It's not just that he looks like a teddy bear. He's always bubbling with enthusiasm. He loves the game and it shows.

Vince Coleman is the fastest man in baseball, whether he's stealing a base or turning a potential "gapper" into a putout.

Shallow or deep, with his quick starts and speed afoot, Kirby Puckett can rob you coming and going.

Right Field

What a difference between how this position is treated when we are kids and how it is filled in the majors. In sandlot pickup games, the right fielder is usually the weakest player and the last one chosen. Indeed, if there are not enough players, you just eliminate right and don't allow any hits there. In the majors, however, no fielding position has produced as many Hall of Famers—a full score, to be exact.

Fewer balls are hit to right field than to any other place on the diamond. The position, therefore, requires tremendous concentration to stay in the game. You've got to hang on every pitch even though you might not touch a ball in play in the course of the game. And when the ball does come your way, it's a good bet that the runner will try for the extra base. To add to your

problems, during a day game, more likely than not, you'll be looking into the sun because that's the way many ball fields are laid out.

The right fielder should have the best arm in the outfield. He's got to be able to stop the runner from going from first to third on a single, or advancing to third or home on a fly. Conventional wisdom has it that a left-handed right fielder is a plus because he can get rid of balls hit down the line more quickly. The other side of that proposition is that a right-handed right fielder will have his glove closer to balls hit down the line. In actuality, I've played with fewer left-handed outfielders. It really doesn't matter what side you throw from as long as you can uncork accurate and long throws. In most parks, the throw from the corner in right to third base is about 400 feet.

There are some superior right fielders in the game today. Before the Pirates moved him, Andy Van Slyke played right as well as anybody in the game, and now he's doing the same in center. Dwight Evans has been a standout for years. And then there is Jose Canseco, charter member of the 40/40 Club and a vastly improved fielder. For my all-star team, though, I went with a player who's always been solid and usually outstanding for almost twenty years . . . Dave Winfield. (It is, after all, *my* book.)

Position and Stance

The factors that affect where you position yourself vary considerably and even change as the count changes on a batter. The large percentage of balls hit fair are pulled, and the tendency to pull increases when the count favors the batter. Knowing this, savvy fielders move laterally according to who is ahead in the count. The inning, score, and number of outs all can provide clues to the best place to play. With the winning run on second, for instance, you may have to gamble by playing shallow, hoping to prevent the run from scoring. You play the percentages until you are forced to riskier play by the state of the game.

The batter at the plate is the greatest single element in deciding where to play. Does he hit to all fields or can you count on him to pull the ball? How much pop does he have to his bat, and once he hits the ball, how fast is he? How and what your pitcher is throwing need to be considered. Hitters often swing late at heat and they tend to pull breaking balls. Tired pitchers often lose location or hang pitches, so play deeper.

Your other teammates also figure in where you play. Shade toward weaker outfielders and away from stronger ones. Play shallower or deeper depending on the skills of the infielders in front of you. You should know your own abilities; if you move to one side markedly better than to the other, plan accordingly. Lastly, consider the field and related conditions. Is the wind or sun a factor? Where are the fences and how far are they off the foul line? With deep fences, you must play deeper.

Along with the consideration and anticipation that go into positioning is the forethought that must attend where to throw the ball if there are runners on base. In between pitches, it pays to review your ''game plan'' for what happens after you catch the ball. Spend the time now, when you can afford to, and have a clear mind in the heat of making the play.

Outfielders commonly use a square stance with feet parallel and even, similar to the standard stance used by infielders. The majority prefers a drop-step stance with the toe of one foot even with or behind the heel of the other. Most outfielders drop the foot on their throwing side back. Some outfielders like to shade their nonthrowing shoulder toward the plate. Regardless of which stance you use, stay up on the balls of your feet in a comfortable crouch. You must be relaxed, your body free from tension that will hinder movement. You do not have to crouch as low as an infielder. If you rest your hands on your knees, drop them or move them forward as the ball approaches the plate. Not only will this give your hands greater freedom, it will also move your weight forward, and you'll be ready to run quickly in any direction.

I have my own trick for staying ready. As the ball approaches home plate, I move my feet up and down slightly. By the end

Once the ball has been pitched, drop your hands off your knees (if you rested them there) and get ready to move.

of the season, there's a well-worn spot out in right where I stand. Some people think it's a nervous habit, but it's just my way of keeping on my toes.

Getting the Jump on the Ball

Those outfielders who can "move at the crack of the bat" exhibit the kind of aggressive play and ability to judge the ball that outfielders need. Getting a good jump on the ball starts with close observation of the pitcher and the batter. Even if you cannot identify the kind of pitch, you should be able to ascertain its location and other details such as whether the hitter swung early or late. At the professional level, the sound the bat makes as it strikes the ball is one way to gauge where the ball will go. Aluminum bats do not resonate in the same way and do not, therefore, provide the same helpful hints to the outfielder.

Balls hit to either side of you allow you a clear line of sight and are usually easy to judge. Keep in mind that balls hit down the line can slice or hook. To move laterally, pivot and push off with the foot nearest the

ball and cross over with your outside foot. This is an explosive move involving your whole body. Rise from your semicrouch as you accelerate and get into proper running form. On balls hit over your head, pivot on both feet. If you must run at an angle to make the catch, take your initial stride with the foot nearest the ball.

Balls hit right at you are the toughest to read. You can't tell immediately whether the ball will rise or fall. Avoid taking false steps. Hold your ground until you can determine the flight of the ball. Balls hit right at you can approach like a knuckleball. If the ball is straight over your head, you might find it easier to turn your glove side away from the ball to pursue it. This way you won't have to reach across your body to catch the ball.

Catching and Throwing the Ball

Once you have taken your first few steps, you usually are able to determine whether you can reach the ball on the fly or whether another fielder has a better chance at the play. But this is not always the case, and you frequently must make decisions on the run and don't know until the last moment which way the play will go. If you need to play it safe, adjust your angle so that the ball will not get by you, but try to do this without taking additional strides. Err on the side of safety if you must. If, on the other hand, you need the play, GO FOR IT! You've got nothing to lose and everything to gain. Make the play!

One key to outfield play is getting to the place where the ball will descend as quickly as possible. This allows you to get into the best position to catch and throw and to make needed adjustments. Don't drift with the ball, running just fast enough to make the catch. If you are coasting, any slight misjudgment or other factor, such as a sudden breeze or a teammate's misreading your intentions, could result in a misplay.

One of the hardest balls to catch is the long drive over the outfielder's head. To begin with, it's harder to go backward than forward. And when you move toward balls in front of you, you can keep your eye on the ball all the way. When you move back for a ball, you might have to turn your back on it, concentrate on running to the spot where you think it will land, and only then glance back up and make the catch. Personally, I find it preferable to keep my eye on the ball all the time. I have such a big body that once I get it going, it's hard to change directions or adjust.

Balls hit far in front of you force you to choose whether to slow up and take the ball on a hop or try to catch it for the putout. If you go for the bounce, you must slow up and bring your body under control. Keep your glove and body in front of the ball so that if you can't catch it, you can at least knock it down. Watch for unusual bounces due to the spin of the ball. Keeping your balance while running and reaching for a shoestring catch is difficult.

You might choose to dive for the ball or slide into the catch so you can keep your eye on the ball all the way and have your glove open and facing up. The bent-leg slide is the best way to bring your body to the ground. It also gives you a measure of safety, because balls you don't reach may bounce off your body and stay close. If you dive or stretch far, consider going right into a roll to prevent injury and to keep the ball from being jarred. If you miss a short fly with the dive, it shouldn't travel far behind you, so going for the ball is usually a

good gamble. As with so many other aspects of the game, practice will keep you sharp and ready to respond to real challenges in the game. Rehearse your slides and dives.

Outfielders need to charge ground balls and return them to the infield quickly. On hard-hit balls, the fielder may elect to drop to his knee. You will not be able to throw as quickly from this position, but you decrease the chance that the ball will slip by or through you.

Occasionally you must charge a ball, field it just with the glove hand, and come up throwing to prevent a runner from advancing or a run from scoring in a tight game. Only in this urgent situation should you field the ball outside your body and with just the glove. I find this method to be the quickest, most coordinated way to field and release the ball. Because of your momentum and the path of the ball, if you don't make the catch, the hitter will be able to run the bases almost at will. A similar situation arises with the bloop hit that dies between you and the infielders. You may have to pick up this ball bare-handed to thwart the runner.

I have combined catching and throwing in this section to emphasize how one action must lead to another. The motions ideally merge. How you move toward the ball facilitates this merger. Take the banana route when you can on balls hit to your side. This will enable you to capitalize on your momentum as you start to go into your throw.

My old Little League coach taught me early on the way to prevent runners from advancing. It is the same technique used by most professional ballplayers. It is called "overplaying the ball." Instead of running in to stand in place or camp under a fly, he taught us to get a bead on the ball, stay

Catching and throwing the ball should usually be a continuous motion for the outfielder. Put lots of mustard on the ball and end your throw with a strong follow-through to keep runners from advancing.

behind it by a few steps, then accelerate toward the ball as it descended. We'd make a catch on the move then, using our momentum, step and fire the ball. This method is a step or two faster than the conventional catch-step-throw sequence.

Up Against the Wall

One of the hardest lessons an outfielder ever learns is how to catch a ball up against the wall. Most parks are pretty well padded and allow you some slack. Others don't allow you to take any liberties with them. They are hard and unforgiving. When I played in the National League, Pittsburgh had iron-hard walls. That was in the time of the Lumber Company, and you could be sure that you'd be bouncing off some fences when chasing their drives.

The shape of the stadium may complicate your life. In Kansas City you can get pinched in the rounded corners while chasing a ball. The most challenging walls are

in Wrigley Field. Balls go into that ivy and sometimes out again. The ivy is a source of deception, not protection. The angles are odd, with the wall sticking out where it shouldn't be. You can get mangled by the angled walls of the Windy City. And if the walls don't get you, the bleacherites will. Not even the fence atop the wall protects the fielder from the fans.

The key to playing the wall or the fence is learning what you can do with it and what it can do to you. The only way to do this is by practice. Touch it. Shoulder it. Crash it. Climb it. Vault off it. If the wall allows you to overreach it, find all the ways you can extend your arm to steal a homer. Study how to use the wall to your advantage. Freddy Lynn plays the wall like a virtuoso, and that comes from practice. You must learn how you will bounce off the wall and how the ball will. Study the angles and the caroms. Knowing your wall allows you to keep the runner from taking an extra base.

Yeah, I got both these balls. Practice climbing the walls. You never know when it will save the game.

You can even decoy runners by faking a catch, then turning to take the ball off the wall. Over the years leftfielders at Fenway have turned this into a "routine out." They deke you into thinking they've got the catch. Then, at the last moment, they turn and play the carom off the "Green Mon-ster," then turn again and throw to a team-mate, often catching a runner. Or they can hold a runner uncertain of whether to ad-vance. Mike Greenwell estimates he uses this play thirty to forty times a year.

Your safety has to be a consideration every time you approach a wall. If you can reach the wall before the ball does, you're a leg up. You can position yourself as far back as necessary or possible. You can gauge the distance to the wall by the width of the warning track (count your strides in practice) or by reaching toward the wall with your throwing hand. If you reach the wall before the ball and see that a great leap will be required to have any chance of a catch, locate yourself near the base of the wall. Turn sideways to the ball and crouch to spring.

Hitting the Cutoff

One of the most important throws you can make doesn't have to result in an assist or a putout. The throw to the cutoff man is successful if it keeps the trailing runner from advancing. If the throw goes all the way through or if your throw is on target and a relay is needed, you can, of course, nail the lead runner. You must hit the cutoff with as accurate and strong a throw as you can muster and still be quick about it. Think of how often a throw from the outfield ends in a bang-bang play at the plate. You're the fuse for that explosion. Make sure your team makes the biggest and last bang with a good throw.

The best story about cutoffs happened to me one night when I accidently struck and killed a sea gull in Toronto with a warm-up throw (and was arrested for cruelty to animals). Billy Martin, trying to milk the incident for all the humor it was worth, said that it was the first time I had hit the cutoff man all season. Outfielders have to do a lot better than that or they will lose runs for their team. Hit the cutoff man consistently. You will save or cost your team many runs a year solely on this ability.

Lack of communication can lead to no catch, possible injury, and loss of game, or even a teammate.

Communications

The outfielder should be an aggressive player who wants the ball to come his way because he knows he will catch it. Anything he can touch, he can catch. This confidence is a necessary component of the outfielder's makeup, his mindset. To be able to play the outfield with this verve safely requires good communications.

When communications fail many things can happen, and most of them are bad—dropped balls, freak extra-base hits, monumental collisions. Two or more fielders converging on a ball is a fearsome sight. Good communications can lessen the chances of such mishaps and the injuries that frequently result. The easiest way to avoid collisions is through loudly and clearly calling for the ball. If two outfielders call for the ball, the center fielder has priority. An outfielder has priority over an infielder.

Another precaution that outfielders can take when they are approaching the ball is for the center fielder to take the inside route, preparing to catch the ball low. The other fielder takes the outside route, ready to catch the ball high.

Outfielders also communicate when they change positions. They usually shift together. Your cohorts will also help you judge flies and shout warnings when appropriate. They will tell you what base to throw to. A lot of your communication is to remind each other of the game situation. Sometimes you simply shout encouragement. You are the last line of defense for your team, a special unit, a team within a team. You may even declare a pact. You are resolute together that nothing will drop in front of you and nothing will get over you unless it's all the way out.

RECOMMENDED RESOURCES

Jim Kaplan. *Playing the Field.* (Algonquin Books, 1987). $12.95.

CHAPTER EIGHT

Coaching and Managing (and Parenting)

THE IDEAL MENTOR

Being a Positive Influence

I've combined coaches, managers, and parents in this chapter because parents frequently are their kid's first unofficial coach at home. And then, when the youngster begins team play, almost inevitably it is someone's parent who becomes the manager. In addition, I believe that good coaches, managers, and parents are cut from the same cloth. The better ones can stimulate, motivate, and nurture young talent. They use the game to develop such life skills and values as fair play, self-esteem, discipline, respect, teamwork, and goal-setting.

Playing ball with a child can begin at quite an early age. Long before bats and gloves and diamonds become part of the picture, kids and parents roll or toss a ball back and forth and just enjoy each other and simple play. All too often, by the time the child is old enough to play organized ball, that innocent enjoyment is replaced by confrontation, competition, and an emphasis on winning; the spirit of play is completely absent.

There is even a frequently encountered type of demanding Little League parent whose desire to see his or her child win causes problems for coaches, umpires, and the children themselves. And some coaches can forget what their real task is and become so intent on winning that the children become just a means to that end. If the kids do not win, they are criticized and made to feel like losers. Kids should be allowed to develop at their own pace. They are only young once and should be able to enjoy their play.

I'm not saying that winning's not great or that there is no place for criticism in youth leagues or that hard work isn't part of playing the game, even at that level. Criticism and work are part of teaching and learning, but there's a time and a place and a way for everything.

One of my first coaches, Bill Peterson, was a tremendous influence in getting me to think about the proper relationship between a coach and his players. He was an

Pushy parents and impatient coaches can ruin the game for a kid.

ex-hockey player who had been a catcher at the University of Minnesota and then joined the marines. After that thumbnail résumé, I probably don't have to tell you that Bill was tough. He sure didn't take any nonsense from us. If we wanted to play on his teams, we learned the rules and the fundamentals and then used them. No showboating with one-handed catches, for instance. He knew that a certain aggressiveness on the base paths, and at bat especially, was essential to winning play. He'd pitch batting practice full speed from forty-five instead of sixty feet all the time, yelling, "Attack! Attack the ball!" He got many a line drive off the shins, but he took them for the team and kept on firing.

In addition to fundamentals, Bill stressed teamwork, appearance, and attitude. At tournaments, people would be amazed at our cohesiveness, neatness, and team spirit. He never criticized us for making a mistake when we had tried our best, but if we let down, didn't hustle, got sloppy, made excuses, or sometimes played like we didn't care, he'd be all over us. Bill taught me

that you can demand that your players strive for excellence, even if some are not yet capable of achieving it. Perhaps, most important for a role model, Bill practiced what he preached.

Sound instruction, praise, and encouragement are at the heart of good coaching. It's far more important to encourage a player in times of failure than to praise him in times of success. To develop as players, kids must be given ample opportunity to succeed, and that means they will fail many times. Good coaches and parents realize and accept this and provide youths with a positive, supportive environment in which they can grow as players and as people.

The Necessary Qualities

The ideal coach has patience, and the younger the player the more patient the coach must be. At all levels of play, the coach is called upon to teach. A coach should know how to spot a mistake and then correct it. He must begin with a sound knowledge of the game, both skills and strategy. Beyond knowing the game, however, he must be able to communicate that knowledge. Specific explanations, clear demonstrations, supervised practice, and positive reinforcement are part of this process.

A good coach can communicate off the field as well. He must be open and truthful. Being able to relate to his players as individuals lies at the heart of successful communication. Different players have different buttons. A sensitive manager will know which buttons to push and when to push them to get the best performance from his players. Even at the professional level, a coach's ability to motivate players is an important factor in a team's success. A combination of positive and negative reinforcement is generally necessary to motivate all the individuals on a team, but the emphasis should be on the positive. Some players need to be coddled, others needled, but all players need praise.

The ideal coach will praise publicly and criticize privately. He will choose judiciously when to criticize. A good rule to follow is to wait until the player has a few good games under his belt. How the criticism is couched is also important to how it will be received. Begin with praise for recent play, move to the criticism, and conclude with optimism that the improvement can be made. Make a sandwich that will be easier to chew for the player. If he can't swallow and digest what you have to say, it will do no good to say it.

Some people refer to a coach's ability to "handle" players. Others object to the term, feeling that you handle a situation or something that isn't human, like a horse. Whatever word you use, the skill it describes goes a long way to determining how successful a coach will be. "Managing" people is fine. This term allows for the mutual respect that should develop between a coach and player. That respect develops to a large extent from a manager's fairness and consistency. If it exists, then team dis-

Knowing which buttons to push to get the best effort from his players is a challenge for coaches at every level of play.

cipline should not be a problem. Discipline on the diamond and off is a reflection of a manager's ability. Games have rules and depend on control. The same holds true for teams. Correct behavior is particularly important for professional teams, adults who travel and live together for seven months of the year.

The ideal coach is also organized. Meetings and practices begin and end on time and are effective. The structure needed to support a team is in place and working. Players have confidence in how they are being evaluated, knowing that an organized, objective approach is being used. A good manager at the upper levels of play surrounds himself with a solid staff and delegates sufficient authority to his coaches so they can make a full contribution to the team. It is easier for a team to achieve cohesion and work toward common goals when responsibilities are shared in this fashion.

There should be no doubt, however, as to who usually has the first and always the final word on matters that affect the team. (Of course, there are situations where the manager defers to the trainer, team doctor, or owner.) The manager must be decisive. Baseball frequently requires you to wait until the last possible moment to make a split-second decision. This is where a sound knowledge of the game comes into play. A good memory helps a coach recall what has happened previously in similar situations. Being observant enables a coach to pick up little tip-offs and recognize patterns that lead to good choices. How the coach uses his expertise is a prime way for a coach to earn the respect of his team.

A successful coach of youngsters is one who can look beyond victories and losses. There are too many factors beyond his control to judge a coach simply on his winning percentage. If a coach has managed to help a player develop physically and mentally, if he has been a catalyst in a person's reaching his potential, that coach has done a good job.

COACHING KIDS

Elementary and Middle School

The coach for children of this age has to stress FUNdamentals. Basic techniques must be learned in an atmosphere that is enjoyable. At this age, kids are facing situations that they have never encountered before—on the baseball diamond and in life. Their anxiety level may never be higher, and a good coach will devote himself to building the players' confidence. This certainly is a time for the fullest participation feasible. Everybody should get a chance to play regularly. The players are beginning to form their attitudes toward athletics, rules, authority, and other issues that they will carry through life. The good coach concentrates on making sure that baseball is a positive experience for all the members of his team. Rewards, recognition, and reinforcement should be constants.

Making practices effective, pleasant, and rewarding is one key to success. For the child to develop an appreciation of work and an awareness of the dividends that practice pays is a lasting legacy. Two other essential qualities that it is easiest to instill at this age are hustle and good sportsmanship. The coach's own behavior is the greatest single factor in how the players and team will behave. You set the standards and establish the norms. Enthusiasm begets spirit. You can ensure that your team sprints to and from their positions and promote chatter and encouragement. How you handle bad calls and losing will be imprinted on these youngsters. It is not reasonable to expect perfect execution from elementary and middle school students. It is incumbent upon you, however, to exemplify and require hustle, spirit, and good sportsmanship.

High School

Adolescence is the age of rebellion, and any coach who is not prepared to face this challenge commits himself and his team to unnecessary conflict. Your players are bound to be testing limits—their own and those of others. Let them know who is in charge and back it up with organization, discipline, and sound fundamentals. Your players may not always appreciate you at the time but they should later on.

The adolescent has a great need for identification. He seeks role models as he tries to establish his own identity, sometimes through unusual ways and odd behavior. At the same time, peer pressure is at a peak and conformity is the norm. Contradictions abound. Surging hormones produce wide swings of mood and sometimes conduct. Coaches who cannot rise to flexibility are going to find their own options limited.

The good news is that skill levels are higher and many players are taking the game seriously. Although coaches still must make sure that players understand and can execute the fundamentals, they will also be able to refine the abilities of others. At this stage, you should be able to spot and groom talent capable of playing the game at higher levels. At the same time you should be using Little League, Boys' Club, and similar youth teams to feed your own program.

MAKING DECISIONS

Strategy

The question frequently arises of how many games a good manager will win for his club. Some managers enjoy a reputation as strategists, and the presumption is that these wily field generals will regularly be able to steal a half dozen or ten games per season from less clever opponents.

I think this is a misconception. I've played for people known as superstrategists, and they play the game like other managers for a simple reason. Baseball is a game of situations and odds that dictate the appropriate play. Almost all managers will call the same play in the same situation. The difference is that winning managers have a team that can deliver and losing managers don't.

Yogi Berra, in typical fashion, hit the nail on the head when he replied to a reporter after losing the first game of the 1964 World Series. The reporter asked him if he intended to do anything differently in the next game. Yogi said, "It ain't football. You can't make up no trick play."

So, while strategy is probably overrated as a source of wins or losses, the manager can be a major factor in his team's success. He does this through his personality and the tone he sets for the club, with the organizational support and confidence he gives his players, but most importantly, by his personnel decisions, whom he chooses to play when and where.

Stop-action videotape machines can provide hitters, pitchers, and their coaches considerable insight into mechanics.

Choosing Players

Although deciding who will be in the starting lineup and who will pitch is a high-profile part of managing, these decisions are only part of the mix as far as personnel matters go. On professional teams that currently play with a twenty-four-man roster, there are usually ten or so pitchers; the rest of the players are fielders (six infielders, five outfielders, and three catchers would be a typical mix). Trades, injuries, and players shuttling to and from the minors ensure that the pool of players a manager can draw from is usually in a state of flux.

Once the manager picks the starting nine fielders and establishes the five-man pitching rotation that is the norm in the majors, ten players are left, equally divided between relief pitchers and the "extra" men. From this latter group will come the pinch hitters and runners, the players who fill in for injured teammates, and those who platoon, or share a position. Some teams that gel and avoid injuries can go through an entire season without calling on these ten players much except for occasional relief. But for most teams, how these ten perform goes a long way to determining how a team ends up. In youth league ball, it is even more important that nonstarters be used regularly and be given the opportunity to contribute on the field.

The Lineup

Composing a batting order that gets runs early and frequently is one of the manager's greatest challenges. Obviously, the kind of team you have determines the kind of game you play. Some of the Yankee teams that I have played on have had four or five long-ball hitters in order and won consistently with power. The Saint Louis Cardinals play a chop-and-run kind of game. They have so many flyers on that club that opposing catchers must have their arm cocked all the time. Most teams play some variation of what Sparky Anderson calls "checkers." You go out and take one base at a time and manufacture your runs.

Naturally, you put your best hitters at the top of the lineup to maximize their number of plate appearances per game. The classic batting order begins with a leadoff man who can consistently get on base. On-base average (OBA) is the key statistic for this player. He should have a good knowledge of the strike zone and enough discipline and patience to work the pitcher for a walk. He should be a speedster so that once he is on

base he's a threat to steal. A good, aggressive base runner with the team's best hitters following him at the plate means runs for your team. Rickey Henderson and Vince Coleman are two outstanding leadoff men.

Many of the same qualities you are looking for in a leadoff hitter pertain to the number-two position. A good OBA and speed are desirable. The player must be able to take a strike or two, allowing the leadoff man to steal. He should be able to hit a fastball, because if your leadoff man is a threat to steal, the batter will see heat. A left-handed number-two hitter is preferable because he will screen the runner from the catcher and he hits naturally to the right side, behind the runner. A right-hander in this position should be able to hit "the other way." This batter should be able to bunt and exercise good bat control so the manager feels confident in calling a hit-and-run.

The number-three hitter is traditionally the best hitter on the team and can hit for power. Again, a left-hander is preferable, but not essential. With a runner on first, it is easier for him to hit the ball through the hole, and he obscures the catcher's view of the runner. By pulling the ball, he can score the runner from third.

Your cleanup hitter can deliver in the clutch and hit for distance. He's the one you have to be able to count on for RBIs. The number-five batter is out of the same mold. Sometimes this position is filled by younger players being groomed to hit fourth or by older players who may have slipped a notch from peak performance but who can still hit the long ball.

The sixth hitter generally goes one of two ways, depending on personnel available. Either he can hit for power and produce runs à la the two batters that precede him or he can be seen as the "second lead-

Mariners' manager Jim Lefebvre exchanges lineup cards with A's manager Tony LaRussa. Between trades, promotions, and injuries, Lefebvre changed his lineup 119 times during 1989.

1989 OFFICIAL BATTING ORDER
SEATTLE

	ORIGINAL	POS.	CHANGE
1	Reynolds	4	B / C
2	Griffey	8	B / C
3	Davis	3	B / C
4	Coles	9	B / C
5	Leonard	DH	B / C
6	Briley	7	B / C
7	Valle	2	B / C
8	Martinez	5	B / C
9	Vizquel	6	B / C
P	Langston	1	B / C / D / E

Manager's Signature *Jim Lf*

1989 OFFICIAL BATTING ORDER
SEATTLE

DATE 10/1/89
ALSO ELIGIBLE

	ORIGINAL	POS.	CHANGE
1	Cotto	7	B / C
2	Griffey	8	B / C
3	Davis	DH	B / C
4	Coles	3	B / C
5	Buhner	9	B / C
6	Valle	2	B / C
7	Martinez	5	B / C
8	Cochrane	4	B / C
9	Vizquel	6	B / C
P	Hanson	1	B / C / D / E

Also eligible: Bradley, Kingery, Briley, Leonard, Presley, Diaz, McGuire, Reynolds, Wilson, Brantley, Jackson, Reed, Wiedenbauer, Swift, Comstock, Powell, Bankhead, Holman, Johnson, Zavaras, Dunne

Manager's Signature *Jim Lefebvre*

Opening and closing day lineups for rookie manager Jim Lefebvre.

off man." Unless your team is incredibly strong, he is the last of your good hitters. It is surprising how often he comes up in crucial situations, such as first inning, bases loaded, and two outs.

The seventh, eighth, and ninth positions are generally filled by your weakest hitters. Number seven should be someone the pitchers won't pitch around number six to face. Number eight is often a defensive specialist, a shortstop or catcher whose main value to the team is not his hitting. It helps if he has speed if you play in a league where the pitcher bats and can advance the runner with a bunt.

The ninth slot used to be reserved for the pitcher. Now that is common only in the National League. In many youth leagues, pitchers often are good hitters. In leagues where the designated hitter is used, this position is often filled by a leadoff-type hitter who, if he gets on base, has a good chance of scoring because your team's best hitters follow him to the plate.

Sparky Anderson is the best manager I've seen over the long term during my career in baseball. No other manager in the 70's and 80's can match Sparky's number of victories and his World Series championships with teams from both leagues.

A new generation of managers, exemplified by Tony LaRussa and Jim Lefebvre among others, are setting new standards of excellence for the 90's. But to share his wisdom on the craft of management, I've called on Sparky.

OBSERVATIONS FROM SPARKY ANDERSON

Umpires

"When I was younger, I'd fight the umpires tooth and nail. I used to actually think some umps were out to get me. Once you learn that they really are out there to do their best—who wants to make the wrong call and look bad?—why scream and blame the ump and get your club riled up? The umpires then become a crutch. Your club looks to them for an excuse. Sure they miss plays, and some mistakes might come at crucial times, but let's go on from there. Study the replays and you'll find that the umps make fewer mistakes than either team does by a long shot. I didn't mellow in my attitude toward umpires, I just grew up."

Early Influence

"I was lucky when I was a kid. For six years, I lived a few blocks away from the University of Southern California campus and was 'adopted' by the baseball team. I was even the batboy when USC beat George Bush's Yale team for the NCAA championship. The head coach, Rod Dadeaux, was a tremendous influence. In all those years, I never heard a negative word from him. As a young guy around older players and coaches, I had the chance to absorb a lot of baseball. When I actually got to play myself, I usually knew more about baseball than those who coached me. The Good Lord touched me when I was young. He didn't give me much of an IQ, but he put me in a place in life where I could do something I know about."

Most Important Lesson

"The most important single lesson I've learned about managing is that I don't win or lose games, the players do. What I get to do is put people in a 'comfort zone' where they can perform at their highest level and then I get out of the way. Don't do anything to prevent good athletes from

Balancing offense and defense, strengths and weaknesses, and picking the best players to put into the lineup is seldom easy.

winning. All good coaches grasp this lesson and help to put the right player in the right spot.''

Coaches

''Coaches and managers are obligated to understand the individuals that make up their team and to have a good work ethic. I've been fortunate to have coaches who are not afraid of work and who get along with the players. Billy Consolo is in charge of all the balls—no small job—and the extra players. Vada Pinson is our hitting coach, and no one else talks to the players about batting. Billy Moffett is our pitching coach, and most of his work is finished before the game, although he then sits with our pitcher in the dugout. Dick Tracewski is our organization man and sets up batting practice,

extra hitting, etc. He's also my first base coach. Alex Grammas is my third base coach. Once the game starts, his decisions are more important than mine. He's got to know the outfielders' arms, how they throw going right or left, whether they charge the ball, how quickly they release it. I've worked with Alex for eighteen years and never had a cross word with him.''

Advice to Young Managers

''When we start out in the majors, we're so thrilled we sometimes forget what brought us here. We love the game and working with young players. We start working with stars and forget that they are humans. Young managers shouldn't worry about getting fired. If you're hung up about keeping your job, you're under stress and it's hard to keep your mind on your work. Try to get the best out of your players and to prepare them for life after baseball. I'd like to manage until I'm eighty-five or I can't make out the numbers on the scoreboard any longer. But the only thing you lose when you get fired is your chance to manage in the majors. There's lots more to life than that.''

RECOMMENDED RESOURCES

Walter Alston. *The Complete Baseball Handbook: Strategies and Techniques for Winning*. (William C. Brown, 1984). $35.95.*

Ken Dugan. *Secrets of Coaching Championship Baseball*. (Parker Publishing Company, 1980).

Ted Kerley. *Leadership Training for Little League Managers and Coaches*. (Little League Baseball, Inc.).

Jerry Kindall. *Sports Illustrated Baseball*. (Sports Illustrated, 1983).*

Ron Polk and Donna Lopiano. *Baseball-Softball Playbook*. (Mississippi State University, 1983).*

A Coaching Clinic: A Training Video for Coaches, Managers, Parents, and Players. (Major League Baseball, 1988). $19.95. (To order call 800-543-7800).

*These are the three best previously published books covering all aspects of baseball.

CHAPTER NINE

Measuring Achievement

BASEBALL AND STATISTICS

Considering the Numbers

Statistics have come in for some pretty rough treatment by writers deemed to be quotable. It has been said, for instance, that there are three kinds of lies: "lies, damned lies, and statistics." Statistics are supposedly "for losers." They have been compared to bikinis in that "what they reveal is suggestive, but what they conceal is vital." Perhaps the best advice is to "not put your faith in what statistics say until you have carefully considered what they do not say." While there is truth to all these evaluations of statistical evaluation, baseball is very much a game where you go with the odds, and the odds are based on numbers.

I am not aware of any other game in which statistics play such a prominent role and are as emblazoned in the very story of the sport. Think of Ty Cobb's lifetime .367 average, Joe DiMaggio's 56-game hitting

streak, Hank Aaron's 755 career home runs, Lou Gehrig's 2,130 consecutive games. Baseball is awash in records. Fans and commentators thrive on statistics, and there is a considerable industry that turns them out. The Elias Sports Bureau has been around since the early part of this century, and since 1975 its computer-assisted analyses have shed a great deal of light on individual and team performance. The annual *Baseball Analyst* is rightly revered as just about the last word in the business, although the *Baseball Abstract* by Bill James is in the same league. There is even a 3,000-member Society for American Baseball Research (SABR) that has spawned a new discipline, sabermetrics, which combines research and statistical analysis of our national pastime.

I caution players not to get too hung up on numbers and comparisons. They are important to professionals when it comes time to negotiate a contract or prepare for arbitration, but in a team setting, focusing on individual statistics can be disruptive or destructive. To help you better understand the

195

Naturally, you should try to put up big numbers, but don't get so hung up on individual statistics that you forget that baseball is a team sport.

numbers professional players put up, or to compute your own statistics and those of your team, use the following methods.

HITTERS

Batting Average

The standard for measuring batting consistency is batting average. The benchmark batting average that divides the best hitters from the rest has traditionally been .300. To compute, divide the total number of hits by the official times at bat. If the batter walks, is hit by the pitch, advances the runner with a sacrifice bunt, scores the runner with a sacrifice fly, or is awarded first base because of the catcher's interference or obstruction, his appearance at the plate is not counted as an official at bat. These appearances do count, however, in calculating total appearances, which are relevant to determining the batting and slugging champion. In the major leagues, a player must have at least 502 appearances at the plate to qualify for the championship. This number is based on the number of regular season games (162) multiplied by 3.1, the approximate number of at bats per game.

Some of the variations on batting average that further refine and define a player's value to the team determine his percentage in special circumstances. These include: at home, on the road, on grass or artificial turf, leading off the inning, with the bases empty, with a runner at first, with runner(s) in scoring position, and the last two categories with two outs.

All these figures can also be calculated according to how the hitter responds to them in late-inning pressure situations. As the game becomes more sophisticated, specialized, and scientific, such data help determine strategy.

On-Base Average

On-base average gauges a player's ability to avoid making an out. To determine this figure, divide the total of hits, walks, and hit-by-pitch by the total of at bats, walks, hit-by-pitch, and sacrifice flies. While it is true that you can also reach base by error, interference, or fielder's choice, these occasions do not figure in the calculations. There can be considerable difference between batting average and OBA, and the principal reason is the number of walks a batter receives. Leaders in OBA are also usually leaders in runs scored. Two of the best in these departments that I have played on the same team with are Willie Randolph and Rickey Henderson. An average of .400 is very good. Ted Williams led the league twelve times in this category (once with a .551) and has a phenomenal .483 career OBA.

Slugging Percentage

Slugging percentage is the best measure of a hitter's power. It is calculated by dividing total bases of all hits by the number of official at bats. A single equals one total base, a double two, a triple three, and a home run four. With his extraordinary ability to stroke extra-base hits, Don Mattingly usually is at or near the top in this category. Heavy hitters exceed a .500 percentage, and the champions sometimes top .600. Babe Ruth's single season record of .837 and lifetime percentage of .670 are two records that will probably stand forever.

Other Offensive Measurements

The number of stolen bases, hits, runs, extra-base hits (especially home runs), and runs batted in are also relevant offensive yardsticks. The triple crown in baseball is won by the player who leads his league in batting average, RBIs, and homers. Games played also indicates value to the team. A player who is in the lineup day after day, overcoming injury and fatigue, is a blessing to a manager. Among the other ways of evaluating players are:

Game-Winning Runs Batted In— GWRBIs are (were) a relatively new statistic and a controversial one to boot. Whoever drives in the run to give his team a lead that is never relinquished is credited with the GWRBI. It can be a 1-0 lead in the first inning with a final score of 13–12. Subsequent action has no bearing if the lead is never lost. Major league baseball made it an official statistic in 1980 and discontinued it in 1988.

Walk-to-Strikeout Ratio—Ideally, you should have more walks than strikeouts. Power hitters will naturally chalk up more whiffs than hitters who reach the fences less often. At bats per strikeout is a similar tool. The players who strike out the very least average about one strikeout every twenty at bats.

Home Runs per at Bat—The modern emphasis on power has made this statistic more important. Anything above one home run in twenty at bats is very good. Ex-teammate Ken Phelps has led the majors several times by getting a home run every fourteen or so times that he comes to the plate.

Runs Produced—This category combines RBIs and runs minus the number of home runs. I am regularly at or near the top in this statistic. Until my back injury forced me out of the entire 1989 season, I led all active players in the last decade in this department.

Total Production—Other than scoring runs and advancing the runner, the two principal aims of a batter are to not make an out and to hit for distance. Adding on-base average and slugging percentage creates a figure that compensates for what each of these individual statistics ignores. Totals around .800 are excellent, over .900 all-star, and over 1.000 Hall of Fame caliber.

Total Average—This measurement, devised by baseball writer Tom Boswell, makes good sense. The total number of bases accounted for by a player is divided by the number of outs he has cost his team. Walks, stolen bases, and hit-by-pitch are added to total bases. Caught-stealing deducts a base and adds an out. Double plays count as two outs.

erages than outfielders. Good players should score over .900. The number of errors is not necessarily the best gauge of a fielder's ability, however. It is roughly analogous to the number of hits yielded by a pitcher. A pitcher may give up several hits but few runs, and the same could be true of a fielder. Many errors are harmless, many are not awarded when they should be, and others are given to the wrong player. Also, a fielder with wide range will go for balls that lesser fielders wouldn't even try for.

For outfielders, the number of assists is a key statistic because it means you are denying the other team scoring opportunities. The strength and accuracy of your throws is cutting down runners or persuading them not to even try for that extra base. I've led both leagues in assists, and that is one of my most satisfying records. The number of double plays a team can turn is also a defensive measure. Ironically, poorer teams sometimes are right at the top in double plays because they allow more men to reach base.

Each year in both major leagues, a Gold Glove is awarded to the player at each position who demonstrates the greatest fielding ability.

FIELDERS

Fielding Average and Other Measurements

One way of determining a fielder's defensive strength is fielding average. You divide the number of putouts and assists by the total chances handled by the player (putouts, assists, and errors). Because they handle more balls and more difficult balls, infielders usually have lower fielding av-

PITCHERS

Won-Lost Percentage

For teams, divide the number of wins by the total number of games played. To calculate the percentage for an individual pitcher, divide the number of losses by the number of wins.

The starting pitcher can be credited with a win only if he has pitched at least five complete innings and if his team is leading when he is replaced and never relinquishes the lead. If the starting pitcher cannot be credited with the win and more than one reliever is used, the following rules apply:

1. If the winning team took the lead while the starting pitcher was in and holds it throughout the game, the reliever judged to have been "most effective" by the official scorer is given the win.

2. Whenever the score is tied, the game becomes a new contest as far as the winning or losing pitchers are concerned.

3. If the opposing team takes the lead, no pitcher up to that point can be given the victory unless the pitcher against whom the opponent took the lead continues to pitch and his team regains the lead for good.

4. The winning reliever is the pitcher of record when his team assumes and holds on to the lead.

Regardless of how many innings the first pitcher has pitched, the loss is his if he is replaced with his team behind or if runners charged to him give the opponents the lead after he has left the game and his team fails to either tie the game or regain the lead.

Won-loss record is to pitchers what batting average is to hitters, the primary tool of evaluation. This is unfair to the pitcher. A hurler on a pennant winner has a tremendous advantage over one on a cellar dweller. There are so many factors beyond the pitcher's control: the defense behind him, the runs his club can get him, the bullpen that backs him up. Some mighty good pitchers can consistently end up on the short end of the score.

Wins are also harder to get in the last decade or so than they were earlier. The

five-man rotation that is practiced today gives a pitcher eight fewer starts than he would enjoy as part of a four-man rotation.

Saves

A relief pitcher is credited with a save when he meets all three of the following conditions:

1. He is the finishing pitcher in a game won by his team.

2. He is not the winning pitcher.

3. He enters the game with a lead of no more than three runs and pitches for at least an inning; or he enters the game with the potential tying run on base, at bat, or on deck; or he pitches effectively for three innings.

Some commentators have labeled saves as the "most easily manipulated stat" because it is totally up to the manager to call whomever he wants out of the bullpen in easy save situations. A pitcher can actually get a save by coming on in the ninth inning and throwing one pitch to one batter. Nevertheless, there are also saves and relievers that live up to their names. In 1986, my teammate Dave Righetti set a major league record for saves with 46. Not bad for a guy who started his career as a starting pitcher.

The best pair of relievers I ever saw in action was Ron Davis and Goose Gossage in 1981. If we held the lead in the seventh inning and then turned the game over to this pair to set up and close, the game was as good as over.

The Phillies and the Orioles have come up with another statistic they apply to relievers that makes a lot of sense. They record "holds" and "squanders," based on whether the reliever keeps or fails to keep his team's lead. The Phillies are also responsible for "scoring ratio," which compares the number of runners a pitcher inherits to the number of runs he allows them to score.

Earned-Run Average

ERA is calculated by multiplying the number of earned runs charged to a pitcher by nine and dividing the total by the number of innings (and fractions of innings) actually pitched. An unearned run is any run that scores because of an error or a passed ball, or any run that scores after there would have been three outs in the inning if an error or passed ball had not occurred.

A more sophisticated version of this statistic is the normalized earned-run average, or NERA, which adjusts the figure by factoring in the league average ERA and the home park impact (some parks are notoriously favorable to either hitters or pitchers). How effective the bullpen is also plays a large role in determining ERA. An ERA under 3.00 is considered superior. League leaders usually come in around 2.25. The best ever recorded in modern times was Bob Gibson's 1.12 in 1968.

Other Pitching Statistics

For just about every offensive category there is a corresponding pitching statistic. The cumulative batting average that hitters amass facing a given hurler becomes that hurler's pitching average. The best PA on record is Luis Tiant's .168 in 1968. Of pitchers still active, Nolan Ryan has an amazing PA of slightly over .200. The guy just keeps on keeping on.

The refinements on batting average that have been facilitated by the computerization of sports statistics also apply in reverse to pitchers. We now can get a handle on not just the number of hits and runs given up by a pitcher but when he yields them. If he scatters them, a hurler can give the other team lots of hits that don't matter. Or he can give up runs early on but not in late-inning pressure situations. Some players get better when it counts. It's not that they are not always trying, it's that they bear down and excel when the game is on the line.

Opponent's on-base-average, home runs or gopher balls allowed, shutouts, the ratio of walks to strikeouts (two K's for every walk is the traditional formula indicating control), and number of strikeouts are additional yardsticks for pitchers. Although strikeouts can be exciting for fans and humiliating for hitters, they are probably overrated as a measure of a pitcher's ability. They certainly are not the most efficient way of retiring a batter. I wish I could impress this on more pitchers, especially the aforementioned Mr. Ryan and his hard-throwing brethren, Roger Clemens and Mark Langston.

An earlier mark of endurance and reliability, complete games, has lost some of its relevance in the wake of the reliever revolution. This is not to say that teams don't benefit from pitchers who can go the distance, just that it doesn't happen as often as it once did, nor is it as important. Innings pitched is still a reliable measure of how much an individual works, and a new statistic, quality starts, has largely replaced complete games. A quality start is one in which the pitcher has gone at least six innings without giving up more than three runs.

INTANGIBLES

Beyond Measurement

All of the above categories end up reducing a player's contribution to numbers. Although commonly accepted objective standards are a necessary component of evaluating performance, they don't tell the whole story of how a player contributes to a team. None of them measure attitude, for instance. How a player approaches the game affects not only his own play but potentially the ability of teammates, coaches, and managers to do their jobs. The effect of a player shirking his obligations, of a veteran sharing his expertise with a younger player, of a teammate whose enthusiasm is contagious, is difficult or impossible to quantify. That doesn't mean that it is not real, however, or that it won't eventually show up in the win-loss column.

Young players, in particular, need to bring to the game a willingness to be coached. You can contribute to your team by always being on time for games and practices, by always hustling and cooperating. Be open to the advice of your coaches. With very few exceptions, their primary goal is to help you become a better player and a better person. Listen up. Pay attention. Help out. You may not have the physical skills to become your team's most valuable player, but everybody on the team has a chance to be named most cooperative or most enthusiastic player.

RECOMMENDED RESOURCES

Seymour Siwoff, Steve Hirdt, and Peter Hirdt. *The Elias Baseball Analyst.* (Collier Books, issued annually). $12.95.

John Thorn and Pete Palmer, with David Reuther. *The Hidden Game of Baseball: A Revolutionary Approach to Baseball and Its Statistics.* (Doubleday, 1984).

Craig R. Wright and Tom House. *The Diamond Appraised.* (Simon & Schuster, 1989). $19.95.

CHAPTER TEN

From the Scouts' Perspective

FIRST THINGS FIRST

Why Stay in School?

If you are a youngster hoping for a professional career in baseball, you may think that the best ticket would be to catch on with a minor league club out of high school and gradually move up. Well, I'd like to begin this section by making a pitch for college as the best way to prepare yourself, not only for a career in baseball but also for life afterward. To begin with, I can speak from firsthand experience.

I was drafted by the Baltimore Orioles as a pitcher right out of high school, but I chose instead to go to the University of Minnesota. The four years that I spent in college were some of the richest in what has already been a very rewarding life for me. I won a scholarship to play baseball, then basketball, for the Golden Gophers and learned a lot about history, political science, and a wealth of other subjects—in addition to getting first-rate instruction in baseball. During the summers I had the opportunity to play against some of the best amateur players in the country. In my last year, Minnesota went on to compete in the

Here I am as a first team All-American pitcher at the University of Minnesota.

NCAA Tournament and eventually the College World Series, and then I was drafted, this time by the San Diego Padres as an outfielder. During my college days, I got to travel, meet a lot of people, and mature. I also went from 6'3" and 195 pounds to 6'6" and 220 pounds and became a much more valuable prospect.

In the years since I attended college, the quality of play and the level of competition

203

and overall talent have dramatically increased. Look at the players who have come out of college play recently: Mark McGwire, Will Clark, Pete Incaviglia, Oddibe McDowell, Cory Snyder, Jim Abbott, Bo Jackson. These are just a few of the players who honed their skills in college and have gone from the campus to the pros. Big league scouts make fewer mistakes on college kids, so frequently the trip to the majors is shorter out of college than if a player goes directly to the minor leagues.

The real reason for going to college, though, is that it's too much to pass up, and right after high school is usually the best time to go. If you have the opportunity and don't exercise it, you may not have that opportunity again, or it will not be as easy. Picking up your studies after a long period of neglecting them, and doing it in an environment where almost everybody is younger and fresher than you are, is difficult. Getting to professional ball is a long shot even for very talented players. And if you get there, the stay is a short one more often than not. Although professional scouts speak of college tuition subsidies as an added inducement to prospects, the reality is that with winter ball and instructional leagues, the likelihood of ever seeing a campus while playing in the minors is slim.

Even if you make it in professional sports, how long a career can you count on? Most players are in, over, and out by the age of thirty. And then what do you do? You get out into the real world and face the reality that most of your peers have a college degree and eight more years of experience in the field you would like to enter. You may also feel physically invincible at the start of your career, but keep in mind that one pitch, a hard slide, or a misjudged fly ball could end that career in

an instant. If you do not go to college, what's your backup in today's society?

Naturally, there are some prospects who have no intention of going to college even if they weren't intent on a career in baseball. And I must conclude this section by saying that my advice runs contrary to that of most professional baseball people, who believe that the earlier they begin to work with a youngster, the sooner they will be able to develop a full-fledged player. Another factor to be considered by an athlete choosing between college or the rookie league is the track record of the specific school. Many athletic programs have pretty dismal records of educating—much less graduating—their "student-athletes."

What College Coaches Look For

Tipped off by high school coaches, former players, and alumni who are part of their network, or alerted by press accounts, college coaches try to catch as many high school and organized league ball games as they can. They'll be there with their stopwatches (and some with radar guns) sizing up athletic potential. They'll check batting averages and ERAs and box scores, but they are just as interested in your grade-point average and your SAT or ACT scores. How you have performed academically is an essential consideration. Before you make the team, you have to make an earlier cut and be admitted to school.

College coaches at good schools will be looking not only at your grades but also at what courses you took to get those grades. Many universities, for instance, require two years of a foreign language and work in a laboratory science. NCAA Division One teams are allowed to award the equivalent of thirteen full-time scholarships. Only on rare occasions are students given a full ride in baseball. The usual procedure is for the scholarship pie to be divided into many smaller pieces.

MAKING IT TO THE PROS

The Major League Scouting Bureau

Professional baseball has access to just about all the resources that college coaches can muster—and then a lot more. Since 1975, the Major League Scouting Bureau (MLSB) has operated under the umbrella of the Commissioner's Office. Based in El Toro, California, it employs a cadre of experienced full-time personnel to assist teams in finding talent. The bureau has divided the United States into seven regions, each with a territorial supervisor who oversees a staff of scouts. Currently the bureau has fifty scouts who take in tens of thousands of games annually, searching for the nation's most promising players. This service is meant to provide the twenty-six major league teams with consistent and reliable data facilitating their decisions on whom to pursue to fill their needs.

Each year the bureau prepares a computerized profile of approximately 800 amateur players. These prospects have been evaluated by the three-man system employed by the bureau. A territorial scout, a territorial supervisor, and a national cross-checker must agree before a prospect is listed with the bureau. The bureau can provide videotapes of the top 150 players. In addition, all prospects are given the Biopter Eye Test to ensure that they do not have undetected vision problems. Each player must also complete the Athletic Motivation Inventory, an effort to measure a player's mental aptitude for the game. The bureau also scouts A, AA, and AAA professional leagues.

The MLSB provides other services. It holds clinics for high school coaches at their annual national convention and sponsors an Inner City Baseball Development Program that since 1986 has sent instructional teams to Los Angeles, Chicago, and Miami. The program, run in the fall, reaches youths who may not otherwise have the opportunity for that level of instruction.

Don Pries, director of the MLSB, summarizes the principal work of his organization:

When we scout a prospect, we focus on mechanics over performance. Good mechanics is, of course, the foundation of good performance, but we're more interested in tools than numbers. We look at a player's faults. At this level, every player has flaws and must make adjustments. That's why we have farm clubs and the minor league system. We try to determine what needs to be corrected and the likelihood of that player making the corrections.

Team Scouts

The MLSB was created to supplement the work of the scouts employed by each team, and as much as some teams have come to rely on the bureau's work, the team's own scouts are a mainstay in discovering new talent. Just as the bureau has a hierarchy that must pass on a prospect before he is offered a contract, so do the individual clubs. The process usually begins when a player is noticed by an associate scout, also called a "bird dog" because he beats the bushes to flush out talent. Bird dogs are rarely salaried, but usually get a commission if one of their prospects pans out. They pass their information on to a part-time area scout, who checks the player out and, if he finds the player promising, will have the player fill out a prospect card. A full-time regional scout is the next step up the ladder. This is sometimes the first person with the authority to actually sign a player or recommend that he be drafted. This happens only rarely, however. In almost all cases, the regional scouting supervisor is the person who makes this decision in conjunction with the team's front office.

If you manage to get as far as the regional supervisor, congratulations, but you've still got a way to go. Up until now, your contacts have been from your area. If the supervisor thinks you have promise, he'll inform the club's director of scouting and a national crosschecker will be assigned to evaluate you. If his report is favorable, the scouting director himself may even come to see you play. Depending on the team's organizational structure, degree of autonomy of various personnel, and how highly you are regarded (that is, how much money may be involved in your signing), several other front office people may be part of the decision, including the head of baseball operations and the team owner.

The June Draft and Undrafted Free Agents

Since 1965 the principal means by which major league teams have acquired the rights to sign prospects has been the annual June draft. The draft was established to overcome the inherent inequality between winning teams with money and extensive farm systems and clubs without these strengths. To help restore equity, teams low in the standings are given preference over teams that finish ahead of them. Based on the recommendations of their own scouts and the work of the Major League Scouting Bureau, approximately 1,500 to 1,800 players are selected each year. Of that number, about half will actually sign a contract to play and be assigned to a minor league club. The average major leaguer spends three and a half years in the minors before coming up to the show.

The round in which a player is drafted helps determine the size of his contract and whether that player receives a bonus. Simply because a player is drafted high does not mean he is destined to break into the majors, however. About half of the first-round draft choices don't last in professional ball. At the same time, several all-stars in the majors today were low-round choices: Jose Canseco went in the fifteenth round. Don Mattingly was drafted in the sixteenth round, as was Buddy Bell. Orel Hershiser didn't go until the seventeenth round. I think Al Cowens must hold the record, however. When he was drafted in 1969, he went in the seventy-fifth round!

Simply because a player is not drafted does not mean that professional ball is out of the question. At any given recent time in the majors, between 10 and 15 percent of the players had not been drafted. Overlooked by the teams in June, they had caught somebody's eye later on and simply signed an undrafted free agent contract. They might have been spotted in a summer league, or shown up for an announced team tryout, or moved up from a semipro team. You could assemble a pretty good team

SEATTLE MARINERS FREE AGENT REPORT

Player: **GRIFFEY** **GEORGE** **KENNETH** Class Start **R** OFP **72**
complete last name first name middle name

Address _____ Phone _____
street/p. o. box city state zip a/c

Parents Name: _____
last name first name middle name

Address _____ Phone _____
street/p. o. box city state zip a/c

Name of School College **MOELLER** City **CINCINNATI** State **OHIO** Team Name _____

Position **C.F.**	NON-PITCHERS	Pres	Fut	PITCHERS	Pres	Fut	EXCEL GOOD FAIR POOR USE WORD DESCRIPTION
Bat **L** Throw **L**	Hitting Ability	4	7	Fast Ball Vel			Personal Habits **GOOD**
Hgt **6'3** Wgt **195**	Power	6	8	Movement			Dedication **GOOD**
Birthdate **11-21-69**	Running Speed	6	6	Curve			Aggressiveness **FAIR**
Grad. Date _____	Base Running	5	6	Control			Emotional Maturity **GOOD**
Date Elig. _____	Arm Strength	5	6	Change			Baseball Instinct **"**
Phase _____	Arm Accuracy	4	6	Slider			Intelligence **"**
Legion Player _____	Fielding	5	7	Knuckler			Coachability **"**
Last Yr. Elig. _____	Range	6	7	Other			Agility **EXCEL.**
Glasses/Contacts _____	Games: This Yr. **1** Total **1**			Fielding			Poise **GOOD**
Married _____	Pull **✓** Str. Away **✓**			Inn: This Yr _____ Total _____			Soc-Econ Status **EXCEL**
Children _____	Opp-Fld **✓** Spray _____			Delivery _____ Arm Action _____ High _____ Low _____ Ave _____			Injuries/Diseases **NONE**

Physical Maturity and Description: *17 YR OLD BOY WITH A MANS BODY. TALL - BROAD SHOULDERS STRONG MUSCULAR ARMS & LEGS - SMALL WAIST.*

Player's Strength: *BIG STRONG KID WITH A LOT OF POWER. TYPE THAT COULD HIT (30) H.R.'S A SEASON SOME DAY. HAS A STRONG ARM AND HE CAN RUN = O.F. INSTINCTS ARE GOOD CAN REALLY GO GET THE BALL. HAS ALL THE TOOLS TO BE A SUPERSTAR.*

Player's Weakness: *HIS WEAKNESSES ARE ALL CORRECTABLE WITH INSTR. AND EXPERIENCE JUST NEEDS TO GO OUT AND PLAY.*

Additional Comments: DOUBLE CHECK **YES** / NO

HAS A LOT OF NATURAL ABILITY EVERYTHING SEEMS TO COME EASY FOR HIM. DOESN'T EXERT HIMSELF IS A VERY LIKABLE KID. JUST SPOILED THEY TELL ME. HAS TO BE A FIRST RD. CONSIDERATION FOR US. IS THE TYPE THAT COULD COME FAST. RAISED O.F.P. (2) POINTS FROM MY FIRST REPORT OF 5-11-87

Ken Griffey, Jr., is my choice as 1989 Rookie of the Year. Above is the scouting report on him fresh out of high school. Note his overall future potential (OFP) rating of 72. The highest OFP ever recorded by the Major League Scouting Bureau was Bo Jackson's 75.

from players who never got drafted. In fact, Al Goldis, the White Sox scouting director, and Rick Wolff, sports editor at Macmillan, have done just that in their book, *Breaking into the Big Leagues*. Their starting pitchers are Bob Ojeda and Rick Mahler, with Jeff Reardon and Dan Quisenberry in the bullpen. Rich Gedman is catching. The infield consists of Andre Thornton, Frank White, Kevin Mitchell, and Ken Oberkfell. In the outfield are Brian Downing, Claudell Washington, and Jeffrey Leonard, with Gary Ward in reserve. With Larry Parrish as designated hitter, you have quite a team—and not a single member was drafted.

GETTING THE SCOUTS' ATTENTION

Physical Skills

Now that you know the process by which a prospect becomes a professional player, let us consider the skills that the scouts will want to see before they seek your name on a contract. To begin with, nonpitchers are evaluated in six basic physical categories: hitting, power, speed, arm strength, fielding, and baserunning. These categories are often broken down to more specific skills (such as fielding range and throwing accuracy), and other qualities (such as aggressiveness and instinct) may be rated. As a batter, you should show the scouts that you are aggressive, have good bat speed, can make contact consistently, and hit the ball hard to all fields. As a fielder, you must be quick, have range and a strong arm, and be able to get the jump on the ball. As a base runner, you need raw speed, quickness, the ability to read signs, and a good slide.

A pitcher should exhibit control, good mechanics, a smooth delivery with full arm extension, a variety of pitches that move, and velocity. The most important of these is velocity. All other components of pitching can be improved through instruction and practice, but you can't teach speed.

If you say, "I'm not that good in all those categories," fear not. If you can score relatively high in two or three of the six physical categories listed, you will probably advance. Most scouts rate players on a double 20-to-80 scale that measures their current and potential major league ability. Regardless of age or experience, the prospect's abilities are compared to those of a major leaguer. How a player compares to his teammates or opponents is absolutely irrelevant to the grading system. Numerical grades and their meanings are: 20–29, poor; 30–39, well below average; 40–49, below average; 50–59, average; 60–69, above average; 70–79, very good; 80, the best. Using this scale, an outstanding high school pitcher with good potential might be given a 30/55 present/future rating.

Typically, pitchers' velocity is also rated on a 20-to-80 scale such as the one shown below.

MPH	Grade
Below 82	20–29
83–84	30–39
85–87	40–49
88–89	50–59
90–92	60–69
93–97	70–79
98 +	80

Running speed is another category in which absolute numbers can be assigned, at least for present abilities. You may be clocked in a 40-yard dash or a 60-yard dash (7.0 seconds is about average; anything below 6.7 is good). Running times to first base are measured from moment of contact between bat and ball to the runner's foot touching the bag, with the following grades applying:

Right-handed Batter	Left-handed Batter	Grade
4.6	4.5	2
4.5	4.4	3
4.4	4.3	4
4.3	4.2	5
4.2	4.1	6
4.1	4.0	7
4.0	3.9	8

Character

Some of the qualities that a scout evaluates, like the speed of a player's fastball, he can be certain about. Other evaluations are based on interpretation or an educated guess. Even though there is great emphasis placed on standardized judgment, scouting is far more an art than a science. Trying to predict how a player will perform five or ten years down the road is a matter of opinion, and that is one reason that some scouts can be high on a prospect whom others don't even consider.

Perhaps the hardest qualities for a scout to get a handle on are those that comprise a player's "makeup." These consist of competitiveness, confidence, dependability, honesty, intelligence, poise, and teamwork. The person you are, not just the athlete you are, is a major factor in determining whether you will make it in professional ball. Although your athletic skills are capable of tremendous development, your character is often largely formed by the time a scout is checking you out. I certainly don't mean to imply that a teenager will not develop mentally, or that a talented player with character flaws isn't going to get scouted, or that baseball is filled with Eagle Scouts. I've played against at least one person who was actually scouted while he was still in prison. What I do want to emphasize, however, is that mental and spiritual qualities are part of the equation that add up to your playing ball at a higher level. If you aspire to being a better ballplayer, work on being a better person.

RECOMMENDED RESOURCES

Al Goldis and Rick Wolff. *Breaking into the Big Leagues: How to Make Pro Scouts Notice You.* (Leisure Press, 1988). $10.95.

Thomas Tutko, Leland Lyon, and Bruce Ogilvie. *Athletic Motivation Inventory.* (Institute of Athletic Motivation, Redwood City, California; first used in 1971).

Kevin Kerrane. *Dollar Sign on the Muscle: The World of Baseball Scouting.* (Avon Books, 1985).

DAVE WINFIELD'S CAREER STATISTICS AND HIGHLIGHTS

STATISTICS

YR Club	AVG	G	AB	R	H	2B	3B	HR	RBI	BB	SO	SB
1973 SAN DIEGO	.277	56	141	9	39	4	1	3	12	12	19	0
1974 SAN DIEGO	.265	145	498	57	132	18	4	20	75	40	96	9
1975 SAN DIEGO	.267	143	509	74	136	20	2	15	76	69	82	23
1976 SAN DIEGO	.283	137	492	81	139	26	4	13	69	65	78	26
1977 SAN DIEGO	.275	157	615	104	169	29	7	25	92	58	75	16
1978 SAN DIEGO	.308	158	587	88	181	30	5	24	97	55	81	21
1979 SAN DIEGO	.308	159	597	97	184	27	10	34	118	85	71	15
1980 SAN DIEGO	.276	162	558	89	154	25	6	20	87	79	83	23
1981 YANKEES	.294	105	388	52	114	25	1	13	68	43	41	11
1982 YANKEES	.280	140	539	84	151	24	8	37	106	45	64	5
1983 YANKEES	.283	152	598	99	169	26	8	32	116	58	77	15
1984 YANKEES	.340	141	567	106	193	34	4	19	100	53	71	6
1985 YANKEES	.275	155	633	105	174	34	6	26	114	52	96	19
1986 YANKEES	.262	154	565	90	148	31	5	24	104	77	106	6
1987 YANKEES	.275	156	575	83	158	22	1	27	97	76	96	5
1988 YANKEES	.322	149	559	96	180	37	2	25	107	69	88	9
N.L. Totals	.284	1117	3997	599	1134	179	39	154	626	463	585	133
N.Y.Y. Totals	.291	1152	4424	715	1287	233	35	203	812	473	639	76
M.L. Totals	.287	2269	8421	1314	2421	412	74	357	1438	936	1224	209

GWRBI: 1980-10; 1981-9; 1982-15; 1983-21; 1984-13; 1985-19; 1986-6; 1987-8; 1988-10.
Total = 111.

DIVISION SERIES RECORD

YR Club, Opp.	AVG	G	AB	R	H	2B	3B	HR	RBI	BB	SO	SB
1981 N.Y. vs Mil.	.350	5	20	2	7	3	0	0	0	1	5	0

CHAMPIONSHIP SERIES RECORD

YR Club, Opp.	AVG	G	AB	R	H	2B	3B	HR	RBI	BB	SO	SB
1981 N.Y. vs Oak.	.154	3	13	2	2	1	0	0	2	2	2	1

WORLD SERIES RECORD

YR	Club, Opp.	AVG	G	AB	R	H	2B	3B	HR	RBI	BB	SO	SB
1981	N.Y. vs L.A.	.045	6	22	0	1	0	0	0	1	5	4	1

ALL-STAR GAME RECORD

YR	Club, Site	AVG	G	AB	R	H	2B	3B	HR	RBI	BB	SO	SB
1977	N.L., N.Y. (AL)	1.000	1	2	0	2	1	0	0	2	0	0	0
1978	N.L., S.D.	.500	1	2	1	1	0	0	0	0	0	0	0
1979	N.L., Sea.	.200	1	5	1	1	1	0	0	1	0	1	0
1980	N.L., L.A.	.000	1	2	0	0	0	0	0	1	0	0	0
1981	A.L., Cle.	.000	1	4	0	0	0	0	0	0	1	0	0
1982	A.L., Mont.	.500	1	2	0	1	0	0	0	0	0	0	0
1983	A.L., Chi. (AL)	1.000	1	3	2	3	1	0	0	2	0	0	0
1984	A.L., S.F.	.250	1	4	0	1	1	0	0	0	0	0	0
1985	A.L., Min.	.333	1	3	0	1	0	0	0	0	0	0	1
1986	A.L., Hou.	1.000	1	1	1	1	1	0	0	0	0	0	0
1987	A.L., Oak.	.200	1	5	0	1	1	0	0	0	1	0	0
1988	A.L., Cinn.	.333	1	3	1	1	1	0	0	0	0	0	0
A.S.G. Totals		**.361**	**12**	**36**	**6**	**13**	**7**	**0**	**0**	**6**	**2**	**1**	**1**

HIGHLIGHTS

Led Minnesota to College World Series with 13–1 record as pitcher, .385 BA and 33 RBIs as hitter; named Series MVP, 1973.

Drafted by four professional teams in three sports; Atlanta Hawks (NBA), Utah Stars (ABA), Minnesota Vikings (NFL), and San Diego Padres (MLB).

One of three players now in major league baseball never to play in minors.

Hit safely in first six games to begin San Diego career.

Led NL outfielders in assists with 15 in 1976.

In 1979, led NL with 118 RBIs, 24 intentional walks, and 333 total bases and was MVP runner-up.

In 1981, first season as Yankee, led the team in games, at bats, hits, total bases, doubles, RBIs, GWRBIs, and sacrifice flies.

Led AL outfielders in assists with 17 in 1982.

Shares Yankee record for most GWRBIs in single season (21 in 1983).

Had three 5-hit games in June to tie Ty Cobb's major league record, 1984.

Won four Silver Bats (1981–84).

Won seven Gold Gloves (1979–87).

First Yankee since DiMaggio to have 100 RBIs in five consecutive seasons (1982–86).

Hit 300th career home run in August 1986.

Set AL and tied major league record for RBIs in April (29 in 1988).

Leads current Yankee players in games, runs, home runs, grand slams, RBIs, and GWRBIs.

Among top five active major league players in hits, home runs, and RBIs.

ALL-STAR STATISTICS

Selected to all-star team twelve
consecutive years.

Tied all-star record for most at bats in
a nine-inning game (5 in 1979).
Tied all-star record for most
consecutive games with hit (7).
Holds all-star record for most doubles (7).